Anne Sexton

Twayne's United States Authors Series

Warren French, Editor

University of Wales, Swansea

TUSAS 548

Anne Sexton
Photograph courtesy of Wide World Photos, Inc.

Anne Sexton

By Caroline King Barnard Hall

Twayne Publishers
A Division of G. K. Hall & Co. • *Boston*

Anne Sexton
Caroline King Barnard Hall

Copyright 1989 by G. K. Hall & Co.
All rights reserved.
Published by Twayne Publishers
A Division of G. K. Hall & Co.
70 Lincoln Street
Boston, Massachusetts 02111

Copyediting supervised by Barbara Sutton
Book production by Gabrielle B. McDonald
Book design by Barbara Anderson

Typeset in 11 pt. Garamond
by Compset, Inc., Beverly, Massachusetts

Printed on permanent/durable acid-free paper
and bound in the United States of America

Library of Congress Cataloging-in-Publication Data

Hall, Caroline King Barnard.
    Anne Sexton / by Caroline King Barnard Hall.
        p.   cm.—(Twayne's United States authors series ; TUSAS 548)
    Bibliography: p.
    Includes index.
    ISBN 0-8057-7538-2 (alk. paper)
    1. Sexton, Anne—Criticism and interpretation.   I. Title.
II. Series.
PS3537.E915Z69   1989
811.'54—dc19   89-30986
                                                                     CIP

To
John and the Kings

Contents

About the Author
Preface
Acknowledgments
Chronology

Chapter One
A Poet's Life: A Story   1

Chapter Two
To Bedlam and Part Way Back   12

Chapter Three
All My Pretty Ones: Confession   32

Chapter Four
Live or Die: "To Endure, Somehow to
Endure"   54

Chapter Five
Love Poems: "A Woman Who Writes"   73

Chapter Six
Transformations: Fairy Tales Revisited   92

Chapter Seven
The Book of Folly: Fire and Ice   113

Chapter Eight
The Death Notebooks: "not to die, not to die"   130

Chapter Nine
Last Volumes, Last Poems   147

Chapter Ten
The Experience Teller   170

Notes and References   175
Selected Bibliography   181
Index   187

About the Author

Caroline King Barnard Hall, who received her Ph.D. in English and American literature in 1973 from Brown University, is the author of *Sylvia Plath* (Twayne Publishers, 1978). Her academic career has included two senior Fulbright lectureships in modern American literature and women's studies, at the University of Klagenfurt in Austria in 1980–81 and at the University of Copenhagen in Denmark in 1986. She currently lives in New Orleans and teaches at Xavier University.

Preface

Anne Sexton's ten volumes of poetry, written in the seventeen years before her suicide in 1974, chronicle this poet's search for an exit from a labyrinth of mundane difficulty, psychological pain, and emotional extremes. Her poetry was the vehicle through which she explored possibilities and recorded both success and failure. The epigraph Sexton chose for her first volume serves well as epigraph for her entire canon, for Sexton is indeed the courageous one who "make[s] a clean breast of it in face of every question," who, "seeking enlightenment . . . , pursues [her] indefatigable enquiry, even when [she] divines that appalling horror awaits . . . in the answer." Sexton's poetry is appropriately framed by this quotation and by the epigraph chosen by her editor for "Beginning the Hegira," a section of *45 Mercy Street,* her last volume: "A journey . . . undertaken as a means of escaping from an undesirable or dangerous environment; or as a means of arriving at a highly desirable destination."

Anne Sexton's poetry invites a chronological reading focusing on the subtle shifts in her perception of three related themes: the nature of the mid–twentieth-century female experience, the lineaments of madness, and the character of confession. Through all her poetry, Sexton offers herself as subject, minutely examining her own psyche, her own emotions, and her own external circumstances, in an enquiry that at once atomizes the personal and transcends it. The destination she reaches is, we hope, desirable for her. The destination the reader of Sexton reaches is clearly desirable for anyone who seeks to know oneself more fully.

By examining Anne Sexton's poetry chronologically, then, this study aims to acquaint the reader with the whole work of an important mid-century American poet. Sexton's journey should be comprehended and experienced in the order in which it occurred, volume by volume, since most of the collections are thematically or conceptually unified. By following the poet's lead, we can best understand Sexton's journey through the labyrinth of madness, love, alienation, guilt, and hope toward her answer. Sexton is, in many ways, the Icarus of her poetry, always "sailing queerly like Icarus" toward disaster ("The Break"), yet most frequently celebrating that flight, as in her sonnet "To a Friend

Whose Work Has Come to Triumph." "Who cares," declares the poem's speaker, "that he fell back to the sea?"

For their advice, counsel, and help in various necessary ways, I wish to thank my husband, John, and also J. B. Wolgamot. I offer special thanks as well to Liz Traynor Fowler of Twayne Publishers, and to my editor, Warren French, who quite literally made all of this possible. A portion of this book appears, in different form, in *Original Essays on the Poetry of Anne Sexton,* ed. Frances Bixler (Conway: University of Central Arkansas Press, 1988).

                                              Caroline King Barnard Hall
New Orleans

Acknowledgments

Grateful acknowledgment is made to Houghton Mifflin Co. for the United States and Canadian rights and to Sterling Lord Literistic, Inc., for the United Kingdom rights to quote from the works of Anne Sexton noted below.

To Bedlam and Part Way Back, © 1960 by Anne Sexton. © 1981 by Linda Gray Sexton and Loring Conant, Jr., executors of the will of Anne Sexton.

All My Pretty Ones, © 1962 by Anne Sexton. © 1981 by Linda Gray Sexton and Loring Conant, Jr., executors of the will of Anne Sexton.

Live or Die, © 1966 by Anne Sexton. © 1981 by Linda Gray Sexton and Loring Conant, Jr., executors of the will of Anne Sexton.

Transformations, © 1971 by Anne Sexton. © 1981 by Linda Gray Sexton and Loring Conant, Jr., executors of the will of Anne Sexton.

Love Poems, © 1967, 1968, 1969 by Anne Sexton. © 1981 by Linda Gray Sexton and Loring Conant, Jr., executors of the will of Anne Sexton.

The Book of Folly, © 1972 by Anne Sexton. © 1981 by Linda Gray Sexton and Loring Conant, Jr., executors of the will of Anne Sexton.

The Death Notebooks, © 1974 by Anne Sexton. © 1981 by Linda Gray Sexton and Loring Conant, Jr., executors of the will of Anne Sexton.

45 Mercy Street, © 1976 by Linda Gray Sexton and Loring Conant, Jr., executors of the will of Anne Sexton. © 1981 by Linda Gray Sexton and Loring Conant, Jr., as executors of the will of Anne Sexton.

The Awful Rowing toward God, © 1975 by Loring Conant, Jr., executor of the estate of Anne Sexton. © 1981 by Linda Gray Sexton and Loring Conant, Jr., as executors of the will of Anne Sexton.

Words for Dr. Y., © 1978 by Linda Gray Sexton and Loring Conant, Jr., executors of the will of Anne Sexton. © 1981 by Linda Gray Sexton and Loring Conant, Jr., as executors of the will of Anne Sexton.

Anne Sexton: A Self-Portrait in Letters, edited by Linda Gray Sexton and Lois Ames. Commentary © 1977 by Linda Gray Sexton and Lois Ames. © 1977 by Linda Gray Sexton and Loring Conant, Jr., executors of the will of Anne Sexton. © 1981 by Linda Gray Sexton and Loring Conant, Jr., as executors of the will of Anne Sexton.

Chronology

1928	Anne Gray Harvey born 9 November, in Newton, Massachusetts.
1934–1945	Attends public schools in Wellesley, Massachusetts.
1945–1947	Attends Rogers Hall, a boarding school for girls in Lowell, Massachusetts. Writes first poems.
1947	Enters The Garland School in Boston.
1948	Marries Alfred Muller Sexton II 16 August.
1948–1950	Returns to Cochituate, Massachusetts.
1950–1953	Moves to Baltimore, then back to Massachusetts. Models for the Hart Agency. Moves to San Francisco; returns to Weston, Massachusetts.
1953	21 July, Linda Gray Sexton born. August, moves to 40 Clearwater Road, Newton Lower Falls, Massachusetts.
1953–1955	Intermittent hospitalization at Westwood Lodge for emotional disturbances and attempted suicide.
1954	Her aunt Anna Ladd Dingley dies 14 July at age eighty-six.
1955	4 August, Joyce Ladd Sexton born.
1956	March, admitted to mental hospital. Attempts suicide 9 November. Sees psychiatrist "Dr. Martin" in December; begins to write poetry.
1957	Enrolls in John Holmes's poetry seminar at Boston University; meets Maxine Kumin.
1958	August, attends Antioch Summer Writers' Conference on scholarship; studies with W. D. Snodgrass. September, enrolls in Robert Lowell's poetry seminar at Boston University; meets Sylvia Plath and George Starbuck.
1959	Mother dies 10 March. Father dies 3 June. August, attends Bread Loaf Writers Conference as Robert Frost Fellow. Undergoes surgery to remove appendix and ovary in October.

1960   March, *To Bedlam and Part Way Back*; father-in-law dies.

1961   Teaches poetry at Harvard University and Radcliffe College. With Maxine Kumin, serves as first scholar in poetry at Radcliffe Institute for Independent Study.

1962   Fall, *All My Pretty Ones*. November, awarded Levinson Prize by *Poetry*; hospitalized at Westwood Lodge.

1963   *All My Pretty Ones* nominated for National Book Award. Receives first traveling fellowship of the American Academy of Arts and Letters. Travels in Europe August–October. Works on *Mercy Street* with Ford Foundation grant for residence at Charles Playhouse, Boston. Moves to 14 Black Oak Road, Weston, in December.

1964   *Selected Poems,* London.

1965   Elected a Fellow of the Royal Society of Literature. Summer, awarded a travel grant from the Congress for Cultural Freedom.

1966   Attempts suicide in July. Travels in Africa with her husband on grant from Congress for Cultural Freedom, August–September. Begins work on novel, never completed. Fall, *Live or Die*. Breaks her hip on thirty-eighth birthday, 9 November.

1967   January, appointed lecturer at Boston University. May, *Live or Die* awarded Pulitzer Prize for Poetry. July, attends International Poetry Festival in London.

1968   Receives honorary Phi Beta Kappa from Harvard. July, forms rock group Anne Sexton and Her Kind. Fall, begins teaching poetry at McLean Hospital.

1969   February, *Love Poems*. Spring, works on "Mercy Street" at American Place Theater, New York. Receives Guggenheim Fellowship and honorary Phi Beta Kappa from Radcliffe. Begins teaching Oberlin College poetry workshop.

1970   Receives honorary doctorate of letters from Tufts University. Attempts suicide.

1971   *Transformations.*

1972   Receives honorary doctorate of letters from Fairfield University. Becomes full professor at Boston University;

holds Crashaw Chair in Literature at Colgate University. 9 November, *The Book of Folly.*

1973 Receives honorary doctorate of letters from Regis College. Serves on Pulitzer Prize jury. February, asks husband for divorce, which is granted in November. 5 May, attends opening of Minnesota Opera Co.'s production of *Transformations.* Is hospitalized for emotional disturbance.

1974 February, *The Death Notebooks.* Dies 4 October.

1975 February, *The Awful Rowing toward God.*

1976 *45 Mercy Street.*

1978 *Words for Dr. Y.*

1981 *The Complete Poems.*

Chapter One
A Poet's Life: A Story

Anne Sexton begins *The Awful Rowing toward God,* the last volume she prepared for publication, with a poem called "Rowing," in which she reviews the events of her life. "A story, a story!" is the poem's opening line.[1] Her life indeed becomes a story, which she tells over and over again throughout her creative work. Anne Sexton believed that the most interesting poetry was written out of personal experience; from the beginning of her career as a poet, Sexton's creative impulse grew from the "need to make form from [the] chaos" of her own biographical and psychological realities.[2] In considering the work of Anne Sexton, then, whose poems so often allude to and evoke personal experience to weave their meaning, one naturally turns to the events of her life. Readers of Sexton's poetry find themselves naming Sexton herself as the speaker of many poems and often find if difficult to discuss subject and theme without referring to her biographical data. For those reasons, even a brief examination of the events of Sexton's life begins to illuminate one's understanding of her work. Indeed, studies of her life and of her work augment one another, since for Sexton, biography and textual analysis are often mutually illuminating.

Childhood and Adolescence

The poet Anne Sexton was born Anne Gray Harvey on November 9, 1928, in Newton, Massachusetts, to Mary Gray Staples and Ralph Churchill Harvey. Her family had been prominent in New England for many years; her maternal great-uncle, Nelson Dingley, had been speaker of the Maine House of Representatives and governor of Maine; his sister, her maternal great-aunt Anna Ladd Dingley, had had a career as a newspaper editor; her mother's father, Arthur Gray Staples, had been editor-in-chief of the *Lewiston* (Maine) *Evening Journal*; her paternal grandfather had been president of the Wellesley (Massachusetts) National Bank. Anne Gray Harvey's mother, who was born in Auburn, Maine, and attended Wellesley College, had intended to be a writer but gave that ambition up when she married Anne's father in 1922. Anne's father, who was from Chelsea, Massachusetts, owned a successful woolen business at the time of Anne's birth. This family, with its long New England tradition, was to become an important motif in Anne Sexton's poetry, as we see, for example, in "Funnel":

> The family story tells, and it was told true,
> of my great-grandfather who begat eight
> genius children and bought twelve almost new
> grand pianos. He left a considerable estate
> when he died. The children honored their
> separate arts; two became moderately famous,
> three married and fattened their delicate share
> of wealth and brilliance. The sixth one was
> a concert pianist. She had a notable career
> and wore cropped hair and walked like a man,
> or so I heard when prying a childhood ear
> into the hushed talk of the straight Maine clan.
> . . . .
> Back from that great-grandfather I have come
> to puzzle a bending gravestone for his sake,
> to question this diminishing and feed a minimum
> of children their careful slice of suburban cake.[3]

"This diminishing" is a major theme for Sexton as well. As Diana Hume George points out, "Sexton speaks here not only of her own heritage but of the diminishing resonance of the American myth itself, one created by (and for) fathers."[4]

Together with her two sisters (Jane, born in 1923, and Blanche, born in 1925), Anne Gray Harvey grew up in the Boston suburbs, living first in Cambridge, then in Wellesley, and then in Weston, Massachusetts. Linda Gray Sexton (Anne's daughter and literary executor, and an editor of Anne's *Letters*) and Lois Ames report on the family's domestic comfort: "The Harvey residence in Weston was . . . spacious. The new house glinted with huge windows and a long terraced green lawn spread from the corner of the fourth garage down to the very edge of the street. Its four stories were complete with maids', cook's, and butler's quarters" (*L,* 4). In the summer, the Harvey family often traveled to the Maine seacoast to be with Mary Gray Staples Harvey's relatives. There were seven large summer houses on Squirrel Island, near Boothbay Harbor, where the Harveys, Dingleys, and Stapleses gathered.

Although Anne's memories of these summers were "happy," as her editors tell us in the *Letters* (*L,* 4), many of her growing years in Boston were more difficult. She was, say Sexton and Ames, "a demanding child":

"It was hard to be Anne's friend," Blanche recalls, "all of her followers were of the slave variety." Even at this early age, she created her own dramatic works and cast herself in the starring roles. Often a source of family irritation, she was forever leaping from room to room with one purpose in mind—to be noticed. Her parents threw up their hands at Anne's pranks. . . . Constantly defying adult authority, she ate cake in her bedroom, threw rotten apples at the ceiling, and rummaged through Blanche's dresser drawers in secret. (*L,* 4, 5)

At an early age, she apparently had established a flamboyant, willful pattern of behavior that reappeared throughout her life. She had also developed a view of herself as outcast and unwanted. "At six," wrote Sexton in a 1963 poem, "I lived in a graveyard full of dolls": "I will speak of the little childhood cruelties, / being a third child, / and last given / . . . / being the unwanted, the mistake. . . ."[5]

From the evidence of her poems, it seems clear that Anne's closest confidante and friend during these early years and into her young adulthood was not a parent or a sister but her great-aunt Anna Dingley, for whom Anne was named. "Nana," as Anne called her, spent long visits at the Sexton home through Anne's childhood. One of the greatest tragedies of Sexton's life was Nana's death in 1954, at eighty-six years of age, after having suffered for years from senility (or madness, as Sexton interprets the ailment in many poems). As Sexton comments in a 1958 letter, "My Nana went crazy when I was thirteen. . . . At the time I blamed myself for her going because she lived with our family and was my only friend" (*L,* 41). One of the principal motifs in Anne Sexton's poetry is her guilt and sense of loss at the departure of Nana: "I knew you forever and you were always old, / soft white lady of my heart" (*TB,* 13).

Anne Gray Harvey attended public school in Wellesley from first through tenth grade. When she was seventeen, she was sent to Rogers Hall, a boarding school for girls in Lowell, Massachusetts; she graduated in 1947 and then, in the fall of that year when she was nineteen, she entered The Garland School in Boston, a finishing school for women. Throughout her school years, Anne was energetic and flirtatious; according to Linda Gray Sexton and Lois Ames, "her classmates remember her as happy, vivacious, and popular, but underneath, she later claimed, lurked exquisite pain which found an outlet in her role as the class rogue" (*L, 6*). She successfully sought the attention of many boyfriends, sometimes to the detriment of her schoolwork. The editors of Sexton's *Letters* report that "Although her carelessness and lack of attention were the qualities most often mentioned by her various teachers, many of her report cards remarked on her verbal ability and intellectual agility as well" (*L, 6*). Anne started writing poetry at Rogers Hall, but apparently gave up the endeavor temporarily when her mother, who also wrote poetry, saw one of Anne's works and accused her of plagiarizing Sara Teasdale ("a notion later confirmed wrong," says Diana Hume George).[6]

Marriage

In the summer of 1948, when Anne was nineteen, she met and married Alfred Muller Sexton II, a sophomore premedical student at Colgate University. Anne and "Kayo," as he was called, met in July. In August, they eloped, leaving on the fourteenth for North Carolina; they were married in Sunbury, North Carolina, on the sixteenth and spent a week-long honeymoon in Virginia Beach.

For the next five years, the couple moved frequently. After returning to Massachusetts, they moved to Hamilton, New York, so that Kayo could continue his undergraduate studies at Colgate. By the late fall of that year, however, the newlyweds found themselves in a difficult financial situation (Sexton and Ames tell us that "Kayo could no longer tolerate their financial dependence on his parents" [*L, 21*]), and so Kayo left Colgate and the couple moved back to Massachusetts, finding an apartment after several months in Cochituate. There, Anne went to work in a bookstore, Kayo in a woolen firm (a job found for him by Anne's father). In 1950, following the onset of the Korean War, Kayo joined the Naval Reserves and was sent to Baltimore; Anne joined him there in November, but returned to Massachusetts in May 1951 when Kayo's ship, the aircraft carrier *Boxer*, left port. Back in Massachusetts, Anne lived alternately with her parents and with the Sextons, supporting herself by modeling for the Hart Agency in Boston. In 1952 she drove to San Francisco to join Kayo, whose ship was docked there for repairs; when Kayo's ship sailed, she returned, now pregnant, to Weston to live with her parents.

On 21 July 1953 Anne gave birth to her and Kayo's first child, Linda Gray Sexton, at the Newton-Wellesley Hospital, where Anne had also been born. Kayo was still in San Francisco, waiting for his discharge papers. By the account of Sexton and Ames, "Motherhood was overwhelming." Anne had found childbirth horrifying and later avoided discussing it" (*L,* 22). A month later, in August, Anne and Kayo purchased a house at 40 Clearwater Road, in Newton Lower Falls, where they were to live for the next eleven years. Kayo now worked in the Sexton woolen business.

For the next two years, Anne suffered several serious emotional setbacks. Sexton and Ames report that during this period Anne "was intermittently hospitalized at Westwood Lodge, in Westwood, Massachusetts, for attempted suicide. Kayo's mother took charge of Linda" (*L,* 22). Equally devastating for Anne was the death in July 1954 of her Nana, Anna Ladd Dingley. This was a loss that she never resolved and that she was to explore again and again in her poetry.

Anne Sexton's second child, Joyce Ladd Sexton, was born on 4 August 1955. According to Sexton and Ames, "Anne was unprepared for the responsibility of another infant, an inquisitive two-year-old, a household, and a husband. . . . Her anger and concomitant depression deepened" (*L,* 22–23). In March 1956 Sexton was again admitted to a mental hospital; Linda was sent to live with her Harvey grandparents, and Joyce went to live with the Sextons. When Anne returned home several months later, Linda returned as well, but Joyce remained with the Sextons for three years and, according to Sexton and Ames, "ceased to recognize Anne as her mother" (*L,* 23). On 9 November 1956 Anne attempted suicide. In December she began seeing a new psychiatrist, Dr. Martin Orne ("Dr. Sidney Martin"), who encouraged her to write poetry. In many poems, Anne refers to Joyce's early separation from her; in "The Double Image," for instance, recalling "The time I did not love / myself," she addresses her child:

> Today, my small child, Joyce,
> love your self's self where it lives.
> There is no special God to refer to; or if there is,
> why did I let you grow
> in another place. You did not know my voice
> when I came back to call. . . .
>
> (*TB,* 54)

In the next two years Anne Sexton became a poet. In September 1957 she enrolled in a poetry seminar at Boston University taught by

John Holmes. There she met Maxine Kumin, establishing a friendship that lasted for the rest of her life. With the support of this seminar, of Kumin, and of her psychiatrist (who recognized, according to Sexton and Ames, "that her therapy progressed as she began to discover and appreciate her talents" [*L,* 29]), she worked energetically on her poetry, often using material from her psychiatric sessions. Between early 1957 and the spring of 1959, she composed the poems that were to appear in her first volume, publishing a number of them in literary magazines. In 1958 she received a scholarship to attend the Antioch Summer Writers' Conference in August, where she studied with W. D. Snodgrass. In September of the same year she was accepted into Robert Lowell's poetry seminar at Boston University, where she met, among the other students, Sylvia Plath and George Starbuck.

During these early years of her career, Sexton experienced personal tragedy along with her professional success. She checked herself in and out of mental institutions, which she called her "summer hotel" and later her "sealed hotel." Her mother was suffering from breast cancer and died on 10 March 1959. Three months later, on 3 June, her father died of a cerebral hemorrhage. Sexton begins her poem "The Truth the Dead Know" with this stanza:

> Gone, I say and walk from church,
> refusing the stiff procession to the grave,
> letting the dead ride alone in the hearse.
> It is June. I am tired of being brave.[7]

Sexton's guilt over these events was to be explored in her poetry and in her letters for years to come: "I am depressed," she wrote in a 1958 letter. "My mother is dying of cancer. My mother says I gave her cancer" (*L,* 40). Her father had revealed to a disapproving Anne his plan to remarry after her mother's death, but he had died before the marriage could take place. Sexton recalls these events in "All My Pretty Ones":

> This year, solvent but sick, you meant
> to marry that pretty widow in a one-month rush.
> But before you had that second chance, I cried
> on your fat shoulder. Three days later you died.
> (*PO,* 5)

In August 1959 Sexton received the Robert Frost Fellowship to attend the Bread Loaf Writers Conference. But in October she contracted pneumonia and underwent surgery to remove her appendix and an ovary, wondering for a time whether she, too, had cancer. The experience provides the occasion for her poem "The Operation":

> After the sweet promise,
> the summer's mild retreat
> from mother's cancer, the winter months of her death,
> I come to this white office, . . .
>
> . . . .
>
> to hear the almost mighty doctor over me equate
> my ills with hers
> and decide to operate.
>
> (*PO,* 12)

Anne Sexton's first volume of poetry, *To Bedlam and Part Way Back,* was accepted by Houghton Mifflin on May 19, 1959, and published in March 1960.

The pattern of professional success, personal tragedy, and emotional difficulty characterized the rest of Anne Sexton's life. In the same month that saw the publication of her first volume of poetry Sexton's father-in-law was killed in an automobile accident. "So many dead," she wrote that month in a letter. "I am tired. But I continue. I am not well yet. But hope I'll make it" (*L,* 101–102). Her second volume of poetry, named *All My Pretty Ones* to commemorate her dead family members, was published in the fall of 1962 and nominated for the National Book Award the following year. In the winter of 1963 she was awarded the first traveling fellowship of the American Academy of Arts and Letters, and in August 1963 she left on a tour of Europe with her neighbor, Sandy Robart. The grant provided her with a stipend to travel for a full year; she returned home, however, after three months, homesick and depressed. About Sylvia Plath's suicide in early 1963, Sexton wrote: "she had the suicide inside her. As I do. As many of us do. But, if we're lucky, we don't get away with it and something or someone forces us to live" (*L,* 261). In December Anne and Kayo moved to a new house at 14 Black Oak Road in Weston. Her *Selected Poems* was published in London in 1964, and in the following year she was elected a Fellow of the Royal Society of Literature.

In the summer of 1965 the Congress for Cultural Freedom awarded Sexton a travel grant, and she and Kayo decided to use it to go on a

safari in Africa the following summer. Linda Gray Sexton and Lois
Ames tell us that "for her husband the safari equaled the fantasy [of
the dream of his childhood], but Anne found it horrible: flies, dirt,
and endless blood" (L, 297). In July 1966 Sexton again attempted
suicide but nevertheless left in August with Kayo for Africa. She
wrote, just before embarking, "I know I'm crazy but knowing doesn't
help. Dr. Deitz wishes I wouldn't try to go to Africa now but it's all
set. Can't back out" (L, 298). The safari experience is frequently al-
luded to in Sexton's poetry, especially of this period. She writes, for
instance, in "Loving the Killer":

> Though I only carried a camera,
> love came after the gun,
> after the kill,
> ....
> While Saedi, a former cannibal,
> served from the left
> ....
> I vomited behind the dining tent.[8]

The Sextons returned to Weston in September after a visit to Italy.

   At about this time Sexton began work on a novel, which she never
finished and which she deprecatingly called "just a woman's story, another woman's story and so what" (L, 349). On her thirty-eighth birthday—9 November 1966—she fell down the stairs at her home and
broke her hip, an experience that provides part of the occasion for her
poem "The Break": "So I fell apart. So I came all undone. / Yes" (LP,
23).

   Live or Die, Sexton's third volume of poetry, was published in the
fall of 1966 and in May 1967 was awarded the Pulitzer Prize for Poetry.
In the previous six years she had received significant recognition for
her work and many awards; she had, for instance, taught at Radcliffe
College and at Harvard University, been awarded the Levinson Prize
from *Poetry* magazine, and been awarded a Ford Foundation grant to
work on a play at the Charles Playhouse in Boston. In July 1967, at
the invitation of Ted Hughes (Plath's husband), she attended the International Poetry Festival in London. According to Linda Gray Sexton
and Lois Ames, "Suicide ceased to be a daily threat [for Anne Sexton]
between 1967 and 1970" (L, 313). In the winter of 1969–70, she
began work on some new kinds of poems, her "transformations from

the Brothers Grimm" (*L*, 352). Sexton was quick to assure a corre-
spondent, however, that "it would further be a lie to say that [these
poems] weren't about me, because they are just as much about me as
my other poetry" (*L*, 362). These poems, Sexton said, were "strange";
"they are kind of a dark, dark laughter. They are very modern. . . .
It's about time I showed some signs of humor" (*L*, 365). She had actually shown a great deal of wry humor in her earlier work and would
continue to do so; one salient characteristic of many Sexton poems is
the straight, sensible voice that lends a hint of absurdity to the poems'
treatment of their subjects. The humor in these "transformations"
works in much the same way, with perhaps a darker and more absurd
emphasis.

Her professional success continued, as Sexton and Ames report: she
received "an honorary Phi Beta Kappa from Harvard in 1968 and Radcliffe in 1969; a Guggenheim Fellowship in 1969; honorary doctorates
of letters from Tufts University in 1970, Fairfield University in 1972,
and Regis College in 1973" (*L*, 313). In the fall of 1968 she began
teaching a poetry class at McLean Hospital in Belmont, Massachusetts,
and in the winters of 1969 and 1970 she taught a poetry workshop for
Oberlin College students. In January 1967 she was appointed a lecturer
at Boston University and, as Sexton and Ames tell us, "she continued
teaching in the graduate creative writing program with George Starbuck, John Barth, and John Malcolm Brinnin until her death in 1974"
(*L*, 349). *Love Poems*, her fourth volume of poetry, was published on
13 February 1969, and that spring she traveled back and forth to the
American Place Theater in New York to complete work on her play
(never published), "Mercy Street." Her fifth volume of poetry, *Transformations*, was published in 1971, and Sexton attended the opening of
the Minnesota Opera Company's production of *Transformations* on 5
May 1973.

The Final Years

In a 1970 letter Anne Sexton wrote, "Yes, it is time to think about
Christ again. I keep putting it off. If he is the God/man, I would feel
a hell of a lot better" (*L*, 368). This was the direction of Sexton's work
between 1970 and 1974, clearly evident in the last three volumes Sexton wrote and prepared for publication: *The Book of Folly*, published on
9 November 1972; *The Death Notebooks*, published in February 1974;
and *The Awful Rowing toward God*, published posthumously in February
1975. The familiar themes of Sexton's previous poetry pervade these

volumes, as one might expect; here we see, as before, poetic consider-
ations of death, particularly the deaths of the poet's close family members (her mother, father, and great-aunt) and of the poet herself; of
guilt over the lives and deaths of those people; of love for husband and
daughters and, I suspect, for others as well; and of anger, especially
toward certain men, chief among them the psychiatrist and the deserting lover. But here we see as well the amplification of a theme that has
been less evident in the earlier work than it becomes here: the theme
of the search for God.

The theme if clearly stated in "Gods," the opening poem of *The
Death Notebooks:*

> Mrs. Sexton went out looking for the gods.
> She began looking in the sky—
> ....
> No one.
> ....
> Then she journeyed back to her own house
> and the gods of the world were shut in the lavatory
>
> At last!
> she cried out,
> and locked the door.[9]

One of the epigraphs to *The Awful Rowing toward God* is a quote from
Kierkegaard: "But above all do not make yourself important by doubting" (*AR,* vi). Although there are notable exceptions, the thematic
weight of these late poems points to Sexton's hope of abandoning
doubt, and indeed to her occasional success in accomplishing that aim.
She most often seems death-directed, but death often represents the
beginning of new life.

Anne Sexton spent the last year of her life as a single woman, having
asked her husband in February 1973 for a divorce. In this she acted,
say Linda Gray Sexton and Lois Ames, "against the advice of her psychiatrist and many of her friends," and "Kayo contested the divorce
until its bitter end in November, convinced that Anne was acting precipitously" (*L,* 389). In fact, the evidence of many of Sexton's last
poems suggests that she herself held ambivalent attitudes toward this
divorce.

Sexton was admitted to McLean Hospital during this last year, suffering still from depression. She wrote poems furiously, especially those

collected in *The Awful Rowing toward God.* "Her life," observe Sexton and Ames, "rapidly spiraled inward." Although she continued to teach and to give guest lectures at universities, "she gave fewer readings, saw fewer friends, used fewer worksheets—blotting out all but the essentials" (*L,* 391). In "The Rowing Endeth," the closing poem of *The Awful Rowing toward God,* the last volume that Sexton planned, prepared, and sent to the publisher, she writes:

> I'm mooring my rowboat
> at the dock of the island called God.
> ....
> "It's okay," I say to myself,
> ....
> I empty myself from my wooden boat
> and onto the flesh of The Island.
> (*AR,* 85)

On Friday, 4 October 1974, at 40 Black Oak Road in Weston, Massachusetts, Anne Sexton ended her life.

Chapter Two

To Bedlam and Part Way Back

"The Courage to Make a Clean Breast of It in Face of
Every Question"

The volume *To Bedlam and Part Way Back* contains poems that Anne
Sexton composed, revised, and sent to various journals for publication
between 1957 and 1959. As she commented in one of her letters, the
period of time in which all the *Bedlam* poems were written and accepted for publication was exactly "2 years and four months" (*L*, 78),
from early 1957 to the spring of 1959. Houghton Mifflin accepted
Sexton's first volume on 19 May 1959, and it appeared in March 1960.

These were years when Anne Sexton was preoccupied with learning
her craft and finding her own voice. She had written some poems during her school years, and now, after her marriage and the birth of her
two daughters, she turned to writing with renewed energy. She enrolled in poetry seminars taught by John Holmes and Robert Lowell
at Boston University and by W. D. Snodgrass at an Antioch Summer
Writers' Conference. She developed friendships and talked about poetry
with George Starbuck, Sylvia Plath, Maxine Kumin, Nolan Miller,
and Carolyn Kizer.

Encouragement from her psychiatrist, Martin Orne, ("Doctor Sidney
Martin"), contributed to her newfound commitment; "Doctor Martin"
considered Sexton's writing good therapy. During the years when she
worked on the poems in the *Bedlam* volume, Sexton saw her psychiatrist regularly and was hospitalized frequently for depression, usually
admitting herself to an institution that she called her "summer hotel"
or her "sealed hotel" for several days or weeks at a time. And the poems
finally collected in this volume were, as Sexton herself observed, "all
about my own madness" (*L*, 80).

Bedlam provides the setting for several of these poems, a bedlam
that is at times actual (whether remembered or anticipated) and at
times symbolic. One has the sense that, for Sexton in this poetry, madness and honesty are inextricably linked, that the impulse to write

honestly at any cost is both a felt need and a positive value. Such an impetus may have its origin in the motion of poem-as-therapy encouraged by her psychiatrist. But it clearly becomes, as she writes more and more poems, an emotional, psychological, and aesthetic imperative. In a 1959 letter to W. D. Snodgrass, Sexton says that she is "just writing what I can, what I *have* to. My stuff is always just what is actually going on. I can't make it up any different" (*L,* 54).

Making a Clean Breast of It

There is a sense of mission bound up in the notion of writing what she has to, a mission that the poet is at once incapable of refusing, glad to pursue, and reluctant to accept. The quotation from Schopenhauer that Sexton chose for the volume's epigraph emphasizes the point:

It is the courage to make a clean breast of it in face of every question that makes the philosopher. He must be like Sophocles' Oedipus, who, seeking enlightenment concerning his terrible fate, pursues his indefatigable enquiry, even when he divines that appalling horror awaits him in the answer. But most of us carry in our heart the Jocasta who begs Oedipus for God's sake not to inquire further. (*TB,* epigraph)

The poet Sexton's role, like the philosopher's, is to seek enlightenment at any cost, at the cost of disapproval, disaffection, madness, death. But the poet also has a bit of Jocasta in her who whispers that the effort is not worth the cost. One may speculate as well that the Jocasta whom the poet carries in her heart speaks also in the person of her family, her friends, and her colleagues.

In fact, the poem "For John, Who Begs Me Not to Enquire Further" iterates the importance Sexton places on writing what she has to. According to the editors of Sexton's *Letters,* John Holmes, Sexton's first mentor, "did not approve of her candor. Early in 1959 he expressed doubts about [the] public confessions" evident in the poems of her *Bedlam* volume, "warning her against exposing both herself and her family" (*L,* 58). In response to this warning, Sexton composed first the poem "For John, Who Begs Me Not to Enquire Further" and then a letter to Holmes. And a few days later, in a letter to W. D. Snodgrass, she wrote, "I am about to write an article in defense of sincere poetry. . . . I guess because I am starting to get attacked on my kind of poetry. I guess this always happens when you do something out of the norm. John Holmes thinks my book is unseemly, too personal, tho talented. So I have been firing the burners in defense of myself" (*L,* 62).

And so this poem, with the volume's epigraph, provides a credo for the *Bedlam* collection and indeed for Sexton's entire oeuvre:

> Not that it was beautiful,
> but that, in the end, there was
> a certain sense of order there;
> something worth learning
> in that narrow diary of my mind,
> in the commonplaces of the asylum
>
> ....
> There ought to be something special
> for someone
> in this kind of hope.
>
>   (*TB,* 51–52)

These, then, are some principal themes of this volume: the "commonplaces of the asylum"; the "sense of order" that can be derived, at least tentatively, from discovering "something worth learning"; the jottings and recordings of the "narrow diary" of the poet's mind. In many of the poems, too, there is "hope," the hope of having found the road part way back after visiting bedlam. And usually, finding the way back comes as a result of having been sincere. Confessional candor provides the key to the discovery of order and meaning or, as Robert Frost put it, to a "momentary stay against confusion." Paradoxically, "mak[ing] a clean breast of it" and "seeking enlightenment" at any cost, even though it may lead to the discovery of a "terrible fate," is the only route to salvation.

"Kind Sir: These Woods" describes the process. The poem's epigraph, a quotation from *Walden,* announces a biblical theme used by other poets as well (among them Robert Frost in "Directive" and Richard Wilbur in "Digging for China"): "For a man needs only to be turned around once with his eyes shut in this world to be lost. . . . Not til we are lost . . . do we begin to find ourselves" (*TB,* 5). The poem's speaker addresses Thoreau ("Kind Sir") as she remembers a childhood game that involved spinning around with her eyes closed, and then, having become dizzy, opening her eyes to see a strange and different landscape. It was a wishing game, the player wishing hard for something as she spun, hoping her wish would come true in her new, dizzy world. The poem's first stanza, comprising four quatrains rhymed *a b a b, c d c d, e f e f, c c g g,* establishes the setting and describes the playing of the game. The second (and last) stanza draws a conclusion:

> Kind Sir: Lost and of your same kind
> I have turned around twice with eyes sealed
> and the woods were white and my night mind
> saw such strange happenings, untold and unreal.
> And opening my eyes, I am afraid of course
> to look—this inward look that society scorns—
> Still, I search in these woods and find nothing worse
> than myself, caught between the grapes and the thorns.
>
> (*TB*, 5)

The speaker has left her familiar landscape; spinning with her eyes closed, she has become dizzy and lost in a nightmare world. And she is now afraid to reopen her eyes for fear that the nightmare has become reality. But the mature speaker's compulsion to "make a clean breast of it," her search for order and meaning, require that she look directly at whatever is there. The child's look outward toward the landscape, reopening her eyes after spinning, becomes the "inward look that society scorns" of the poet. And it is that which saves her. The landscape that she sees is nothing worse than the woods that were there before, nothing worse than her familiar self. Such a conclusion offers a "kind of hope," as Sexton writes in "For John, Who Begs Me Not to Enquire Further": "This is something I would never find/in a lovelier place, my dear" (*TB*, 52). The place of this poem, "Kind Sir," is woods, and the woods have thorns in them. There are probably old, dead branches and mosquitoes and patches of swampy ground as well. But they are her woods; they are her landscape. And there are grapes there too; there is cool, sweet fruit. There is, in fact, hope that the inward look will help to point the way back from bedlam.

If "Kind Sir: These Woods" describes the process of searching for order and hope, it also exemplifies the sort of development in most of these *Bedlam* poems. As we have seen, Sexton presents the materials of "Kind Sir" in a two-part, two-stanza structure, the first stanza establishing the setting and the dramatic situation of playing the children's game and the second stanza drawing the mature conclusion. In a 1959 letter to Nolan Miller, Sexton comments on her preference for this type of organization: "I do have a feeling for stories, for plot, and maybe the dramatic situation. I really prefer dramatic situations to anything

else. Most poets have a thought that they dress in . . . imagery. . . .
But I prefer people in a situation, in a doing, a scene, a losing or a
gain, and then, in the end, find the thought (the thought I didn't
know I had until I wrote the story)" (*L,* 61).

Additionally, "Kind Sir," with its reference to the "inward look that
society scorns," reflects Sexton's determination to write her "kind of
poetry" and simultaneously a certain defensiveness about doing so.
John Holmes was perhaps not alone in warning Sexton against the
confessional quality of her poems. To be sure, some of these *Bedlam*
poems present themes that were no doubt shocking at the time of
writing, dealing with such material as madness, abortion, the birth of
an illegitimate child, and suicide. As Sexton says in a 1969 letter, "The
stuff I write is so controversial. NO ONE WILL LIKE IT" (*L,* 68).
But as she points out as well in another letter, "The difference between
confession and poetry? is after all, art" (*L,* 44).

Bedlam

Five poems deal directly and literally with bedlam, with finding
order there, and with at least the limited hope that the order can be
carried back into the outside world. The opening poem of the volume,
"You, Doctor Martin" (*TB,* 3–4), introduces much of the thematic and
technical material of the poems to follow. It explores the nature of the
"summer hotel," evoking its sounds and sensations, describing its rou-
tines, and tracing its conflicts, frustrations, and hopes. The poem also
suggests a way back, or at least part of a way.

We find here a kind of ruminative dramatic monologue; the speaker,
a woman patient in a psychiatric hospital, addresses her doctor:

> You, Doctor Martin, walk
> from breakfast to madness. Late August,
> I speed through the antiseptic tunnel
> where the moving dead still talk
> of pushing their bones against the thrust
> of cure. And I am queen of this summer hotel
> or the laughing bee on a stalk
>
> of death.

The prominent placement of the verb "walk" at the end of the first
line, together with the following juxtaposition of "breakfast" with

"madness," suggest both Doctor Martin's involvement in this scene and his distance from it. No inmate himself, he has breakfast first, somewhere in the outside world, and then he walks to the place where his patients are. He is an authority figure ("Doctor") who has perspective, who is composed (he "walks"), sane, and in control. The speaker, on the other hand, is characterized by contrast with Doctor Martin. She has no name. Her motion is "speed," a word that connects, by means of internal rhyme, with "queen" in line 6 and "bee" in line 7, to suggest the brittle meaninglessness of her position in this "antiseptic tunnel" among the "moving dead." The end rhymes "walk," "talk," and "stalk" contrast Doctor Martin's purposeful action ("walk") with the lassitude and immobility of the patients ("talk") and with the frenetic but directionless activity of the speaker, who, speeding around, is a "laughing bee on a stalk/of death." The enjambment emphasizes the word "death."

One thing to note about this poem (and about the majority of poems in this volume) is its traditional structure. Clearly whatever private materials are expressed here have been ordered and worked into strict form. "You, Doctor Martin" comprises six seven-line stanzas, each with the diagonal left margin that we have seen in the first stanza, each with the end rhyme *a b c a b c b* (except for the first stanza, which employ the slight variation *a b c a b c a*). Throughout the poem as in the first stanza, end rhymes and internal rhymes enhance the sense. Enjambments surprise us and dramatize the meaning. The rhythm is basically iambic; the occasional spondee ("I speed") demands attention.

Thematically, the speaker sets herself apart from the other patients, since she is from the outset both a member of the "moving dead" and one who "speed[s]." She observes that "we stand in broken / lines and wait while they unlock / the door." Like the others, she is given therapeutic work to do—making moccasins. Unlike the others, however, she has seen herself from the beginning as "queen of this summer hotel," and her ability to place herself above the other patients in this way prefigures her slow movement back to health. By the final stanza she has become "queen of all my sins / forgotten." "Now," she says, "I am myself."

"Am I still lost?" asks the speaker in the closing stanza. Throughout the poem, she has been lost, one of the damned who stands "in broken lines . . . at the frozen gates of dinner," who is given "no knives/for cutting your throat," who eats mechanically and makes moccasins with her hands, absentmindedly. Lostness here, as elsewhere, involves a flawed or diminished sense of self. In this poem we are told nothing of how the speaker has become lost; but we do learn, as the speaker herself learns, how she may begin to find herself.

Doctor Martin helps; his presence is felt among the patients even when he is absent. His "third eye" sees them always, or so they feel, encouraging and controlling their behavior, lighting "the separate boxes where we sleep or cry." The speaker and her fellow inmates are his "children," and under his tutelage, the speaker "grow[s] most tall / in the best ward."

The closing stanza offers hope. The speaker has learned that self-acceptance must be founded more on inner strength than on outward appearance, that lasting security must not depend upon beauty and glamour. "Once I was beautiful. Now I am myself." She remains in the hospital, however, "counting this row and that row of moccasins / waiting on the silent shelf." Repeating the queen imagery of the first stanza, the speaker now claims that "I am queen of all my sins / forgotten." Yet there is meaningful ambiguity in this sentence: when reading it, shall we pause after "all"? If so, the speaker's success is far from assured, since the implication is that she has triumphed over this present difficulty only by repressing the problems that had sent her to the hospital in the first place. Or shall we, when reading that sentence, pause in the more traditional place, at the end of the line, after "sins"? In this case, the speaker's emotional gains are more substantial, for she has dealt with repressed material, with "forgotten sins," and has emerged triumphant, a queen. The ambiguity is, I believe, intentional, for some uncertainty seems meant to remain. This sentence is followed by the question: "Am I still lost?"

"You, Doctor Martin" offers at least qualified affirmation, then, and shows the road at least "part way back" from bedlam. The speaker has temporarily conquered her difficulties, accepted herself as the woman she is, become a queen. This conclusion is reinforced by the poem's time perspective. Typically, many poems in this volume offer two voices in the person of one speaker: one voice that is involved in the dramatic situation of the moment, and another voice that describes the experience from a later point in time, when she has achieved fuller understanding of it. When the speaker of "You, Doctor Martin" claims, at the poem's close, that "now I am myself," we may assume that "now" designates both the near-end of the hospital stay and the later time of the poem's composition.

Many poems in *To Bedlam and Part Way Back* extend motifs that we see in "You, Doctor Martin": the outside male authority figure; the patient as prisoner, as one of the damned, and as one of the "moving dead"; the patient as alternately childlike, simpleminded, bewildered, and angry; and, above all, the speaker's sense of loss. Further, as Diana Hume George observes, the "tightly condensed father-god figure of 'You, Doctor Martin' fragments into his component parts in subsequent poems of *Bedlam,* becoming father, great-grandfather, Apollo, and, in a transcultural and quasi-mythic incarnation, a dead Arabian father buried with his daughter."[1]

There are four additional poems in this volume that clearly employ the mental hospital as a setting. Unlike "You, Doctor Martin," however, which exemplifies the meaning of the volume's entire title in that it both explores the experience of bedlam and suggests the way back from it, these other poems focus only on a particular aspect of bedlam. Like "You, Doctor Martin," however, these poems are typical of this volume in their traditional structure and in their use of a speaker who is both involved in the poem's experience and reflecting upon it from a distance.

"Music Swims Back to Me" (*TB,* 8–9) recreates the consciousness of speaker-as-patient. The speaker is childlike, lost in the dark of the asylum, and trying to find the way home. She speaks in the vocabulary and cadences of a child:

> Wait Mister. Which way is home?
> . . . .
> La la la, Oh music swims back to me
> and I can feel the tune they played
> the night they left me
> in this private institution on a hill.
>
> (*TB,* 8)

"Mister" is an authority figure who offers the guidance and perspective that at least potentially can aid the speaker in finding "home." Yet in this poem, in contrast to the psychiatrist in "You, Doctor Martin," he fails to fulfill that potential. At the poem's opening, the speaker, bewildered, can find "no sign posts." She is so disoriented that her consciousness registers only impressions. And her one recurring impression points backward, not forward, in time; it is that of the music she heard on the radio the day she was admitted.

In this poem, music is more helpful than "Mister," for it helps the speaker to remember. And memory is something, indeed is the only

thing, that the speaker can use to stay her confusion. With the help of
the music, she gains at least temporary perspective, for she can remember that "everyone here was crazy" when she first arrived.

> Imagine it. A radio playing
> and everyone here was crazy.
> I liked it and danced in a circle.
> Music pours over the sense
> and in a funny way
> music sees more than I.
> I mean it remembers better; . . .
>
> (*TB*, 8)

The experience evoked here is familiar to all of us. We know how a
sudden musical phrase, or a sound, or a smell, can remind us in a flash
of momentary recognition, of the way we felt, or of where we were,
when we heard or smelled it sometime in the past. For this poem's
speaker, the music fleetingly reminds her of her admission day. And
in the third and final fourth stanzas, the music connects briefly with
"a singing in the head," engendering images of shock-treatment therapy with its aftermath of forgetfulness.

Along with the poem's thematic emphasis on confusion and forgetfulness, its circular structure (note, as well, the word *circle* in the third-
from-last line) implies that there will be no answer to the speaker's
opening question, "Wait Mister. Which way is home?" The poem
ends, then, on an interrogative note that, referring to the music and
the circle, echoes its beginning: "Mister?"

The three other poems place the speaker even more firmly in bedlam
and even farther from the discovery of a way back, focusing on isolated
experiences and feelings. In "Noon Walk on the Asylum Lawn" (*TB*,
39), the speaker is threatened, paranoid, hearing voices. The three six-
line stanzas present three examples of this condition. In the first stanza,
"The summer sun ray / shifts through a suspicious tree. . . . It sucks
the air / and looks around for me." "The grass speaks" in the second
stanza, and "the blades extend / and reach my way." In the third line
of each stanza, italicized refrains from the Twenty-third Psalm, offered
as desperate talismans to ward off the assailing environment, interrupt
the description of the menacing landscape: "*Though I walk through the
valley of the shadow*" (stanza 1): "*I will fear no evil*" (stanza 2); "*in the
presence of mine enemies*" (stanza 3).

Through the ironic use of its title, "Lullaby" (*TB,* 41) offers a series of images to describe the speaker's slipping from consciousness after taking a sleeping pill. A nurse comes to "the TV parlor / in the best ward at Bedlam," "walks on two erasers, / padding us one by one." The image of the nurse's rubber-soled shoes is apt; they sound like erasers, and they in fact become erasers, as a pill erases consciousness. The patients, in padded cells, lose sensation as the pill takes effect. It "floats me out of myself" until the speaker's body becomes "alien" and her head "woolen." There is small comfort in such a lullaby; the speaker is reduced to being grateful for the temporary erasing of herself. Perhaps the speaker is grateful as well for the temporary erasure of the fear described in "Noon Walk on the Asylum Lawn."

Common to most of these "bedlam" poems is a childlike persona. "What large children we are," exclaims the speaker of "You, Doctor Martin." "Wait Mister," begs the lost child of "Music Swims Back to Me." Lullabies are for children, and the speaker of "Lullaby" uses short, simple, juvenile phrasing. To be mad is to be like a child, suggest these speakers. When one is in bedlam, one has no authority, no circumspection, and little or no ability to help oneself.

The poem "Ringing the Bells" (*TB,* 40) employs this childlike quality as its organizing principle, borrowing for its structure the cadences of the nursery rhyme "This is the house that Jack built." As in that nursery rhyme, there are no stanza or sentence breaks here. The poem's content concerns one of bedlam's activities, bell ringing: "And this is the way they ring / the bells in Bedlam / and this is the bell-lady . . ."

Memory and Loss

In a 1959 letter to W. D. Snodgrass, Anne Sexton confessed that "I want everyone to hold up large signs saying YOU'RE A GOOD GIRL" (*L,* 68). That desire is clearly manifested in the childlike persona of these "bedlam" poems, as is the awareness that such an attitude works counter to the speaker's drive to stay permanently out of bedlam. And yet, reading through all the poems in this volume, one infers that the past is alive even for the adult speakers, even in the act of letting it go.

On the whole, the poetry of this volume is very affecting, melancholy, and despairing; the *Part Way Back* of the title seems only seldom realized. Sexton wrote in 1969, "I rather like being slugged; to walk away from the poem with old wound reopened and . . . let the poem bruise me. Without the damn *goose* I walk away unchanged and even bored" (*L,* 69). And these poems *do* bruise. An immense sense of sadness and loss pervades nearly all of them. Whether the poems' themes concern lost friendship, lost innocence, lost love, lost time, lost connections, or lost happiness, they convey the sense that the speaker, surviving, is diminished, and that survival is not, or is barely, worth the effort.

This theme of loss is closely tied to the theme of memory, which also pervades most of the poetry of this volume. One senses that the speaker of these poems is trying to live more wholly in the present by remembering and coming to terms with the past, with only limited success. She remembers love she denied or feared to accept; she remembers people, some of them now dead, whom she failed or who might have made her present more meaningful. Through loss, the present is diminished, and memory cannot exorcise either the ghosts or the pain.

For this speaker, memory is often tinged with guilt. When Anne Sexton was a schoolgirl, her beloved great-aunt Anna Ladd Dingley became senile and was taken to a nursing home. Later, in a 1958 letter, Sexton wrote, "My Nana went crazy when I was thirteen. . . . At the time I blamed myself for her going because she lived with our family and was my only friend. Then at thirteen I kissed a boy . . . and I was so pleased with my womanhood that I told Nana I was kissed and then she went mad. . . . At thirteen, I was blameful and struck" (*L,* 41). During the writing of the *Bedlam* poems, both of Sexton's parents died, her mother in March 1959 and her father in June of the same year. About her mother's illness, she wrote in a 1958 letter, "I am depressed. My mother is dying of cancer. My mother says I gave her cancer (as though death were catching—death being the birthday that I tried to kill myself, nov. 9th 1956). Then she got cancer . . . who do we kill, which image in the mirror, the mother, ourself, our daughter?????" (*L,* 40). And the next year, she wrote in a letter, "My life is falling through a sieve . . . I'm dropping out of myself. Partly because my mother is dying now and I . . . I know it's crazy, but I feel like it is my fault. . . . My father, since his shock, is not the same; he acts about ten years old, and keeps crying and begging my mother not to die. . . . (Remember the letter I wrote you about hating her) . . . What do we do with our old hate?" (*L,* 51).

Much of the poetry in this volume, then, reflects and gives expression to the speaker's perception of a diminished present, a remembered, happier past, and a sense of guilt at having survived. Many of the poems focus on loss, whether it be the loss of Nana ("Some Foreign Letters," "Elizabeth Gone," "The Waiting Head"), or mother ("The Division of Parts"), or father ("The Bells," "The Moss of His Skin"), or innocence ("The Expatriates," "Where I Live in this Honorable House of the Laurel Tree"), or children ("Unknown Girl in the Maternity Ward"), or youthful joys ("The Kite," "Funnel," "The Road Back"), or friends ("For Johnny Pole on the Forgotten Beach," "A Story for Rose on the Midnight Flight to Boston"). If the speaker of this volume has gone *To Bedlam,* it is, at least in these poems, her guilty, "crazy" feeling of blamefulness and loss that has sent her there.

A closer look at one of these poems underlines this point and shows specifically how Sexton blends the materials of past and present to advance the themes of loss and guilt. In "Some Foreign Letters" (*TB,* 13–15), the speaker uses the life of Nana ("soft white lady of my heart") as revealed in some of her letters to express and dramatize her own present distress. Three time periods alternate here as a way of emphasizing the disconnection between memories: the youthful Nana (the Nana who wrote the letters while in Europe), the old Nana (whom the young speaker knew), and the speaker's own present time. The poem's opening line, through tone and content, introduces the middle time period; Nana is old, and the speaker is young. For a child, an older relative or parent does seem known forever, does seem "always old":

> I knew you forever and you were always old,
> soft white lady of my heart. Surely you would scold
> me for sitting up late, reading your letters,
> as if these foreign postmarks were meant for me.
> . . . .
> . . . I
> see you as a young girl in a good world still,
> writing three generations before mine. I try
> to reach into your page and breathe it back . . .
> but life is a trick, life is a kitten in a sack.
>
> (*TB,* 13)

Nana's youth is caught in an unalterable and unrecoverable past, as a kitten is trapped in a sack. Although it may seem alive in the letters, this appearance is only a trick of time, since the past is irretrievable. A kitten in a sack is a drowned kitten; Nana, or her reality as a young woman, is also dead.

The second, third, and fourth stanzas further develop the interplay of memory, contrasting the youthful, letter-writing Nana with the older Nana whom the youthful speaker knew. The second stanza's first line sets the mood and theme to follow: "This is the sack of time your death vacates." Because of this trick of time that life has played on me, observes the mature speaker, my present is poorer. The aunt is dead; the speaker has known her only as an old woman; and the aunt's death makes any further knowing, except through letters, impossible.

Additionally, in these and other stanzas, structure advances and expresses sense. The lines and phrases that describe the youthful Nana's journeys and activities are written in free verse with syllabic emphasis. Many of the sentences are complex, or compound-complex, comprising several lines, to give the impression of breathless pleasure and joyous activity: "How distant you are on your nickel-plated skates / in the skating park in Berlin, gliding past / me with your Count, while a military band / plays a Strauss waltz." Contrasted and interspersed with these long, flowing lines are short, simple declarative sentences, often containing multiple, closely spaced stresses. One of these, "The Count had a wife," calls attention to itself for thematic reasons that are worked out in the closing stanza, as do the other short sentences having to do with the Count. Even more frequently, the speaker's own memories are expressed in short sentences: "I loved you last." Or, "You were the old maid aunt who lived with us." Or, "when you were mine you wore an earphone." Or, "When you were mine they wrapped you out of here / with your best hat over your face. I cried / because I was seventeen. I am older now."

The fifth and last stanza demonstrates the ultimate irresolvability of the time contrasts that have been developed throughout the poem:

> Tonight I will learn to love you twice;
> . . . .
> Tonight I will speak up and interrupt
> your letters, warning you that wars are coming,
> that the Count will die, . . .
> . . . .
> . . . And I tell you,
> you will tip your boot feet out of that hall,
> . . . .
> . . . letting your spectacles fall
> and your hair net tangle as you stop passers-by
> to mumble your guilty love while your ears die.
>   (*TB*, 15)

The speaker already loves the old woman, the great-aunt she knew; now, by reading the letters, she has also learned to know and love the young woman the aunt had once been. Desperately, the speaker wishes that she could overcome the trick of time by warning the great-aunt of the 1890s about her future, of which the speaker has learned from the letters and from experience. But she cannot save Nana: as the first stanza declares, "life is a trick." And so neither can she save herself. Memory has emphasized the finality of loss, and the speaker is left alone in the painful present.

The phrase "guilty love" in the poem's closing line is intentionally ambiguous and exemplifies the way memory and guilt combine in these poems. On one level, the great-aunt's love is "guilty" since "the Count had a wife." On another level, however, the guilt also belongs to the speaker, who remains unable to rescue Nana from her own diminished future. And finally, on a third level, the guilt belongs to the girl who felt, and to the woman who still feels, "blameful and struck" for the much-loved great-aunt's lapse into mad, deaf senility. Both the great-aunt and the speaker remain caught in their "guilty love." There is real pathos in the speaker's realization that rather than exorcise loss and guilt, memory can only perpetuate them.

"The Double Image": Part Way Back from Bedlam

Although most of the poems of this volume appear to emphasize a present impoverished by loss and diminished by memory, one poem, perhaps the major work of the volume, shows the potential of memory to come to terms with the past in a positive way. In "The Double Image," the speaker moves beyond loss to at least qualified affirmation, and in the process the poem clearly dramatizes the entire movement named in the volume's title—not only *To Bedlam,* but also *Part Way Back.* Significantly, Sexton has commented that "I don't think I like any poem of mine [in this volume] as well as 'The Double Image'" (*L,* 72).

Sexton has called this poem "two-hundred odd lines of confession and art" (*L,* 44), and indeed its original title (the second half was deleted upon publication) was "The Double Image: A Confession." The poem takes the form of a long dramatic monologue in which a thirty-year-old mother speaks to her four-year-old daughter; it is probably valid to suggest that the mother is Sexton herself and that the daughter is Joyce. In the poem's seven sections, the mother speaks at times directly to her daughter in the present, and at other times ruminatively, her attention directed toward her own past.

The poem's occasion is the reuniting of mother and daughter after the mother's four-year absence. During this period of time, she twice attempted suicide, was hospitalized, and stayed with her own mother in an effort to recover her physical and mental health. The mother-speaker's purpose is to understand and explain those four years to herself; it is also, although incidentally, to offer explanation and love to her child. In this connection, we note Sexton's own stated intention in writing this poem: its "reason for being written," she said in a 1958 letter, is to fill "my own need to make form from chaos" (L, 43).

In the first stanza, the mother speaks to her daughter, trying to explain something that the four-year-old is still too young to comprehend and will perhaps "never really know." The speaking voice is calm and conversational; in its easy cadences we hear maturity and self-understanding.

> I am thirty this November.
> You are still small, in your fourth year.
> We stand watching the yellow leaves go queer,
> flapping in the winter rain,
> falling flat and washed. And I remember
> mostly the three autumns you did not live here.
> They said I'd never get you back again.
> I tell you what you'll never really know:
> all the medical hypothesis
> that explained my brain will never be as true as these
> struck leaves letting go.
>
> (TB, 53)

This stanza establishes a metaphor that becomes the controlling image of the poem's first section; the suicide attempts of the mother-speaker (tenor) are identified with the falling of a few last winter leaves (vehicle). As the leaves, "yellow" but tenacious to have stayed so long on the tree, "go queer, / flapping in the winter rain, / falling flat and washed," so the speaker suggests the inevitability of her own drive to attempt suicide. Like the leaves still holding on to the winter tree, she had resisted her suicidal impulses for longer than one might have expected. But like the yellow leaves, she was already dying, already condemned. As the winter rain finally forced the leaves to let go, so some force finally precipitated the speaker's "letting go." Both leaves and speaker are "struck": wounded, marked, doomed. It is interesting to recall in this context Sexton's use of the word *struck* in the 1958 letter, quoted above, in which she describes her guilt over her great-aunt's death: "At thirteen, I was blameful and struck" (*L, 41*).

The second stanza develops the meaning of the tenor of the metaphor. The mother-daughter relationship is more complex than the opening stanza implies: the force that precipitated the "letting go" was the mother's guilt, her feeling blameful for having somehow caused the daughter's infant illness. Color imagery advances the meaning as well; the mother of the first stanza may be dead like the yellow leaves, but the "ugly angels," the "witches" who plague her with guilt, are actively alive and "green":

> I, who chose two times
> to kill myself, had said your nickname
> the mewling months when you first came;
> until a fever rattled
> in your throat and I moved like a pantomime
> above your head. Ugly angels spoke to me. The blame,
> I heard them say, was mine. They tattled
> like green witches in my head, letting doom
> leak like a broken faucet;
> as if doom had flooded my belly and filled your bassinet,
> an old debt I must assume.
>
> (*TB, 53*)

End and internal rhymes reinforce and enrich the meaning, here as elsewhere in the poem. For example, "rattled" and "tattled" connect the daughter's sickness with the mother's voices of doom. "Bassinet" and "debt" connect the daughter's birth with the mother's guilt.

The third stanza recapitulates the "witches" motif, names the speaker's feeling ("guilt"), and offers further development of the controlling metaphor:

> Death was simpler than I'd thought.
> The day life made you well and whole
> I let the witches take away my guilty soul.
> I pretended I was dead
> until the white men pumped the poison out,
> putting me armless and washed through the rigamarole

of talking boxes and the electric bed.
. . . .
Today the yellow leaves
go queer. You ask me where they go. I say today believed
in itself, or else it fell.

(TB, 53–54)

Here, the daughter is well again, and the mother (having let go) experiences, along with an actual death attempt, figurative death and
resurrection. The color here is white, the whiteness both of forgetting
and of cleansing. The poison is "pumped . . . out," both literally and
figuratively; the straitjacketed ("armless") speaker is "washed" (extending the meaning of the "washed" leaves of stanza 1), connoting at once
that she is finished with one life-phase (washed out), forgetful as a
result of electroshock therapy ("electric bed"), and cleansed. So that
"today," in the poem's present time, the speaker is able to draw a
conclusion from her experience, for her daughter, thereby extending
the metaphor: Where do the leaves go? Why do people go away? Why
did I fall and leave (pun no doubt intended) you? One must believe in
oneself.

The fourth and final stanza of the poem's first section completes the
meaning of the metaphor:

Today, my small child, Joyce,
love your self's self where it lives.
There is no special God to refer to; . . .
. . . All the superlatives
of tomorrow's white tree and mistletoe
will not help you know the holidays you had to miss.
The time I did not love
myself, I visited your shoveled walks; you held my glove.
There was new snow after this.

(TB, 54)

The child is here exhorted to share her mother's insight and "love your
self's self." As the mother-speaker has learned, this is a task one must
face alone: "There is no special God to refer to." There is neither God
nor any god on whom to lean, not for the mother and not for the
motherless daughter. The color white in this stanza assumes new meaning; it is the white of Christmas snow that covers the winter tree and
suggests new birth, the possibility of a new beginning, a tabula rasa.

The mother who "did not love myself" is rejoined with her daughter and once again holds her hand.

In the poem's second section, the voice becomes tighter, the enjambments jarring, and the cadences and end rhymes more patterned: "Too late, / too late, to live with your mother, the witches said. / But I didn't leave. I had my portrait / done instead" (*TB*, 55). Each of the four stanzas in this section ends with a variation on the closing refrain "I [she, they] had my portrait / done instead." The careful, formal voice and structure appropriately expresses content; the section concerns the speaker's return to her own mother's house after being hospitalized for her first suicide attempt. This voice and structure continue in sections 3, 4, and 5.

Stanza 2 opens with the lines "Part way back from Bedlam / I came to my mother's house in Gloucester" (*TB*, 55). Unable, however, to make the same loving, restorative connection with her mother that she is attempting in present time, by writing this poem, to make with her own daughter, the speaker and her mother remain locked in their own worlds. "I cannot forgive your suicide, my mother said" (stanza 2). The speaker, who is truly an "angry guest" (stanza 3), is for the mother only a smiling portrait with her "hair restyled" (stanza 3).

The third and fourth sections recount the denouement of the speaker's and the speaker's mother's story and develop the poem's title image. In the third section the speaker's mother "turned from me, as if death were catching, / . . . / and said I gave her cancer." At the same time the portrait freezing the troubled daughter-speaker in a smile is hung on a north wall in the mother's house (*TB*, 56). In section 4, returning uncured from the hospital, the mother now comes "part way back" and has "her own portrait painted" to hang "on the south wall": "matching smile, matching contour. / And you resembled me; unacquainted / with my face, you wore it" (*TB*, 57). Hearing the voices of her "witches," and the feeling the guilt of her mother's accusations and of her distance from her own child, the speaker attempts suicide and tries "the sealed hotel" a second time. Yet the end of section 4 suggests movement toward real connection between the speaker and her mother. Both now have been ill; both have come "part way back"; their portraits hang on opposite walls. And finally the mother reaches out to the speaker in a way unspecified in the poem, with healing laughter. The lines echo the words of the writer of Genesis: "On April you fooled me. We laughed and this was good" (*TB*, 57).

In section 5 the speaker recovers from the second suicide attempt:

"All that summer I learned life" (*TB,* 58). Here she turns again to speak to her own daughter, reassuming the dramatic posture of the opening section, where her purpose in speaking was principally to reach self-understanding and nominally to justify her actions, motivations, and feelings to her daughter. With the return to this rhetorical posture, maintained to the end of the poem, the voice becomes calmer and the structure appropriately less formal, approaching the verbal realization of maturity and self-understanding we have heard in the poem's opening lines: "And I had to learn / why I would rather / die than love, . . . / and how I gather guilt like a young intern / his symptoms" (*TB,* 58).

The closing lines of this section ("and two portraits hang on opposite walls") provided the transition to section 6, where the speaker muses on the two smiling portraits, the double image. The mother's portrait is the speaker's "mocking mirror, my overthrown / love, my first image" (*TB,* 60). The two portraits together form in "the mirror, / that double woman who stares / at herself, as if she were petrified / in time" (*TB,* 60). Sexton comments in a 1959 letter that this poem is "entirely about the 'mother-child' relationship" (*L,* 56). And in a 1958 letter to W. D. Snodgrass, she asks: "Who do we kill, which image in the mirror, the mother, ourself, our daughter????? Am I my mother, or my daughter? Snodsy, I am afraid to love" (*L,* 40). In the double image of section 6, the speaker finds both identity and maturity. She has twice tried to kill herself; her portrait freezes in time that stage of her life. But she has changed; in the portrait, "I rot on the wall, my own / Dorian Gray" (*TB,* 60). "Gray" is both her own name and her mother's. The speaker is not the smiling person whom the portrait captured; she was "rotten" at the time of its painting, with one suicide attempt behind her and another to come, and even now she has found her way only part way back. Neither is her mother the smiling person in her portrait, for the mother of the portrait could not forgive and was herself ill with cancer. And so the two portraits merge, as a "mirror." The speaker looks like her mother; she is like her mother, being the daughter; and yet the mother is her "overthrown / love." The speaker expresses at once the tugs of love and of guilt, as if to say "I was like you, I loved you, I made you ill. You were like me, you loved me, you made me ill. We are like each other, and yet to survive I must grow away from you and from the me which the portrait captures." And so "the artist caught us at the turning; / we smiled in our canvas home / before we chose our foreknown separate ways" (*TB,* 60).

In section 7, the poem's final section, the speaker turns again to her daughter, creating a triple image of mother-speaker-daughter, recalling the awkward reunion of speaker with daughter after the four-year absence. The themes of identity, guilt, and self-knowledge combine in the poem's closing lines:

> I, who was never quite sure
> about being a girl, needed another
> life, another image to remind me.
> And this was my worst guilt; you could not cure
> nor soothe it. I made you to find me.
>
> (*TB*, 61)

In making the daughter she has found some of herself; in trying to make sense of her relationship with her own mother she has reached at least provisional understanding; in trying to explain her experience of bedlam to her daughter she has managed to explain it also to herself.

The speaker has been in this poem *To Bedlam*, both literally and figuratively, and she has come *Part Way Back*. The movement of "The Double Image" parallels, to some degree, the movement of Robert Lowell's "Skunk Hour": the speaker has experienced the dark night of the soul and has emerged from it with at least limited success. In "The Double Image," it is guilt that brings darkness, guilt for having caused the illness both of daughter and mother. And it is love that heals. The speaker is finally able to explain to her daughter the necessity to "love your self's self."

Chapter 3
All My Pretty Ones: Confession

Comparing her first and second volumes of poetry, Anne Sexton commented that in *To Bedlam and Part Way Back,* "I was giving the experience of madness"; in *All My Pretty Ones,* "the causes of madness."[1] In fact, there is much thematic similarity in the two volumes: Sexton composed some of the poems that appear in *All My Pretty Ones* at the same time that she was completing work on her first volume. But although the major themes of *Bedlam* are continued into the second volume, new thematic concerns are evident here as well. Also apparent is a certain evolution in Sexton's approach to poetic form and tone. Sexton herself pointed out the apparent paradox in *All My Pretty Ones* of "a little more restraint" in tone (*L,* 94) coupled with a "loosen[ing] up" of form.[2]

To Bedlam and Part Way Back was published in March 1960; in January 1962 *All My Pretty Ones* was accepted by Houghton Mifflin for publication, and it appeared in the fall of the same year. By this time Sexton had begun to enjoy recognition as an experienced poet. Acceptances in journals of her poems came more easily; she employed a literary agent and a lecture agency; and she was awarded grants, was invited to give interviews, and was offered television appearances and teaching positions. She may have felt that such recognition validated her work in some way; the poems of *All My Pretty Ones* do evince a certain new confidence. In a January 1962 letter, Sexton quoted a letter she had received from Robert Lowell:

The best thing about your book [*All My Pretty Ones*] is its unstoppered fulness. I get an impression of increasing supply and weight; indeed your first book, especially the best poems, spills into the second and somehow adds to it. . . . my favorite still is the *Hudson* one on your father ("All My Pretty Ones"). I feel a passion and concentration here. I'm glad you've tried new things, the religious poems and character sketches. They are variously successful, I guess, but give the book a professional air of not just confessing, but of liking to write poems. (*L,* 133)

Confessional

In a 1973 interview Anne Sexton remarked that "it's a difficult label, 'confessional.'"[3] And indeed it is difficult, since that label is widely used and variously interpreted. The term does, however, require attention in a discussion of poems like Sexton's. By remarking in his letter to Sexton that the poems of her second volume give the impression of "not just confessing," Robert Lowell both points to and validates the term, as have many other poets and critics of the mid–twentieth century. Certainly one finds it difficult to discuss the thematic content of Sexton's poems without referring to biographical data, and one finds it difficult to analyze the speaker of these poems without acknowledging the urge to name that speaker as Sexton herself. Is "confessional" a valid, meaningful critical designation? Does it designate a significant development in twentieth-century poetry?

The critic M. L. Rosenthal is perhaps responsible for the label, writing in 1967 that "The term 'confessional poetry' came naturally to my mind when I reviewed Robert Lowell's *Life Studies* in 1959. . . . Whoever intended it, it was a term both helpful and too limited, and very possibly the conception of a confessional school has by now done a certain amount of damage."[4] Rosenthal explains that he intended the term to signify the sort of poetry he saw in *Life Studies,* which is "usually developed in the first person and intended without question to point to the author himself." He remarks that "Because of the way Lowell brought his private humiliations, sufferings, and psychological problems into the poems of *Life Studies,* the word 'confessional' seemed appropriate enough."[5] The widespread appearance of this sort of poetry within a decade of Lowell's 1959 *Life Studies* certainly did seem to signal the arrival of a new movement. Allen Ginsberg's *Howl* was published in 1956, W. D. Snodgrass's *Heart's Needle* in 1959, Anne Sexton's *To Bedlam and Part Way Back* in 1960 and *All My Pretty Ones* in 1962, Theodore Roethke's *The Far Field* and John Berryman's *Dream Songs* in 1964, Sylvia Plath's *Ariel* in 1965, and Sexton's *Live or Die* in 1966.

Reception of this "new" poetry was mixed. One critic, reviewing Sexton's *Live or Die,* wrote that these "are not poems. They are documents of modern psychiatry and their publication is a result of the confusion of critical standards in the general mind."[6] In 1965 the critic Ralph J. Mills, Jr., wrote that he saw confessional poetry as that which deals with "the more intimate aspects of life, areas of experience that

most of us would instinctively keep from public sight."[7] In the same
year critic A. R. Jones defined the confessional poem as a "dramatic
monologue in which the persona is naked ego involved in a very personal world and with particular, private experiences."[8] Anne Sexton
reports that John Holmes, in the late 1950s, "told me that I shouldn't
write such personal poems about the madhouse. He said, 'That isn't a
fit subject for poetry.'"[9] Such definitions and objections may be valid
as far as they go, but they do not go far enough.

To his own description of this kind of poetry, M. L. Rosenthal
added, "These poems seemed to me one culmination of the Romantic
and modern tendency to place the literal Self more and more at the
center of the poem in such a way as to make his psychological vulnerability and shame an embodiment of his civilization."[10] It is perhaps
this very intimacy of revelation that shocked critics into declaring
confessional poetry unfit in subject or merely documentary in nature.
Yet the phenomenon of personal poetry is not new; it is rather an idea
whose time has come—again. It is a modern reapplication of a romantic mode, a contemporary relative of the works of Byron, Whitman,
and Dickinson.

This poetry may represent, as well, a reaction against the Eliotic
school of extinction of personality that so dominated the early decades
of the twentieth century. As Eliot wrote in "Tradition and the Individual Talent," "poetry is not a turning loose of emotion, but an escape
from emotion; it is not the expression of personality, but an escape
from personality."[11] The confessional poetry of midcentury is just the
opposite of Eliot's symbolist mode. In its use of apparently biographical personae and speakers and in its themes of sexual love, oedipal
hate, personal anguish, unbearable suffering, and emotional breakdown, this poetry represents not an escape from personality but an
expression of it.

It is important to note, further, that when we discuss Anne Sexton's
poetry, we are turning our attention to the biography and personality,
to the *voice,* of a woman poet. Gender is a significant dimension here.
Anne Sexton, the heir of Emily Dickinson, was the first female confessional poet; arguably, she was the "mother" of the confessional school.[12]
As Diana Hume George points out,

If the response of her contemporaries to "confessional poetry" was sometimes
sharply negative, it was specially inflected with contempt for "her kind."
When Lowell confessed, at first we slapped his patrician hand and told him

to shape up and put back the stiff in his upper lip. When Sexton confessed, we sharpened the knife and heated the pot.[13]

About these confessional themes and concerns, Rosenthal comments:

Confessional poetry is a poetry of suffering. The suffering is generally "unbearable" because the poetry so often projects breakdown and paranoia. Indeed, the psychological condition of most of the confessional poets has long been the subject of common literary discussion—one cannot say gossip exactly, for their problems and confinements in hospitals are quite often the specific subjects of their poems. It is not enough, however, to relegate the matter to the province of the mentally disturbed. A heightened sensitivity to the human predicament in general . . . has led to a sharper sense, as a by-product perhaps, of the pain of existence under even "normal" conditions.[14]

The issues of breakdown and paranoia demand attention and yet resist easy answers. All the confessional poets suffered mental illness. Most spent time in mental hospitals. Some committed suicide. According to Rosenthal, breakdown and suicide are part of the "imaginative risk" that poets who are "sensitive enough to the age and brave enough to face it directly" must take.[15] Sexton makes a similar point, commenting that "there are so many people who are mentally disturbed who are not writers, or artists, . . . that I don't think genius and insanity grow in the same bed. I think the artist must have a heightened awareness. It is only seldom this sprouts from mental illness alone."[16] It may be, in fact, that the imaginative artist's breakdown and madness are at once uniquely contemporary gestures and not new at all. It may be that these mid–twentieth-century poets simply discuss such matters more openly and frankly than their romantic forebears and that the "imaginative risk" has always been a necessary feature of personal poetry.

For poetry is what the successful work of the confessionals must finally be considered. It is, after all, more than mere documentation. James Merrill has observed that "Confessional poetry . . . is a literary convention like any other, the problem being to make it *sound* as if it were true."[17] Robert Lowell has said of *Life Studies* that although "there's a good deal of tinkering with fact, . . . the reader was to believe he was getting the *real* Robert Lowell."[18] Anne Sexton contends that it "is necessary" to "distort the literal facts of [one's] life to present the emotional truth that lies under them." The poet does not "have to include everything to tell the truth. You can even lie (we can confess and lie forever). . . . It's something that an artist must do to . . . have the effect of the axe."[19] Says Rosenthal, referring as well to Sexton's epigraphs in her first two volumes, "'To make a clean breast of it in the face of . . . appalling horror' and to write a book that is 'the ax for the frozen sea within us' is not just a matter of intention but one of art. Force of character, clarity of line . . . would seem essential."[20]

Further, as Marjorie Perloff points out, confessional poetry fuses the romantic with the realistic mode, and it is Lowell's "superb manipulation of the realistic convention, rather than the titillating confessional content, that is responsible for the so-called breakthrough of *Life Studies*." Lowell's "metonymic structure is far from artless." And "the style born of this fusion" of metonymic realism with the "romantic lyrical 'I' . . . marks a turning point in the history of twentieth-century poetry."[21]

Confessional poetry is, then, a specific and legitimate movement in twentieth-century poetry; it is at once a modern manifestation of an ongoing tradition, a reaction against a previously dominant mode, and a unique development. We should not be surprised that its advent provoked such violent and emotional reaction among critics and readers alike. Such responses were no doubt motivated and inspired in part by the very personal, violent, and emotional nature of the poetry itself and in part by the uncompromisingly feminine perspective on which Anne Sexton insisted. It is indeed impossible to discuss the themes of Sexton and of other confessional poets without referring to biographical data, and it is difficult to analyze the poems' speakers without thinking of the poets themselves.

Perhaps, however, if we feel some distaste for the critical use of biographical materials, or reluctance to breach the hermetic inviolability of poetic texts, we should consider the possibility that such timidity is itself a manifestation of the masculine, New Critical aesthetic against which the confessional poets rebelled. We should remember, as well, Sexton's own comment that neither tradition nor rebellion motivated her art: I "can't write any other way," she said. "The writer is stuck with what he can do."[22] The analysis of new poetry requires the use of new tools.

In fact, critical justification hardly seems necessary when we hear the poet herself discussing in the first-person singular the speaker of one of her poems. In a March 1960 letter to Louis Simpson, she writes:

I have written a new longish poem called "The Operation" which is (damn it as I really don't *want* to write any more of them) a personal narration about my experiences this fall. . . . Toward the end, when I decide I will live after all, I say "All's well, they say. They say I'm better. / I lounge in frills or, picturesque, / I wear bunny pink slippers in the hall. / I read a new book and shuffle past the desk / to mail the author my first fan letter" . . . and it goes on. (*L,* 99)

A closer look at this poem may reveal the ways in which the confessional poet employs admittedly biographical materials and then distorts these "literal facts . . . to present the emotional truth that lies under them."[23]

In "The Operation," Sexton dramatizes the feelings and thoughts prompted by her abdominal surgery, an operation to remove an ovarian cyst. While acknowledging the validity of Sexton's comment in another letter that "letters are false really—they are expressions of the way you wish you were instead of the way you are . . . (poems might come under this same catagory [*sic*])" (*L,* 122), we can nevertheless deduce the salient biographical facts from her letters. "I just got out of the hospital," she writes in a letter of October 1959, "having had an operation. . . . They . . . took out my appendix . . . and an ovary and a cyst the size of a grapefruit. . . . So here I am . . . not knowing if I have cancer or not" (*L,* 88). A month later, in November, the experience has become material for a poem. "I was awful sick," she writes in a letter. "I had pneumonia and a major operation (removal of one ovary, one tube, an appendix)." And now, "I am working on a new thing that may not work (an operation, death, cancer, mother, me). . . . I could really write it if I could just die at the end. Full Cycle. Mother dies her ugly death and now Anne follows, trailing her guilty gowns down the last aisle" (*L,* 91, 92).

The "literal facts" of this case, then, are Sexton's hospitalization, her abdominal surgery for the removal of an ovarian cyst, a fallopian tube, and an appendix, and her momentary uncertainty about the cyst's carcinogenic properties. The "emotional truth," which we can see developing in the November letter, involves Sexton's association of herself with her mother by means of their shared experiences (Sexton's hospitalization and feared cancer associated with her mother's hospitalization for breast cancer, and Sexton's anticipated death associated with her mother's actual death). Fear, then, is one controlling emotion that grows from the daughter's reflection upon this shared experience. Guilt is another, more central one.

One way the poem expresses and informs this emotional truth is through metonymy.

> After the sweet promise,
> the summer's mild retreat
> from mother's cancer, the winter months of her death,
> I come to this white office, its sterile sheet,
> its hard tablet, its stirrups, to hold my breath
> while I, who must, allow the glove its oily rape,
> to hear the almost mighty doctor over me equate
> my ills with hers
> and decide to operate.
>
> (PO, 12)

We see here several metonymic transfers that function throughout the poem. In the mention of summer and winter, there is a shift from actor to setting. The "promise" of "the summer's mild retreat / from mother's cancer" was "sweet." Here the rhyme of "sweet" with "retreat" points up the pleasant and quiet qualities of the time preceding the operation; for the daughter, the season before the surgery was fertile summertime. Since Sexton's mother died in March 1959, the daughter was freed in the following summer from the pain of her mother's dying but was unaware during that same summer of her own approaching pain. In this opening stanza, however, the doctor "equate[s]" the daughter's illness with the mother's, and this equation of experience continues in the following stanzas. In stanza 2, the setting of sweet, fecund summer becomes a generalized yesterday whose promise is both sweet and menacing: "It grew in her / as simply as a child would grow, / as simply as she housed me once, fat and female" (PO, 12). Here the image becomes more complex; in the setting of summer, mother grows the daughter in her uterus, mother grows the cancer in her body, daughter grows the cyst in her ovary. In stanza 5, the speaker comments again, "tomorrow the O.R. Only the summer was sweet" (PO, 13).

Other seasons in the poem extend this metonymic shift from actor to setting; as the poem's speaker comments in stanza 4, "woman's dying / must come in seasons" (PO, 13). Autumn and winter are used to express their traditional meanings of dying and death. The mother's final cancer and death occur in "the winter months"; the daughter-speaker remembers, in stanza 3, that "there was snow everywhere. / Each day I grueled through / its sloppy peak" to visit her mother at the hospital (PO, 12). And now, through the connection of color, the daughter finds herself in a wintry, deadly setting: "I come to this white office, its sterile sheet" (PO, 12). During her own operation, the daughter's perception of an autumn setting expresses her emotional and physical condition: "I hear limbs falling / and see yellow eyes flick in the rain" (*PO*, 13).

We can also recognize in these same materials a metonymic transfer from actor to action. Although the intense personal feelings of the poet herself are at the center of this poem, the feelings are expressed not so much directly as through a system of images that demonstrate feeling by means of action. The qualities of feeling that the speaker imposes on her mother's death (fear, reluctance, horror) are realized by a nightmarish environment: "winter months," "snow everywhere" through which the speaker "slop[s]" and "gruel[s]" on her way to visit the hospital, in a season of sleeping, of "fear / where the snoring mouth gapes / and is not dear" (*PO*, 12). Leaving the hospital after a visit to her mother, the speaker "walk[s] out, scuffing a raw leaf, / kicking the clumps of dead straw / that were this summer's lawn" (*PO*, 13).

The guilt to which Sexton refers in her November 1959 letter ("Mother dies her ugly death and now Anne follows, trailing her guilty gowns down the last aisle" *L*, 92) is also realized metonymically in this poem. The complex combined image of daughter-as-fetus and mother's cancer and daughter's feared cancer reflects the speaker's association of her life with her mother's death and implies, through setting, a sort of guilty causation. In stanza 5, the speaker flatly observes: "Fact: death too is in the egg" (*PO*, 13). In stanza 2, she comments:

> It grew in her
> as simply as a child would grow,
> as simply as she housed me once, fat and female.
> Always my most gentle house before that embryo
> of evil spread in her shelter and she grew frail.
>
> (*PO*, 12)

The mother's cancer is "evil," and by implication, the daughter who also "grew" in her mother is evil as well. The fetus-daughter shares a setting with the evil cancer, thereby sharing responsibility for the mother's death.

In fact, the operation in this poem does signal a kind of temporary death for the speaker. After surgery, the speaker floats between life and death. The setting contrasts her condition with that of the other patients, emphasizing the sterility of her body and once again connecting that sterility with death and with mother: *just a daughter*

> I soar in hostile air
> over the pure women in labor,

over the crowning heads of babies being born,
I plunge down the backstair
calling *mother* at the dying door,
to rush back to my own skin, tied where it was torn.

(*PO*, 14)

During the postoperative period, the speaker, helpless, disembodied, "thick with shock" (*PO*, 15), calls for her mother.

In the poem's resolution, we see another way that literal facts are manipulated to express emotional truth, as well as a way that the poet can change her idea of what the emotional truth of the experience really is. In Sexton's November 1959 letter, she indicates, as we have seen, that the emotional truth of this surgical experience involves the "ugly death" of her mother followed by the "guilty" death of herself, coming "full cycle" (*L*, 92). We have also, however, seen that in Sexton's March 1960 letter to Louis Simpson, she comments that at the end of this poem she decides she "will live after all" (*L*, 99). From this letter we can deduce a few additional "literal facts." She writes "You are *there* in my mind and told me to get well, that there was life and great beauty left. Let me dare say what my 'Operation' doesn't. . . . After nothing but pain and fear and the problems of guilt, your book burst over me and made me want to live" (*L*, 99). We can assume that sometime between November 1959 and March 1960, Simpson sent Sexton a book that changed, for her, the emotional truth of her surgical experience. Therefore, here is how "The Operation" concludes:

All's well, they say. They say I'm better.
I lounge in frills or, picturesque,
I wear bunny pink slippers in the hall.
I read a new book and shuffle past the desk
to mail the author my first fan letter.
Time now to pack this humpty-dumpty
back the frightened way she came
and run along, Anne, and run along now,
my stomach laced up like a football
for the game.

(*PO*, 15–16)

The cadences of these closing lines recapitulate the mother-daughter theme ("run along, Anne, and run along now," *PO*, 16), as the imagery of the opening lines had established it. In a sense, therefore, the speaker has come "full cycle." But instead of joining her mother in death, she has moved beyond the whiteness of oblivion to wearing pink slippers, and though still "frightened," she re-enters "the game."

"The Operation," then, demonstrates the specific characteristics of a confessional poem and in doing so typifies Sexton's early work. Exemplifying M. L. Rosenthal's description of the confessional mode, "The Operation" is clearly "developed in the first person and [is] intended without question to point to the author [her]self." It is "poetry of suffering" that makes the poet's "psychological vulnerability . . . an embodiment of [her] civilization."[24] Furthermore, the experience that forms the center of this poem may be personal and private indeed, but it is also typical and indicative of the modern experience. In mid–twentieth-century America, reproductive surgery and cancer have become more common than ever before and also a fit subject for poetry. And the emotional atmosphere of such psychological and physical suffering, manifested and explored by the poet in combination with an examination of the mother-daughter relationship, expresses the suffering of many and creates new realities as well.

Sexton herself declares that "I write very personal poems but I hope that they will become the central theme to someone else's private life." She aims to give her poems "a rather authentic stamp; that's always my hope."[25] We see in "The Operation" not only the "culmination of the Romantic and modern tendency to place the literal Self more and more at the center of the poem," as Rosenthal observes,[26] but also the fusion of metonymic realism with the "romantic Lyrical 'I'" noted by Marjorie Perloff.[27] And finally, in Sexton's predilection first to die, at least imaginatively, at the poem's close, and then later to live, "The Operation" demonstrates the "imaginative risk" that confessional poets must and do take. In this poem there is indeed, as Robert Lowell has said of his own confessional work, "a good deal of tinkering with fact."[28] But the reader does believe, finally, that she is "getting the *real*" Anne Sexton. As Sexton herself comments, this creation of emotional truth is "something that an artist must do to . . . have the effect of the axe."[29]

The Ax for the Frozen Sea

A principal confessional quality of the poems in *All My Pretty Ones* is reflected in the epigraph that Sexton chose for the volume. These poems, which reflect and express private suffering, personal crisis, psy-

chological difficulty, and emotional upheaval, are intended to move
beyond the pure expression of anguish and to have, as Sexton declares
"the effect of the axe." The epigraph is a quotation from a letter of
Franz Kafka:

. . . the books we need are the kind that act upon us like a misfortune, that
make us suffer like the death of someone we love more than ourselves, that
make us feel as though we were on the verge of suicide, or lost in a forest
remote from all human habitation—a book should serve as the ax for the
frozen sea within us.

Diana Hume George observes that "'the frozen sea within us,' as Sexton
knew, is always iced by consciousness, which keeps us from the depths
of both pain and pleasure that arise from breaking the surface and
plunging into the past that creates the present."[30] Sexton's intention
of breaking that surface and plunging into that past is announced in a
companion to this epigraph, a quotation from *Macbeth,* from which the
volume derives its title:

> All my pretty ones?
> Did you say all? O hell-kite! All?
> What! all my pretty chickens and their dam
> At one fell swoop? . . .
> I cannot but remember such things were,
> That were most precious to me.

This volume derives its thematic weight from Sexton's "pretty ones";
the majority of the poems express and explore her grief, her guilt, and
her sense of loss over the death of those who were "most precious" to
her. Turning to literal facts, it is remarkable that so many of Sexton's
loved ones and casual acquaintances died in such a short span of time.
Nana died in July 1954; her mother died of cancer in March 1959; her
father died from a stroke in June 1959; her father-in-law, whom she
called her "best friend" (*L,* 101), was killed in an automobile accident
in March 1960. She reveals in a letter that "the girl across the street
died of cancer" in August 1960. "*I* said that she ought to die," writes
Sexton. "Why don't I keep my big mouth shut!" "I seem," she says,
"to specialize in dead people. Guilt. Guilt" (*L,* 115). The father of her
close friend, poet Maxine Kumin, died in the fall of 1962. "It was
expected," Sexton writes, "but is hard just the same. Me. I'm tired of
all these dead. There are getting to be too many of them" (*L,* 151).

Sexton considered naming this volume *The Survivor* (*L*, 135). After having decided to call it *All My Pretty Ones*, she commented in a 1962 letter that "it is mostly about the dead . . . and love . . . and sin . . . but mostly the dead" (*L*, 137).

And indeed this volume is, thematically, "mostly about the dead," about the death of people and of things that were "precious." The volume's opening poem, "The Truth the Dead Know," dedicated to Sexton's mother and father, describes the speaker's diminished present, "where the sun gutters from the sky, / where the sea swings in like an iron gate." "I am tired of being brave," declares the speaker (*PO*, 3). The poem "Lament" focuses on the speaker's guilt over the death of an unspecified person or people. "Someone is dead," she says. "I think . . . / I could have stopped it" if she had only done something differently (*PO*, 7). Other poems explore a daughter's fear and guilt connected with her own illness and the death of her mother ("The Operation"), the loss of a loved one ("Flight"), the death of a fetus ("The Abortion"), death in general ("The Starry Night"), and lost youth ("Young," "I Remember").

In these poems and in others, Sexton's grief, her guilt, and her sense of loss are woven into various poetic structures, demonstrating the "imaginative risk" taken by one who chooses not to suppress pain but rather to use painful materials as an impetus for poetry. Sexton describes and endorses the process in a May 1960 letter:

> I think that writers must try *not* to avoid learning what is happening. Everyone has . . . the ability to mask the events of pain and sorrow. . . . But the creative person must not use this mechanism anymore than they have to in order to keep breathing. . . . Writing is "life" in capsule and the writer must feel every bump edge scratch ouch in order to know the real furniture of his capsule. . . . creative people must not avoid the pain they get dealt. . . . Hurt must be examined like a plague. (*L*, 105)

Here, then, is the further relevance of Sexton's chosen epigraph. This book, these poems, are meant not only to "act upon" the reader "like a misfortune," to cause the reader to "suffer like the death of someone we love," to make the reader "feel as though [she] were on the verge of suicide, or lost in a forest." The book is also meant to act upon the writer in those ways as she faces misfortune, death, suicide, and loss— as she examines them and grows from having creatively conducted the examination. This "book should serve as the ax for the frozen sea within us," both for reader and for writer.

Nor should the shock value of such poetry be ignored. The very quality to which some critics of confessional poetry in general and of Sexton's poetry in particular object is an essential part of its intention. As Sexton comments in a 1960 interview, poetry "should be a shock to the senses. It should almost hurt." The reader needs to be jolted out of everyday complacency and triteness; "we need something to shock us, to make us become more aware." For Sexton the poet, both biographical materials and the writings of others provide the shock ("Kafka's work certainly works upon me as an axe upon a frozen sea"), and then "writing . . . puts things back in place . . . . things are more chaotic, and if I can write a poem, I come into order again, and the world is again a little more sensible, and real. I'm more in touch with things."[31]

The title poem of *All My Pretty Ones* exemplifies the volume's thematic center, the creative process of transmuting painful materials into art, and the effect of the ax. As the editors of Sexton's *Letters* tell us, "While in letters Anne could bear to mention the loss of her parents only in passing [pun probably not intended], in 'All My Pretty Ones' . . . she mourned within the strict walls of her art" (L, 64). And as Sexton herself observes, "'All My Pretty Ones' was the name for my dead. I began badly with raw emotion and bitterness, with no good lines at all, and no form, nothing but the need to give reality to feeling."[32]

The poem comprises five ten-line stanzas, each with the end rhyme *a b a b c d c d e e*. In its strict form, "All My Pretty Ones" resembles some of the poems of this volume and most of those in *To Bedlam and Part Way Back*. As Sexton comments,

In *Bedlam,* I used very tight form in most cases, feeling that I could express myself better. I take a kind of pleasure, . . . especially in *Bedlam,* in forming a stanza, . . . and then coming to a little conclusion at the end of it, a little shock, a little double rhyme shock. In my second book, *All My Pretty Ones,* I loosened up and in the last section didn't use any form at all. I found myself to be surprisingly free without the form which had worked as a kind of superego for me.[33]

No doubt this reliance on form is a function of theme. Sexton observes that madness was for her a subject that she needed most to deal with in form,[34] and as we have seen, the subject of madness, combined with the intention of making "a clean breast of it," constitute the thematic center of her first volume. As Sexton developed as a poet, she herself notes, she developed the confidence to shed her reliance on form even when dealing with emotionally difficult themes.[35] In "All My Pretty Ones," however, we find the stanza formation and the "little double rhyme shock," that are typical of her early work.

The speaker opens this title poem by addressing her father:

> Father, this year's jinx rides us apart
> where you followed our mother to her cold slumber;
> a second shock boiling its stone to your heart,
> leaving me here to shuffle and disencumber
> you from the residence you could not afford:
> a gold key, your half of a woolen mill,
> twenty suits from Dunne's, an English Ford,
> the love and legal verbiage of another will,
> boxes of pictures of people I do not know.
> I touch their cardboard faces. They must go.
>
> (*PO,* 4)

In an interview Sexton comments at length on the genesis and development of this opening stanza, describing multiple revisions in which she struggled to sound less "prosy" and "angry," worked to make the poem sound less as though she were "talking to [her]self, which is what you do when you write a poem, I'm afraid," and experimented to find a form "that will help me find my voice."[36] The result is this stanza, which sounds more as though the speaker were talking to her father than to herself, where end and internal rhymes and enjambment of lines four and five enhance sense, and where the voice's expression of nostalgia and love as well as anger is realized both through diction and through the abrupt cadences of the final rhyming *e e* lines.

The speaker is sorting through her dead father's things, deciding what to keep and what to throw out, musing on what she did and did not know of his experience, trying to come to terms with his life and with his death. At the center of the poem's meaning is the speaker's relationship with her father, offered in the particular perspective of this present attempt to understand it and to understand him. The speaker's emotion is complex (love, admiration, bewilderment, anger, guilt), and it is occasionally expressed directly ("leaving me here to shuffle and disencumber / you from the residence you could not afford"; "My

father, time meanwhile / has made it unimportant who you are looking
for"). More often, however, emotion is conveyed through structure (the
"little double rhyme shock" at the end of each stanza) and through
imagery; objects closely associated with the father are metonymically
substituted for various characteristics of the father himself.

In stanza 1, the speaker tries to "disencumber" herself of valuable
objects that her father had owned. In spite of the fact that he "could
not afford" them, the father is represented here by "a gold key, . . .
half of a woolen mill, / twenty suits from Dunne's, [and] an English
Ford." They are objects and possessions of value, suggesting at once
the father's value to the daughter-speaker (golden, precious), the father's estimate of himself (wealthy, substantial), and the daughter's
assessment of the father (acquisitive, insufficiently concerned about
consequences). And in the same way that her father could not afford
these expensive possessions but owned them anyway, the speaker now
finds that she must "disencumber" herself of the emotions that they
recall, since, angry now at being left alone, she can no longer afford
them. The abrupt, strongly stressed sentence that completes the double rhyme at the end of the stanza expresses this felt need for divesti-
ture: "They must go."

The "boxes of pictures" of stanza one provide a unifying motif for
the next three stanzas, where the daughter-speaker turns from examining valuable possessions to studying old scrapbooks. In stanza 2, she
muses over a photograph of her father as a young boy. The images she
sees there (a boy in a "ruffled dress," a man wearing a military uniform,
a lady wearing velvet) suggest that her father's expensive tastes have
been acquired from his family and also that he failed in some way to
live up to his youthful promise. Recognizing none of the faces except
her father's in these photographs, however, as she has also failed to
recognize any of the "cardboard faces" of stanza 1, the speaker wonders
if the adults in these pictures are her father's grandparents; she wonders
"who [he is] looking for" (*PO, 4*); she wonders why her father's boyish
eyes, "thick as wood in this album, / hold me." Again, the abrupt
rhymes and monosyllabic diction of the rhymed declarative sentences
that conclude the stanza express the speaker's anger and frustration:
"I'll never know what these faces are all about. / I lock them into their
book and throw them out." (*PO, 4*).

In stanza 3, the "yellow scrapbook that you began / the year I was
born" (*PO, 4*) has become, like her relationship with her father, brittle

and crumbling. The speaker feels a guilty responsibility for her father's death; perhaps she wanted to keep him old, and "wrinkly," and hers. But "this year, solvent but sick, you meant / to marry that pretty widow in a one-month rush. / But before you had that second chance, I cried / on your fat shoulder. Three days later you died" (*PO,* 5). The father is still spending money, but he is sick. This speaker disapproves of what she views as his precipitous attachment to a "pretty widow." Sexton has commented that she "felt that" her "opposition to [her] father's marriage" had something to do with his death. "Not rationally, but I felt it . . . in the poem I don't want him to marry and he dies . . . . it's distinctly there, my guilt."[37] It is also clearly emphasized by the double rhyme that concludes the stanza.

The photographs in stanza 4 have as their subjects the father's leisure activities during his marriage to the speaker's mother. Again, they catalogue a life of privilege and wealth (speedboat races, formal dances, dog shows, horse shows) and objectify the speaker's love and admiration for her father (he holds "the winner's cup"; he "take[s] a bow"; he "stand[s] like a duke" *PO,* 5) as well as her judgment of him (he is vain). This catalogue is, however, offered in the context of what the speaker presents as her father's weaknesses. It is by now clear that he has lived beyond his means, and we are told in the double rhymed lines that conclude this stanza that he drank too much: "Now I fold you down, my drunkard, my navigator, / my first lost keeper, to love or look at later." (*PO,* 5)

In this context of ambivalent emotion, of love and admiration coexisting with anger, bewilderment, and guilt, we come to the fifth and final stanza. The object that the speaker holds here is a diary that, extending the drunkard motif of the preceding stanza, emphasizes one of the father's negative character traits and stresses the difficulty both daughter and mother had in living with him.

> I hold a five-year diary that my mother kept
> for three years, telling all she does not say
> of your alcoholic tendency. You overslept,
> she writes. My God, father, each Christmas Day
> with your blood, will I drink down your glass
> of wine? The diary of your hurly-burly years
> goes to my shelf to wait for my age to pass.
> Only in this hoarded span will love persevere.

> Whether you are pretty or not, I outlive you,
> bend down my strange face to yours and forgive you.
>
> (*PO*, 5)

Even in her diary the mother explains the father's alcoholism euphe-
mistically; although neither she nor any other family member con-
fronted the issue while the father lived, the daughter-speaker is doing
it now. "My God," she says in a meaningfully ambiguous exclamation;
her father is both her "god" and her possible nemesis. Symbolically at
Christmas, the daughter both celebrates her father and fears his alco-
holic legacy. And in the sacramental imagery, celebration and fear are
joined; drinking the father's blood, the daughter becomes one with
him for good and for ill. Yet the attempt to understand the father that
pervades the poem remains incomplete; the speaker's face, bent to the
father's, remains "strange."

This is a complex concluding image. Clearly, the speaker's face is
"strange" because she has been only partially successful in compre-
hending the father and her relationship with him. The line's phrasing
implies that the father's face is also "strange," extending the meaning
of incomplete understanding and completing the motifs of strangers
and of unknown people and places from earlier stanzas ("boxes of pictures of people I do not know"; "I'll never know what these faces are
all about"). There is also a suggestion that the speaker's face is strange
to the father because she is now grown beyond the child he knew in
the "snapshots" of stanza 4. And Sexton apparently means even more
by this image; she comments in an interview that she is "strange" also
to herself: "I would say it's also got a kind of sexual thing there . . .
to kiss him then, to kiss death itself. My *strange* face. It was always
pretty strange to him. Only now I was trying to love him, and to
forgive him for actually not being pretty."[38]

"All My Pretty Ones," then, typifies many poems of this volume
and extends the formal and thematic preoccupation of Sexton's first
volume. In this poem Sexton confronts, through the materials of her
art, a painful and emotionally complex experience that it was difficult
for her to explore in any other way. In that sense, this poem does "serve
as an ax for the frozen sea" within her and perhaps touches the "frozen
sea" in the lives of her readers as well. Thematically and formally, "All
My Pretty Ones" grows from Sexton's earlier work; the themes of guilt,
love, loss, and memory and the relatively strict, patterned form are

extensions of methods and concerns we have seen in *To Bedlam and Part Way Back.*

New Directions

New thematic concerns and new approaches to form and tone, however, are also evident in this second volume. Foreshadowing Sexton's later work, some poems in *All My Pretty Ones* are love poems ("I Remember," "Letter Written on a Ferry While Crossing Long Island Sound," "Love Song for K. Owyne," "Letter Written During a January Northeaster"), and some reveal her growing fascination with religion ("With Mercy for the Greedy," "In the Deep Museum," "For God While Sleeping," "For Eleanor Boylan Talking with God"). Some poems, as well, demonstrate the loosening up of form that Sexton herself has pointed out, accompanied by a new, freer, more joyful tone.

Both "Young" and "I Remember" are poems that consist of one long, breathless sentence. The lines of both are short and the diction simple; "Young" comprises twenty-three lines, and "I Remember" twenty-two. The form of each appropriately expresses the subject matter; "I Remember" recollects a summer of love and joy ("and we had worn our bare feet / bare since the twentieth of June and there were times / we forgot to wind up your / alarm clock and some nights / we took our gin warm and neat" *PO,* 11). In "Young," the speaker declares the wonder of youth and recollects the wide-eyed delight of discovery ("and it was summer / as long as I could remember, / I lay on the lawn at night, / clover wrinkling under me" [*PO,*6]). It is a poem of uninterpreted sensation, expressing, in words chosen by a mature woman, the immediate and unexamined pleasure of a young girl. Sexton has commented that these "are supposed to be breathless poems, . . . said in *one breath.* They are each one sentence because I only try to capture an instant in them."[39]

The poem that opens the volume's last section (where Sexton observes that she "loosened up and . . . didn't use any form at all"[40]) is "Letter Written on a Ferry While Crossing Long Island Sound." This is, as Maxine Kumin tells us, a "'given' poem" that "began at the instant Anne sighted the nuns on an actual crossing. The poem was written much as it now appears on the page, except for minor skirmishes required to effect the closure in each stanza."[41] The poem's seven stanzas, of varying lengths (from nine to seventeen lines), are like paragraphs, some addressed to a lover from whom the speaker has just parted and some expressing spontaneous feelings or observations inspired by the ended affair, the windswept ferry, the nuns. None of the stanza closures use end rhyme. Although the poem's subject might be expected to have inspired expressions of sadness and loss, it does not; rather, the speaker finds joy and inspiration, somehow, in the sight of these nuns in their windblown habits. The speaker is stunned by the end of her love affair:

> These are my eyes:
> The orange letters that spell
> ORIENT on the life preserver
> that hangs by my knees;
> ....
> Oh, all right, I say,
> I'll save myself.
>   (PO, 55–56)

Feeling numb ("I have ripped my hand / from your hand as I said I would / and I have made it this far / as I said I would" [PO, 55]), the speaker sees the word on the life preserver and knows spontaneously that she will take its advice. Then she sees the nuns: "Over my right shoulder / I see four nuns / . . . / The wind pulls the skirts / of their arms" (PO, 56). There is unexpected joy here, and lightness, and inspiration. In some way, the nuns become the speaker's life preserver, and at the poem's close, the speaker fantasizes that the nuns fly up in the blowing wind in a surreal image:

> There go my dark girls,
> ....
> See them rise
> ....
> They call back to us
> from the gauzy edge of paradise,
> *good news, good news.*
>   (PO, 57–58)

These new, freer aspects of theme and tone are realized in this volume in a poem paradoxically expressed in a quite traditional form, the sonnet. In a 1957 letter Sexton observed that "there are no sonnets" in

To Bedlam and Part Way Back. "I am not ready for sonnets yet" (*L,* 32). In January 1960, however, Sexton did write a sonnet. "To a Friend Whose Work Has Come to Triumph" represents quite a different manifestation of Sexton's experimentation with form and tone. If some poems in *All My Pretty Ones* demonstrate a loosening up of form, this sonnet shows quite the opposite. Yet both tendencies exhibit what Sexton, in a November 1959 letter, called her "new tone": "I don't want my next book to be as boomy as the Bedlam one. A little more restraint and never a false shriek. I wish my poems were gay sometimes. I am tired of my gloom and death" (*L,* 94).

"To a Friend Whose Work Has Come to Triumph" is a Shakespearean sonnet in which the three quatrains (with end rhyme *a b a b c d c d e f e f*) state the situation, and the concluding couplet (*g g*) imposes an epigrammatic turn. Although we may initially be surprised to see Sexton employing a form with such strict requirements, we should note that the tendency, indigenous to the sonnet, to close with a terse, ingenious turn of thought is typical of Sexton's other poetry. It is not very different from the "little conclusion" with which Sexton prefers to end most of her poems, the "little rhyme shock."[42]

"To a Friend Whose Work Has Come to Triumph" uses a portion of the Icarus myth for its development, referring, in the three quatrains, to certain particulars of Icarus's flight from the moment he straps on his new wings to the moment he falls. One may think of the poem's short imperative sentences as being addressed to a general audience, and certainly such an interpretation works. Sexton probably also had a specific audience in mind; she comments in a February 1960 letter to W. D. Snodgrass that she has written this poem to him: "I was thinking about your problem (the one that has to do with being a success). Thinking that it was important to have touched the sun. That what you've done is all that matters, no matter what happens next" (*L,* 97).

The poem's first twelve lines focus on the delight and joy of Icarus as he flies. Imperative clauses direct the audience to "consider Icarus," to feel with him, to see the world from his point of view. Diction directs us also to identify with Icarus's experience; the words are childlike and simple, such as he might have chosen.

> Consider Icarus, pasting those sticky wings on,
> . . . .
> and think of that first flawless moment over the lawn
> of the labyrinth. Think of the difference it made!

There below are the trees, as awkward as camels;
. . . .
. . . Admire his wings!
Feel the fire at his neck and see how casually
he glances up and is caught, wondrously tunneling
into that hot eye. Who cares that he fell back to the sea?

(*PO*, 8)

As we read, we experience simultaneously Icarus's flight and the poem's evaluation of it. Words and phrases like "pasting those stick wings on" and "trees, awkward as camels" suggest ways in which Icarus might verbalize the experience and reinforce the strangeness and wonder of flying. Earth seems an awkward, dark place, with its fog and its labyrinthine confusions, from which innocent, spontaneous Icarus has been freed. The imperative exclamations encourage us to assess Icarus's flight. The vocabulary of excitement, hyperbole, and joy leads to the question that concludes the third quatrain: "Who cares that he fell back to the sea?" The answer, clearly, is that no one should care; Icarus himself doesn't care. What matters to him, and what should matter to the audience, is not that Icarus fell but that he flew.

The sonnet's concluding couplet offers a traditional epigrammatic turn: "See him acclaiming the sun and come plunging down / while his sensible daddy goes straight into town" (*PO*, 8). These lines introduce another element into the poem; Daedalus, the "sensible daddy" (as Icarus might call him and as the poet does call him) is offered as a measure of Icarus's actions. Daedalus represents the safe, conventional view, not flying too high but rather going "straight into town" to complete his business. But as the "sensible daddy" would reproach Icarus for his folly, the value systems of the poem in turn condemns such a "sensible" attitude. These closing lines declare that risk and daring and a brief, blazing life ("acclaiming the sun") are preferable to sensible, unrisking behavior, for Icarus has lived more fully, though more briefly, than his "sensible daddy." The concluding couplet, then, offers a commentary on the preceding quatrains, draws a conclusion toward which the mood and tone of the quatrains have been leading, and provides a twist of meaning that furnishes an evaluative frame for the entire poem.

A sonnet is in many ways the opposite of a typical confessional poem. While the confessional poem is developed in the first-person singular and is meant to point to the poet herself, the sonnet is commonly developed in a more impersonal voice that focuses on the situation of the poem. Both kinds of poem are lyric in nature, but the confessional poem has a strong dramatic tendency, usually developed as a monologue in which the speaker sometimes addresses an identifiable but silent listener. The sonnet, on the other hand, is brief and subjective in nature and shows a tendency toward the didactic with its epigrammatic close. And while the confessional poem is formally fluid, with rhyme, meter, and stanza patterning used to express content, the sonnet's formal brevity and rigidity require concentrated expression of idea or feeling.

"To a Friend Whose Work Has Come to Triumph" demonstrates Sexton's growing versatility and sophistication as a poet. Partly by contrast, it helps to define the nature and characteristics of the confessional mode in which she wrote the majority of the work of her first two volumes. And yet this sonnet also shows the great adaptability of the confessional mode. Like any confessional poem, the lyric "To a Friend Whose Work Has Come to Triumph" expresses the individual and personal emotion of the poet and offers, in its imaginative phrasing, personal expression of subjective emotion.

Chapter Four
Live or Die: "To Endure, Somehow to Endure"

Live or Die, Anne Sexton's third published volume of poetry, comprises poems written between January 1961, when *All My Pretty Ones* was accepted for publication, and February 1966. In January 1963 *All My Pretty Ones* was nominated for the National Book Award, and in May 1963 the American Academy of Arts and Letters awarded Sexton its first traveling fellowship. Houghton Mifflin accepted *Live or Die* for publication in March 1966, and it appeared in the fall of that year. In May 1967 *Live or Die* was awarded the Pulitzer Prize for Poetry.

Live or Die is the only volume in which Anne Sexton intentionally arranged the poems in chronological order of composition. It is also the only volume in which Sexton chose to offer completion dates for each work. In an author's note, Sexton indicates this method of arrangement, "with all due apologies for the bad case of melancholy," and comments that she "thought the order of [the poems'] creation might be of interest to some readers" (*LD,* xi).

Indeed, the order of creation is interesting precisely because the chronology denotes a "fever chart" on which the impulses suggested by the volume's title alternate, interact, and strive with one another for preeminence. Perhaps because of the dramatic nature of the alternatives offered in the title, however, the reader is tempted to perceive more than mere chronology as the structural principle of this volume and to ask, as Barbara Kevles did in a 1968 interview with Sexton, "The whole book has a marvelous structured tension—simply by the sequence of the poems which pits the wish to live against the death instinct. Did you plan the book this way?" Yet chronology is almost the only plan here; Sexton responded to Kevles's question that she "didn't plan the book any way." She simply began collecting new poems after finishing her previous volume and got the title from an early draft of Saul Bellow's *Herzog,*[1] about which she had corresponded with Bellow:

> With one long breath, caught and held
> in his chest, he fought his sadness over
> his solitary life. Don't cry, you idiot!
> Live or die, but don't poison everything.
>
> (*LD*, vii)

This quotation from *Herzog* provides not only the volume's title but also its epigraph and unifying principle. Although there is much sadness in these poems, the speaker who emerges from them appears determined not to cry and "poison everything" but to make a decision. And that decision, ultimately, as the final poem's title declares, is to live.

Together with Sexton's next volume, *Love Poems* (1969), *Live or Die* represents a culmination of the sort of poetry Sexton had been writing since 1957, the time of her *To Bedlam and Part Way Back* poems. The themes, images, formal strategies, explorations, and incantations continue and develop from one volume to the next; as critic Robert Boyers observes, *Live or Die* is "the crowning achievement of the confessional mode which has largely dominated American poetry in the last decade [mid-1960s to mid-1970s]."[2] Anne Sexton herself views this progression and culmination in similar terms:

in the first book [*TB*], I was giving the experience of madness; in the second book [*PO*], the causes of madness; and in the third book [*LD*], finally, I find that I was deciding whether to live or to die. In the third I was daring to be a fool again—raw, "uncooked," as Lowell calls it, with a little camouflage. In the fourth book [*LP*], I not only have lived, come on to the scene, but loved, that sometime miracle.[3]

The poems of *Live or Die* (and of *Love Poems*) do indeed explore intimate aspects of experience, placing the literal self at the center of the poem's encounter and using biographical evidence as the raw materials for the finished poem. Sexton herself sees "even more confession" in the poems of *Live or Die* than in those of the earlier volumes, and in these works she offers such themes (some by now familiar, some new) as madness, death, guilt, love, cancer, sex, suicide, and menstruation. Again, critical response varies. One reviewer of *Live or Die*, Charles Gullans, comments that "these are not poems at all and I feel that I have, without right or desire, been made a third party to her conversations with her psychiatrist. It is painful, embarrassing, and irritating." This particular reviewer sees in Sexton's work either a "monstrous self-indulgence," which is "despicable," or the "documentation of a neurosis, in which case to pretend to speak of it as literature at all is simply silly." He concludes that these things in *Live or Die* "are not poems, they are documents of modern psychiatry and their publication is a result of the confusion of critical standards in the general mind."[4] On the other hand, Robert Boyers, who calls *Live or Die* "the crowning achievement of the confessional mode," observes that "We are grateful to Miss Sexton as we can be to few poets, for she has distinctly enlarged and enhanced the possibilities of endurance in that air of lost connections which so many of us inhabit."[5] Sexton herself declares that "reviews are bad for us" (*L,* 279).

Taken as a whole, *Live or Die* presents a four-year record of struggle, of obstacles overcome, and of insights achieved. The effect of the chronological arrangement of poems is to show these concerns, difficulties, and successes in the sort of natural progression that daily or monthly experience brings, so that the reader becomes witness to a sort of continuous musing on life and death, on hope and despair, and on love and failure. Through repetition and thematic emphasis, the motif that becomes preeminent in this volume is that of endurance. Because of the placement of "Live" as the volume's closing poem, the thematic direction of the whole collection is given an affirmative cast. In keeping with the musing, developmental quality of the poems' arrangement, the voice that speaks in most of these poems sounds reflective, contemplative, and mature. And this newly mature speaker offers newly evocative and memorable images that, expressed most often in free verse, are both more appropriate and more surreal than before.

Sequences and Structures

The long poem "Flee on Your Donkey," third in the volume, indicates just how far Sexton has come, both personally and poetically. It is, as Sexton says in a letter, a poem that she first wrote in 1962 in a mental institution and then reworked for four years until its publication in 1966 (*L,* 295). The poem's title and epigraph come from a Rimbaud poem that had appealed to Sexton. A comparison of "Flee on Your Donkey" with an earlier poem that deals with many similar materials, "You, Doctor Martin" (*TB*), dramatizes several aspects of Sexton's development. The jaunty tone of the earlier work has been replaced by a kind of tired acceptance; the desperate hope of becoming the conquering queen has become the urge simply, somehow, to flee this place, and the imagery of the later poem, typical of many poems in *Live or Die,* echoes the order of the dream.

In the poem's present time, the speaker is readmitted to a mental hospital (unlike the "You, Doctor Martin" experience, where incarceration seems new): "Because there was no other place / to flee to, / I came back to the scene of the disordered senses, / . . . / without luggage or defenses" (*LD,* 4). The tone is flat and factual: "this is a mental hospital, / not a child's game" (*LD,* 4). (Contrast the Jack and Jill imagery of "You, Doctor Martin," or the child's game of "Kind Sir: These Woods" in *TB.*) Here there is no joking, no "laughing bee" as in "You, Doctor Martin": "Once I would have winked and begged for dope. / Today I am terribly patient" (pun probably intended) (*LD,* 4). The image of "curtains, lazy and delicate," which "billow and flutter" (*LD,* 4) at the barred window of the speaker's room, signals the poem's narrative present and reappears, like a refrain, between the speaker's dreamlike, associative musings in related times and situations.

The poem's fifth stanza displays the kind of associative dream-sequence imagery that characterizes not only parts of this poem but also many other poems in *Live or Die.* (Later in the poem, in fact, the speaker addresses her psychiatrist directly, revealing that the examination of dreams has become part of her therapy and suggesting, by extension, that she now uses dream-structures in her art: "You taught me / to believe in dreams; / thus I was the dredger. / . . . / sweet dark playthings, / and above all, mysterious" (*LD,* 8–9)). In stanza 5, the speaker muses about hornets she sees on her window-screen:

> Hornets, dragging their thin stingers,
> hover outside, all knowing,
> hissing: *the hornet knows.*
> I heard it as a child
> but what was it that he meant?
> *The hornet knows!*
> What happened to Jack and Doc and Reggy?
> Who remembers what lurks in the heart of man?
> What did The Green Hornet mean, *he knows?*
> Or have I got it wrong?
> Is it The Shadow who had seen
> me from my bedside radio?
>
> (*LD,* 5)

The actual hornets remind the speaker first of flowers, then transmogrify into stinging, hissing, threatening things that recall frightening radio programs of the speaker's youth: "*The hornet knows.*" (The Green Hornet and The Shadow were principal figures in radio-mystery serials in which men of social position worked secretly and incognito to right injustices.) The Green Hornet, The Shadow, and the stinging, hovering, yet ultimately helpful psychiatrist merge here with the question asked by the deep-voiced announcer who opened the "Shadow" radio program: "Who knows what evil lurks in the hearts of men?" The speaker's sense of her own evil (guilt, blame, failure) is diffuse but clearly present; the "bedside radio" of the child connects with the bedside radio of the woman-speaker in present time, thus bringing us back to the 1962 mental hospital and providing a transition into the present time of the next stanza.

The poem proceeds by going backward and forward in time through various associative processes, the speaker musing upon the deaths of her mother and father, her relationship with her therapist, her hospitalizations, her suicide attempts. That the speaker's therapy has failed her is clear from the poem's beginning and is stressed throughout: "Six years of shuttling in and out of this place!" (*LD*, 5). "But you, my doctor, my enthusiast, / were better than Christ; / you promised me another world / to tell me who / I was" (*LD*, 6). The speaker's exclamation "O my hunger! My hunger!" becomes the poet's refrain. The speaker has come to know the asylum well and shocks us in stanza 8 with the notion that she has become so familiar with the place: "In here / it's the same old crowd, / the same ruined scene" (*LD*, 6). The repetition of that idea in stanza 20 is offered in two similes, the first a bit bothersome (evidence that Sexton's images are not always appropriate), and the second quite excellent and illuminating:

> I have come back,
> recommitted,
> fastened to the wall like a bathroom plunger,
> held like a prisoner
> who was so poor
> he fell in love with jail.
>
> (*LD*, 10)

Anticipating the thematic thrust of the entire volume, however, the speaker of "Flee on Your Donkey" concludes with the urge to live. Even though the sort of health anticipated in earlier years may not be possible, even though the hope of becoming "queen of all my sins" may be discarded, still the speaker wants to get out of this place in any way she can: "Anne, Anne, / flee on your donkey, / flee this sad hotel, / . . . any old way you please!" (*LD,* 11).

Finally, "Flee on Your Donkey" displays a significant formal contrast with the earlier "You, Doctor Martin." Sexton remarked upon the gradual loosening up of form from *To Bedlam and Part Way Back* to *Live or Die* and *Love Poems,* moving from "tight form" to "free verse,"[6] and a glance at both "You, Doctor Martin" and "Flee on Your Donkey" illustrates the point. As we have already seen, "You, Doctor Martin" offers tightly structured stanzas and carefully patterned lines and end rhymes; "Flee on Your Donkey," on the other hand, is written in free verse with no visible, external patterning of lines or stanzas. In a 1968 interview, Sexton comments that although madness was for a long time a subject that she needed to deal with in form, "in *Live or Die,* I wrote 'Flee on Your Donkey' without that form and found that I could do it just as easily in free verse. That's perhaps something to do with my development as a human being and understanding of myself, besides as a poet."[7]

The sequence of "Flee on Your Donkey" and the two poems that follow exhibit the natural, chronological treatment of "Live" and "Die" topics that make the organization of this volume so appealing and that lend it an air of continuous musing, making the volume appear to serve as a chronological record of the speaker's thoughts, feelings, and insights. "Flee on Your Donkey" is dated June 1962, as is the poem that follows, "Three Green Windows." One of the finest poems in this volume, "Three Green Windows" demonstrates again the free verse and the calm, reflective tone that typify the poems of *Live or Die.* And "Three Green Windows" extends the "live" motif that closes "Flee on Your Donkey" by taking it in a completely different direction. "Three Green Windows" offers a dreamy, whimsical affirmation of simple, immediate, sensuous pleasure.

"Three Green Windows" is a triumph of poetic mood. The speaker, "Half awake in my Sunday nap," sees "three green windows." The trees outside the windows, "yeasty and sensuous, / as thick as saints," dominate the speaker's trancelike consciousness, creating within her a feeling of peace and safety: "The trees persist," and the "leaves . . . are washed and innocent" (*LD,* 12). Thus protected and dominated, the speaker is freed for the moment from having to care about the pain and difficulty of the real world: "I have forgotten that old friends are dying. / I have forgotten that I grow middle-aged" (*LD,* 12). In her peaceful,

suspended state, the speaker, "on my bed light as a sponge," feels
innocent and childlike, aware of unpleasant realities but untouched by
them:

> I have misplaced the Van Allen belt,
> the sewers and the drainage,
> the urban renewal and the suburban centers.
> I have forgotten the names of the literary critics.
> I know what I know.
> I am the child I was,
> living the life that was mine.
> I am young and half asleep.
> It is a time of water, a time of trees.
>
> (LD, 13)

"Three Green Windows" is followed by another excellent poem, the
elegy "Somewhere in Africa," dated 1 July 1962. This poem, inspired
by the death of Sexton's friend the poet John Holmes, is addressed
directly to him and manifests an abrupt change in theme, mood, and
form. As it concerns Holmes's death from cancer at age fifty-eight, it
develops one aspect of the volume's "die" motif. Since the poem is an
elegy, the speaker's meditations upon Holmes's death are offered in a
formal setting unusual for this volume: the poem comprises seven four-
line stanzas with the end rhymes *a b a b, c d c d,* and so forth and a
concluding rhymed couplet. Exhibiting many aspects of the pastoral
elegy, this poem expresses the speaker's grief at the loss of her friend
and praises Holmes as a sort of modern-day shepherd ("mourned as
father and teacher, / mourned with piety and grace under the University Cross" LD, 14). In a striking image at once memorable and horrible, the poem employs the flower symbolism typical of the pastoral
elegy:

> . . . cancer blossomed in your throat,
> rooted like bougainvillea into your gray backbone,
> ruptured your pores until you wore it like a coat.
>
> The thick petals, the exotic reds, the purples and whites
> covered up your nakedness and bore you up with all
> their blind power.
>
> (LD, 14)

And the pastoral elegy's declaration of belief in some form of immortality becomes the finely wrought image from which this poem derives its title, awarding to Holmes, the critic of Sexton's very female poetry, salvation at the hands of a timeless, original female god:

> Let God be some tribal female who is known but forbidden.
> Let there be this God who is a woman who will place you
> upon her shallow boat, who is a woman naked to the waist,
> moist with palm oil and sweat, a woman of some virtue
> and wild breasts, her limbs excellent, unbruised and chaste.
>
> Let her take you.
>
> (*LD*, 14–15)

Very few poems of *Live or Die* exhibit such formal structure. We have seen Sexton's own comment on the "raw, uncooked" quality of the poems in this volume, and we may speculate that Sexton's general abandonment of traditional forms here results from her growing self-confidence in her craft and in her subject matter and from her therapeutic focus on the materials of dreams. As we have noted, the speaker of "Flee on Your Donkey" makes direct reference to such concerns; midway through that poem, she observes, "Awake, I memorized dreams. / . . . / I stared at them, / concentrating on the abyss. / . . . / my hands swinging down like hooks / to pull dreams up out of their cage" (*LD*, 7).

Dream structure is evident, then, in many poems in this volume, where the progression of associations defies ordinary, waking, common sense; where images are surreal; where, indeed, we must abandon our by-now-familiar way of reading, since using biographical materials as a gloss offers little or no help. Such poems are "Imitations of Drowning," where the speaker alternately evokes, dreamlike, the experience of fear (in stanzas of short lines) with explanations of the occasions of fear (in stanzas of long, proselike lines); "Mother and Jack and the Rain," where rain provides the dream-connection among remembered experiences; "Consorting with Angels," and "To Lose the Earth," both of which appear to be dreams remembered, verbalized, and recorded as they occurred; and "For the Year of the Insane," where dream-logic and the experience of electroshock therapy merge as the various stages of the electroshock experience become the progressions of a prayer to Mary (the name of both the speaker's mother and Christ's mother).

In diverse and unique ways, each of these poems explores and realizes
as well the two thematic motifs named in the volume's title. "Die"
may be represented by drowning, by destructive memory, by the forgetfulness of electrical voltage; "live" may be found in prayer, Mary,
angels, and in the notion of losing oneself to find oneself. As we have
seen, both "live" and "die" are realized in "Flee on Your Donkey" and
"Somewhere in Africa," and "live" finds unique expression in "Three
Green Windows." Other treatments in the volume of these motifs de-
serve some attention.

Die

In the four-year psychological and imaginative record of *Live or Die,*
death and life are balanced against one another, tested, inspected, and
scrutinized with painstaking attention. The poet re-examines many of
the materials of earlier poems, as if she were trying to settle these
troublesome subjects once and for all; her involvements with important
people in her life reappear in *Live or Die,* so that we find here, as in *To
Bedlam and Part Way Back* and *All My Pretty Ones,* poetic assessments
of her relationships with her mother, her father, her Nana, her children, her husband, and her psychiatrist.

Whether the impulses to live and to die strive with each other
within the poem, one ultimately giving way to the other, as in "Flee
on Your Donkey," or whether the poem focuses principally upon one
motif, as in "Three Green Windows," most of the poems explore these
motifs confessionally, in relation to the speaker herself. Thus, as we
have observed, treatments of the "die" motif connect literal or figurative death with such personal experiences as fear and drowning ("Imitations of Drowning"), electroshock therapy ("For the Year of the
Insane"), and return to the mental hospital ("Flee on Your Donkey").

This speaker-centered, confessional aspect of the "die" motif is further illustrated and defined by other poems. One such is "The Sun."
The sun has been a source of great pleasure for the speaker; Sexton
herself loved to sunbathe—note the photograph of her, entitled "the
Sun worshipper—1962" on page 274a of *Letters.* But the sun has now
become a source of sickness ("O yellow eye, / let me be sick with your
heat, / let me be feverish" *LD,* 3). There may have been a medical
cause for this problem; perhaps Sexton was referring here to the fact
that Thorazine, an antidepressant she was taking, made her sensitive
to the sun's rays. Another such poem is "Menstruation at Forty," in
which the speaker muses on the approaching end of her fertility ("I

hunt for death, / the night I lean toward, / the night I want. / . . . / It was in the womb all along" *LD,* 51) and on the additional children she will not have ("I was thinking of a son . . . / You! the never acquired, / the never seeded" *LD,* 51).

Several suicide poems also extend the "die" motif. In July 1966 Sexton attempted suicide, and the poems "Wanting to Die," of 3 February 1964 and "Suicide Note" of June 1965 perhaps anticipate that event. "Wanting to Die" is one of the few poems of this volume written in regular patterned-stanza form ("And One for My Dame," "Somewhere in Africa," "Imitations of Drowning," "Mother and Jack and the Rain," "Two Sons," "Self in 1958," and "Cripples and Other Stories" are the others: eight of thirty-four, though only five of those, "One for My Dame," "Somewhere in Africa," "Mother and Jack and the Rain," "Two Sons," and "Cripples and Other Stories" also employ a regular pattern of end rhymes). "Wanting to Die," like so many of Sexton's poems, adopts the form of a dramatic monologue; in its first line, the speaker addresses "you," a person whom we may guess is the speaker's therapist: "Since you ask, most days I cannot remember." The speaker, responding to a question that we the readers are not given, replies ambiguously; either she cannot remember whatever "you" has asked her, or more likely, she cannot remember "most days," when "I walk in my clothing, unmarked by that voyage." The only memorable days are the ones when "the almost unnameable lust returns," the lust for death. In a letter of 9 February 1964 (having completed "Wanting to Die" on 3 February 1964) Sexton writes that "When (to me) death takes you and puts you through the wringer, it's a man. But when you kill yourself it's a woman" (*L,* 231). So in "Wanting to Die," the speaker makes this distinction of gender between death imposed or chosen: "Twice I have so simply declared myself, / have possessed the enemy, / eaten the enemy, / have taken on his craft, his magic"; "and yet she waits for me, year after year" (*LD,* 58–59). The poem closes with a series of despairing, death-affirming images, one of them reminiscent of Sylvia Plath's imagery: "leaving the page of the book carelessly open, / something unsaid, the phone off the hook / and the love, whatever it was, an infection" (*LD,* 59).

Two "die" poems in this volume, however, remember and elegize the death of others. One of them is "Somewhere in Africa," written on the death of John Holmes, discussed earlier. The other, toward which "Wanting to Die" provides an effective transition, is "Sylvia's Death," dedicated to Sylvia Plath. Invited by Charles Newman, editor of the *Tri-Quarterly,* to write an essay on Plath following her 1963 suicide,

Sexton wrote "The Barfly Ought to Sing." In a 1966 letter to Newman Sexton noted that she had included the poem "Wanting to Die" in the piece, commenting that "It fits in perfectly and is right DIRECTLY to the point of the whole thing. . . . It has such pertinent lines as 'But suicides have a special language. / Like carpenters they want to know *which tools.* / They never ask *why build.*' I feel the wanting to die poem is needed in order to further show the desperately similar need that Sylvia and I share" (*L,* 280). In her sketch "The Barfly Ought to Sing," Sexton introduces "Wanting to Die" this way:

We talked death and this was life for us. . . . I know that such fascination with death sounds strange (one does not argue that it isn't sick—one knows it *is*—there's no excuse), and that people cannot understand. They keep, every year, each year, asking me 'why, why?' So here is the Why-poem, for both of us. . . . I do feel somehow that it's the same answer that Sylvia would have given.[8]

"The Barfly Ought to Sing" concludes with the *Live or Die* poem of 17 February 1963, "Sylvia's Death."

Clearly a "die" poem, "Sylvia's Death" can also be read as a "live" poem, since its speaker expresses regret at Plath's death while simultaneously showing understanding of it. If the death-suicide-sex distinction elucidated in Sexton's "Wanting to Die" comment applies as well to "Sylvia's Death," then Sexton views Plath's suicide as at least untimely. Death in this poem is male: "him," "he," "our boy," the deathly male visitor of Emily Dickinson's "Because I Could Not Stop for Death." Such a view is realized in the poem; death is also a "thief," and in the poem's next-to-last stanza, Sexton cries parenthetically that she and Plath ought not to give up even when things seem hopeless:

> (O friend,
> while the moon's bad,
> and the king's gone,
> and the queen's at her wit's end
> the bar fly ought to sing!).
>   (*LD,* 40)

Sexton has made a comment about her composition of this poem that points to both a major strength and a major weakness of the works in *Live or Die.* About "Sylvia's Death," she writes that "I tried to make it sound like her but, as usual, this attempt was not fruitful; the spirit of imitation did not last and now it sounds, as usual, like Sexton. One of these days I will learn to bear to be myself" (*L,* 170). In fact, *Live or Die* reveals that Sexton *has* learned to bear to be herself and shows that she is at her best when she *is* being herself. On the other hand, a few poems of this collection that are reminiscent of the work of others fail in their "spirit of imitation" and generally pale by comparison with their models.

"Sylvia's Death" is, actually, not one of these failures; it does indeed, as Sexton notes, "sound like Sexton." There are two other poems in *Live or Die,* however, where Sexton's attempt to adopt Plath's style and tone is unsuccessful. In a 1968 interview,, Sexton commented on several ways in which Plath's *Ariel* had influenced her writing. Plath, she said, "had dared to write hate poems, the one thing I had never dared to write. I think the poem, 'Cripples and Other Stories,' is evidence of a hate poem somehow, though no one could ever write a poem to compare to her 'Daddy.' There was a kind of insolence in them. . . . I think the poem, 'The Addict,' has some of her speech rhythms in it."[9] A number of Plath's *Ariel* poems, including "Daddy," do project insolence in the expression of powerful emotion; comparison with the poems Sexton mentions reveals the relative strengths of Plath's work.

Sylvia Plath's "Daddy" adopts a nursery-rhyme rhythm to express the speaker's stark confrontation with her hate-love of Daddy and husband. Power derives from the combination of tight form (five-line stanzas of anapestic trimeter, many lines with the end rhyme "oo"), ironic use of the nursery rhyme, and astonishing content; the voice we hear is hard and jaunty:

> You do not do, you do not do
> Any more, black shoe
> In which I have lived like a foot
> For thirty years, poor and white,
> Barely daring to breathe or Achoo.
> . . . .
> There's a stake in your fat black heart
> And the villagers never liked you.
> They are dancing and stamping on you.
> They *always knew* it was you.
> Daddy, daddy, you bastard, I'm through.[10]

Sexton's "Cripples and Other Stories" is also written in regular form (four-line stanzas of basically iambic trimeter with matching end

rhymes in the second and fourth lines). Its subject is no doubt as difficult for Sexton to deal with as the subject of "Daddy" is for Plath; in
"Cripples and Other Stories," Sexton confronts her perception that her
parents, mother as well as father, never loved her, and mixes therapist
with father in the poem. Yet the hard-edged power of Plath's "Daddy"
is missing here, and Sexton appears not to dare Plath's insolence:

> God damn it, father-doctor.
> I'm really thirty-six.
> I see dead rats in the toilet.
> I'm one of the lunatics.
> . . . .
> Though I was almost seven
> I was an awful brat.
> I put it in the Easy Wringer.
> It came out nice and flat.
>   (LD, 80–81)

Similarly, "The Addict," in which Sexton tries to capture "some of
[Plath's] speech rhythms," pales by comparison. When reading "The
Addict" one thinks less of Plath's "Daddy" than of her "Lady Lazarus":

> Dying
> Is an art, like everything else.
> I do it exceptionally well.
>
> I do it so it feels like hell.
> I do it so it feels real.
> I guess you could say I've a call.[11]

Sexton expresses a similar idea in "The Addict":

> Don't they know
> that I promised to die!
> I'm keeping in practice.
> I'm merely staying in shape.
> The pills are a mother, but better,
> every color and as good as sour balls.
> I'm on a diet from death.
>   (LD, 85)

Another example of a poem in *Live or Die* that seems unsuccessfully
reminiscent of someone else's work is "Man and Wife" (May 1963).

Reading it, one thinks of Robert Lowell's great poem of the same name from *Life Studies* (1959). Both "Man and Wife" poems explore the theme of loss of passion in a long-married couple; both poems tie the experience to similar Boston locales (Marlborough Street in Lowell's poem; the North End, Louisburg Square, the Common in Sexton's); Sexton's poem uses for its epigraph the title of Lowell's poem that follows "Man and Wife" in *Life Studies:* "To Speak of Woe That Is in Marriage." The similarities are too many and too obvious to be ignored, though Sexton's "Man and Wife" would fare better without Lowell's to compare it with. The tranquillizing alliteration of "m" in Lowell's opening cadences, expressing and joining the words' meaning, render the lines memorable: "Tamed by *Miltown*, we lie on Mother's bed."[12] Here are Sexton's opening lines: "We are not lovers. / We do not even know each other." It is a similar idea but much less richly expressed.

It must be said, however, that there are far more poems in *Live or Die* in which Sexton does "bear to be [herself]" than poems that are weakly derivative. Some fine poems may be found in this volume; we have already looked at a few of them ("Flee on Your Donkey," "Three Green Windows," "Somewhere in Africa"), and we will examine others. One of the great successes of *Live or Die* is the clear, focused, structurally effective imagery that Sexton often employs. In "Crossing the Atlantic," for example, the imagery is evocative and on-center. "Being inside [the steel staterooms where night goes on forever] is, I think, / the way one would dig into a planet / and forget the word *light*" recreates exactly the feel and association of being in a small, windowless stateroom. "The Wedding Night" offers an elaborate, clever, poem-long conceit on the theme of deflowering, metaphorically comparing the wedding night to the opening and falling of magnolia blossoms.

Live

Other successful poems realize and extend the other thematic motif named in this volume's title, "live." These "live" poems appear to fall into three general categories: those that reveal the speaker's attempt to survive through self-understanding; those that express the speaker's love for her daughters; and the volume's closing poem, "Live," which retrospectively sets the direction of the entire volume's poem-sequence.

There are four poems in *Live or Die* where the speaker strives to understand the woman she has become by focusing on earlier life ex-

periences. Although these poems may not seem as obviously positive
as the other "live" poems or as affirmative as the closing of "Flee on
Your Donkey," they are life-affirming in their very impulse of trying
to understand and connect self with self. "Those Times . . ." explores
recollections of "the year I was six," reworking the idea of "being the
unwanted, the mistake / that Mother used to keep Father / from his
divorce." Although the poem is full of prisoner and exile imagery ("I
was locked in my room all day behind a gate, / a prison cell. I was the
exile"), it concludes with the notion of blooming into womanhood and
motherhood. "Protestant Easter," subtitled "eight years old," is an excellent poem that offers fresh, affecting, childlike perceptions. It is
written entirely from the point of view of an eight-year-old and reveals
the associations a child might make of the Easter season with Jesus and
the resurrection with her parents with the Easter church service. The
stream-of-consciousness structure appealingly recreates the child's
mind:

> *Alleluia* they sing.
> They don't know.
> They don't care if he was hiding or flying.
> Well, it doesn't matter how he got there.
> It matters where he was going.
> The important thing for me
> is that I'm wearing white gloves.
> I always sit straight.
> I keep on looking at the ceiling.
>   (*LD*, 43)

The dates appended to "Self in 1958" reveal this as a poem begun
when Sexton was thirty and completed seven years later (June 1958–
June 1965); it begins and ends with the question "What is reality?"
"Christmas Eve" is another fine poem in which the thirty-five-year-old
speaker sits alone musing on her mother's portrait:

> Later, after the party,
> after the house went to bed,
> I sat up drinking the Christmas brandy,
> watching your picture,
> letting the tree move in and out of focus.
> The bulbs vibrated.
> They were a halo over your forehead.
>   (*LD*, 54)

Peace is achieved as the speaker sees herself as both daughter and mother and invokes the forgiveness of Mary (also Sexton's mother's name): "then I said Mary— / Mary, Mary, forgive me / and then I touched a present for the child, / the last I bred before your death." (*LD*, 55).

Two poems of *Live or Die* are addressed directly to Sexton's daughters: "Little Girl, My String Bean, My Lovely Woman" to eleven-year-old Linda, and "A Little Uncomplicated Hymn" to ten-year-old Joyce. "Little Girl" opens with a simile that establishes the poem's controlling imagery: "My daughter, at eleven / (almost twelve), is like a garden" (*LD*, 62). Following these lines, the speaker addresses her daughter directly in love and pleasure; images of ripening fruit and vegetables describe whimsically the daughter's ripening into womanhood. The daughter Joyce is just as lovingly and joyfully addressed in "A Little Uncomplicated Hymn." Although the poem recapitulates some material of earlier poems (notably "The Double Image" and "Unknown Girl in the Maternity Ward" in *To Bedlam and Part Way Back*), in which Sexton expresses guilt at having left this infant daughter to spend time in a mental institution, love and joy dominate this poem. Oversentimentality is avoided by the freshness of imagery, realism, and colloquial expression that undercut what might otherwise seem mawkish.

About the poem "Live," Sexton has observed in a 1968 interview:

Some [poems] were negative and some were positive. . . . I knew that I was trying to get a book together. I had more than enough for a book, but I knew I hadn't written out the live or die question. I hadn't written the poem "Live." This was bothering me because it wasn't coming to me. . . . and then suddenly our dog was pregnant. I was supposed to kill all the puppies when they came; instead, I let them live and I realized that if I let *them* live, that I could let *me* live, too, that after all I wasn't a killer, that the poison just didn't take.[13]

Clearly, then, the conclusion that Sexton sought for her volume, and the answer she wanted to give to the question posed by the volume's title, was "Live." The volume's closing poem, dated "February the last, 1966," repeats as its epigraph the last line of the volume's epigraph from *Herzog*: "Live or die, but don't poison everything. . . . ," indicating that "the live or die question" is indeed settled, at least for now.

The poem comprises two sections, the first (stanzas 1 and 2) describing and summarizing the death with which the speaker has long been

living, and the second (stanzas 3, 4, and 5) offering the discoveries
that allow her to discard death and affirm life.

By "death" in this poem, the speaker means all of the developmental
traumas and psychological difficulties that she perceives to have crippled her; one might specify these by re-examining not only this volume's "die" poems but also most poems of the first two volumes.
"Well," begins the speaker of "Live," "death's been here / for a long
time" (*LD*, 87). She now has a "dwarf-heart"; "the chief ingredient /
is mutilation." Existence has become empty and mechanical:

> Even so,
> I kept right on going on,
> a sort of human statement,
> lugging myself as if
> I were a sawed-off body
> in the trunk.
>
> (*LD*, 87)

"Is life," she asks, "something you play? / And all the time wanting
to get rid of it?" (*LD*, 88). The speaker's tone projects exhaustion and
defeat.

The third stanza, by contrast, offers an abrupt change: "Today life
opened inside me like an egg / and there inside / after considerable
digging / I found the answer" (*LD*, 88). With this image of fertility
and rebirth, the speaker reveals three epiphanies, three commonplace
situations in which she suddenly perceives her existence in a new light,
all of them involving intuitive discoveries of events outside of herself.
The first, extending the egg-fertility image, is simply that there is an
ordinary and real world outside of her that in her despair and depression she has neglected to notice:

> There was the sun,
> . . . .
> I'd known she was a purifier
> but I hadn't thought
> she was solid
> hadn't known she was an answer.
>
> (*LD*, 88)

The speaker's second and related discovery has to do with her family.
In her deathly, introverted perspective, she has failed to realize that

her husband and children do not see her in the extreme, desperate light
in which she views herself:

> God! It's a dream,
> ....
> a husband straight as a redwood,
> two daughters, two sea urchins,
> picking roses off my hackles.
> If I'm on fire they dance around it
> and cook marshmallows.
> And if I'm ice
> they simply skate on me
> in little ballet costumes.
>
> (*LD,* 88–89)

In the saving ordinariness of everyday life, her family thinks of her not
as "a killer, / anointing myself daily / with my little poisons" as she
sees herself, but as wife, mother, poet, as *female:* "I wear an apron. /
My typewriter writes" (*LD,* 89). The speaker's third epiphany is trig-
gered by the birth of the Dalmatian puppies she chooses to let live:
"So I say *Live* / and turn my shadow three times round / to feed our
puppies as they come, / the eight Dalmatians we didn't drown" (*LD,*
89). In images that echo some of Sylvia Plath's but which are this time
completely successful in their realization, the speaker knows that

> in spite of cruelty
> and the stuffed railroad cars for the ovens,
> I am not what I expected. Not an Eichmann.
> The poison just didn't take.
> So I won't hang around in my hospital shift,
> repeating The Black Mass and all of it.
> I say *Live, Live* because of the sun,
> the dream, the excitable gift.
>
> (*LD,* 90)

"Live" is a marvelously affirmative poem that, as we have seen, establishes the thematic direction that Sexton intended for *Live or Die.*
Ultimately, however, the theme that strikes one as preeminent in this
volume is not "live" but "endure." The evidence of the entire volume's
four-year chronology of "live" and "die" poems tempers the wholly
positive note of the conclusion; "die" is clearly not the dominant

theme, one feels, but many compelling "die" poems remain in the mind even after one has finished reading. Indeed, endurance is a dominant theme in *Live or Die;* the speaker of "Walking in Paris" observes that "to be occupied or conquered is nothing— / to remain is all" (*LD,* 49). So that finally, with the speaker of "Mother and Jack and the Rain" (*LD,* 19), we can say that the thematic weight of this volume is "to endure, / somehow to endure."

Chapter Five
Love Poems: "A Woman Who Writes"

By the time of the writing of *Love Poems*, Anne Sexton had become both a well-known and widely recognized poet. Having been awarded the Pulitzer Prize for Poetry for *Live or Die* in 1967, she continued to receive prestigious awards: an honorary Phi Beta Kappa from Harvard University in 1968 and a Guggenheim Fellowship and an honorary Phi Beta Kappa from Radcliffe College in 1969. She became actively involved in the teaching of poetry, aided by a National Endowment for the Humanities grant in 1967–68; she began reading her poetry to musical accompaniments, an activity that led to the formation of a rock group, "Anne Sexton and Her Kind." She gained new confidence, and according to Linda Gray Sexton and Lois Ames, "suicide ceased to be a daily threat between 1967 and 1970" (*L, 313*).

Anne Sexton's fourth published volume of poetry, *Love Poems,* was accepted by Houghton Mifflin in the summer of 1968 and published in February 1969. Its twenty-five poems were written between the summers of 1966 and 1968. Reviewing her work up to this time, Sexton observed in an interview that in her first two volumes (*To Bedlam and Part Way Back* and *All My Pretty Ones*) she had dealt with madness; in her third (*Live or Die*) she had become more poetically daring; and in *Love Poems,* "I have not only lived but loved, that sometime miracle."[1] She may have long anticipated such a volume; remarking upon the contents of *To Bedlam and Part Way Back* in a 1959 letter, Sexton observed that "there isn't one (not even a little one) love poem. Imagine! A woman, her first book, and not a love lyric in the lot" (*L,* 80).

One hears at least a hint of irony in that remark, a subtle indication that Sexton recognized—and was undercutting—the traditional and sexist assumption that love is one of the few subjects fit for the consideration of female writers. For these are love poems with a difference, clearly consistent with the intimate revelations and flamboyant atti-

73

tudes of Sexton's earlier work, and just as clearly not the sweet, sentimental lyrics that might mollify such male critics as those who
believed Sexton's confessional subjects unfit for poetry, who contended
that her work achieved no more than psychological documentation, or
who found the *Live or Die* poems "painful, embarrassing, and irritating."[2] Many critics of Sexton's first three volumes recoiled from what
they saw as this poet's indecorous treatment of madness, suicide, family
relationships, and sex; *Love Poems* might have (and may have) sent them
running.

Love's Violence, Love's Joy

Sexton's own perception of her fourth volume is instructive and revealing, both in what she does and in what she does not say. It is, she
claimed in a 1968 interview, "a happier book than the others. . . . In
some ways the love poems are a celebration of touch—that's the name
of the first poem—but physical and emotional touch. It is a very physical book."[3] In another interview of the same year, Sexton observes that
although "the subject of therapy was an early theme—the process itself
. . . , the people of my past, admitting what my parents were really
like, the whole Gothic New England story," the poetry in *Love Poems*
is different: "One can say that my new poems, the love poems, come
about as a result of new attitudes, an awareness of the possibly good as
well as the possibly rotten. Inherent in the process is a rebirth of the
sense of self, each time stripping away a dead self."[4] Reading this volume, one marvels at Sexton's description of it. A "happier book than
the others" it may be, but one would hesitate to call it happy in any
ordinary sense of the word. It is indeed "a very physical book," but to
see in it "a celebration of touch," one must read for "celebration" both
"praise" and "commemoration." These poems do evince "an awareness
of the possibly good as well as the possibly rotten," but the "sense of
self," where there is any "rebirth" at all, is reborn in peculiar ways.
These love poems are fierce, intense, desperate, tormented, and angry
more than they are tender or joyful.

"The Touch," the poem that opens the volume, offers an appropriate
introduction both in the way which Sexton suggests (establishing the
notion that all of these love poems are "a celebration of touch") and in
a way that she perhaps does not consciously intend. In the poem's
opening stanzas, the speaker, represented by her hand, is isolated,
blind, and motionless: "It lay there like an unconscious woman. / . . .

/ An ordinary hand—just lonely / for something to touch / that touches back" (*LP*, 1). Her lover's touch brings life to this hand:

> Then all this became history.
> Your hand found mine.
> Life rushed to my fingers like a blood clot.
> Oh, my carpenter,
> the fingers are rebuilt.
>
> (*LP*, 2)

What we should notice here is not only the "celebration of touch" but also the relationship of speaker to lover and the lover's relative power. The lover is the actor here; the speaker is passive and waiting ("Your hand found mine"). It is the lover who makes "Life [rush] to [her] fingers." The lover is a "carpenter," a builder; all power of creation is his. Yet the simile for life is "blood clot"; there is animating blood, but "clot" connotes death.

These themes, of male lover as both life-giver and destroyer, and of speaker as passive and acted upon, are either implied, realized imagistically, or stated openly in most of this volume's poems. Related themes are developed as well; love brings torment, anger, and even death as well as joyful life. In "Barefoot," images of love and murder are linked: "You do / drink me. The gulls kill fish" (*LP*, 35). Other poems anticipate the fairy-tale mythology of *Transformations*. The speaker may be a fairy-tale heroine, waiting for her prince to awaken her; in "The Kiss," she reveals that "before today my body was useless," but now "my mouth blooms like a cut" (*LP*, 3). (Notice how alike the two similes are, "like a blood clot" and "like a cut.") This speaker's prince is a creator: a "carpenter" in "The Touch," and a ship builder in "The Kiss" ("Once [my body] was a boat, quite wooden / . . . / . . . But you hoisted her, rigged her" [*LP*, 3]).

Other poems offer imagery and relationships similar to those of "The Touch" and "The Kiss." For example, in "The Breast" the speaker exclaims that "the child in me is dying, dying. / . . . / But your hands found me like an architect" (*LP*, 4). In "Moon Song, Woman Song," the speaker is "alive at night" and "dead in the morning" (*LP*, 31). The lover in "Now" should "turn me over from twelve / to six," and the lovers' room is "a shoe box . . . a blood box" (*LP*, 39). In "Mr. Mine," the lover "constructs" the speaker. "From the glory of boards he has built me up" (*LP*, 43).

"The Break" is a kind of psychodrama that extends these images and offers new ones. Because it is both a love poem and a poem to commemorate Sexton's breaking of her hip in a fall on her thirty-eighth birthday in 1966, and perhaps because it is longer than the poems cited above, "The Break" extends the female / passive and male / active motif while realizing in greater detail the imagery of violence that links love or its absence with torment, anger, and death. From the poem's opening stanzas, one recognizes the meaningful ambiguity of the poem's title and occasion; "The Break" signifies emotional as well as physical disaster, both a broken hip and a broken heart:

> It was also my violent heart that broke,
> falling down the front hall stairs.
> It was also a message I never spoke,
> calling, riser after riser, *who cares*
>
> *about you, who cares,* splintering up
> the hip.
>
> (*LP*, 23)

Complex relationships are realized here. The speaker's physical break is a correlative of her emotional one, and her actual fall is made an expression of anger at a lover for having left her. Suppression of anger precipitates a cataclysmic event; since anger is "a message I never spoke," the consequence of silence is destruction. Both sadness and violence break the speaker's heart. She "explode[s] . . . like a pistol." Such a psychological condition is one to which women are particularly susceptible. The poet Adrienne Rich has commented on its sources; the destruction of unexpressed anger, she observes,

is crucial because for women to dissemble anger has been a means of survival, and therefore we turn our anger inward. Women's survival and self-respect have been so terribly dependent upon male approval. I almost think that we have a history of centuries of women in depression: really angry women, who could have been using their anger creatively, as men have used their anger creatively.[5]

Actually, in "The Break" Sexton the poet reveals her awareness of this female dilemma. She *is* using her anger creatively by realizing its effects in this poem. Yet here the anger works both ways; its suppression destroys the poem's speaker at the same time as its release creates the poem.

Following the fall, the explosion, the speaker is broken and helpless: "The ambulance drivers" (presumably men) "placed me, tied me up on their plate, / and wheeled me out to their coffin" (*LP*, 23). The ambulance is a "hearse." The speaker is stripped both of her clothing and of what remains of her identity: "At the E. W. they cut off my dress" (*LP*, 23). The speaker seeks her last chance at help and validation from a man, to no avail. Nor does the woman standing by offer help. The tiny, witty drama played out here reveals the poet's awareness that the speaker will find no aid from any source: "I cried, 'Oh Jesus, help me! Oh Jesus Christ!' / and the nurse replied, 'Wrong name. My name / is Barbara,' and hung me in an odd device" (*LP*, 23). The speaker's passionate cry to Jesus is undercut by the abrupt cadence of the nurse's reply: "Wrong name." In these lines, diction, mood, and sense combine to create meaning; there is no Jesus here, and besides, Jesus is a man who cannot help. There is only Barbara. As feminist critic Alicia Ostriker points out, such subversion of mythic material is a salient feature of poetry by women: "With women poets we look at, or into, but not up at, sacred things; we unlearn submission."[6]

The rest of the poem emphasizes the break's twin nature: "The fracture was twice. The fracture was double" (*LP*, 24). Both the heart and the body of the speaker have become corpses, but only one of them will heal: the bones "will knit," but "the other corpse, the fractured heart" (*LP*, 25) will not. Images of death objectify the speaker's condition. Life and death here and elsewhere in these poems are red flowers or blood. It is particularly interesting to note that one of these images extends a reference we have seen in "The Touch." If life is a "blood clot" in "The Touch," suggesting at once animating blood and death, in "The Break" death prevails: "My one dozen roses are dead. / They have ceased to menstruate. / They hang / there like little dried up blood clots" (*LP*, 24).

Related to "The Touch" and "The Break" with its blood clot imagery, the short poem "Again and Again and Again" further defines the speaker's anger. Here, anger is at first artificial, unconnected with the speaker's self because she is unaccustomed to expressing it: "I have a black look I do not / like. It is a mask I try on" (*LP*, 29). Her "good look," however, is "like a blood clot." Although she has "made a vocation of [love]," it both animates and destroys. And finally, genuine anger breaks out with annihilating force:

> Oh the blackness is murderous
> ....

and I will kiss you when
I cut up one dozen new men
and you will die somewhat,
again and again.

(*LP*, 29)

These are the poems where Sexton powerfully and affectingly expresses anger and hate toward men. We have seen (in chapter 4) Sexton's comment that Plath's *Ariel* influenced her, especially in its
daring: "Plath had dared to write hate poems, the one thing I had
never dared to write. I'd always been afraid, ever in my life, to express
anger."[7] Strangely, in the 1968 interview where Sexton makes these
remarks, she offers the *Live or Die* poems "Cripples and Other Stories"
and "The Addict" as examples of poems that do express hate and anger.
Yet as we have seen, the emotion of these poems does not ring as true
as it does in such *Love Poems* as "The Break" and "Again and Again and
Again." It is peculiar indeed that Sexton failed to mention these in her
August 1968 interview, since *Love Poems* was accepted for publication
at about that time. Perhaps she dared not.

In any case, Plath's influence is apparent in two other *Love Poems*,
which also express hate and anger. The Nazi imagery so familiar in
Ariel is evident here as well. In "December 2nd," the second section
of "Eighteen Days Without You," the speaker, whose lover has left her,
has a dream: "you dragged me off by your Nazi hook. / I was the piece
of bad meat they made you carry" (*LP*, 47). The arresting title of another poem, "Loving the Killer," reveals the speaker's ruinous ambivalence. The occasion of this poem is an African safari on which Sexton
and her husband went, made possible by a travel grant awarded Sexton
by the Congress for Cultural Freedom. For Sexton's husband, the safari
was a "dream come true," as she observes in a 1966 letter (*L*, 300).
For her, it was a horror, "watching the animal die slowly and then be
served it that night for dinner" (*L*, 299). In "Loving the Killer," then,
the obvious reference is to the lover as a killer of animals. The submerged reference is more devastating. Love itself is murderous: on safari, "love came after the gun, / after the kill" (*LP*, 18). In lines
reminiscent of Plath, the speaker of "Loving the Killer" exclaims: "Oh
my Nazi, / with your S.S. sky-blue eye— / I am no different from
Emily Goering" (*LP*, 19).

Although such images of destruction and anger, victimization by
men, and complicity and hate are evident in a substantial number of
the poems in this volume, there are also poems that move in other

directions. Some declare the theme we have seen of female as passive and acted upon, of lover as life-giver or life-withdrawer, without expressing or suggesting anger. Sexton's friend and collaborator, poet Maxine Kumin, observes that "a good case might be made for viewing [Sexton's] poems in terms of their quest for a male authority figure to love and to trust. . . . in Sexton's poetry the reader can find the poet again and again identifying herself through her relationship with the male Other."[8] We see this relationship developed in such poems as "The Touch," "The Kiss," "The Breast," "Moon Song, Woman Song," "Mr. Mine," and "The Break." In two other poems, the speaker specifically addresses the departure of the "male Other" and the resulting lapse of the speaker into insignificance and lifelessness. "You All Know the Story of the Other Woman" concludes with these lines: "when it is over he places her, / like a phone, back on the hook" (*LP,* 30). The "other woman," the speaker, is an inanimate thing, a plastic object to be placed "on the hook" after use.

One of the finest poems in the volume, "For My Lover, Returning to His Wife," explores the situation more richly. Here, the roles of the wife and the other-woman speaker are contrasted. Although this poem defines both the wife and the speaker in relation to the husband-lover, the speaker chooses to create for herself the position of lesser value: "She is all there. / She was melted carefully down for you / and cast up from your childhood, / cast up from your one hundred favorite aggies" (*LP,* 21). Both wife and speaker are female objects for the lover's use, yet the wife occupies a position of relative solidity while the speaker is an interloper. The wife is "as real as a cast-iron pot"; the speaker is "momentary." The wife is "all harmony"; the speaker is "an experiment." The wife "has always been there"; the speaker is a brilliant but transient "luxury," a "bright red sloop in the harbor." Red is by now a familiar color in these poems, connoting at once animation and death. The speaker perceives her value to the lover as only temporary: She is "littleneck clams out of season" (*LP,* 21). The imagery of this poem is clear and precise as the speaker expresses, in quiet, drained tones, her loss and insignificance. Here is how the poem closes:

> She is solid.
>
> As for me, I am a watercolor.
> I wash off.
>
> (*LP,* 22)

Love Poems shows Anne Sexton at her confessional best. She seems clearly in control of her craft here; her feeling is genuine, and it is realized effectively in precise, expressive imagery, convincing tone, and poetic structure. In a 1968 interview, Sexton noted:

> In *Bedlam*, I used tight form in most cases, feeling that I could express myself better. . . . In my second book, *All My Pretty Ones*, I loosened up. . . . I found myself to be surprisingly free without the form which had worked as a kind of superego for me. In the third book I used less form. In *Love Poems*, [with a few exceptions] all of the book is in free verse, and I feel at this point comfortable to use either, depending on what the poem requires.[9]

This comfort is evident; these poems express feeling in appropriate forms and express it passionately and powerfully.

All that feeling, however, is not anger, torment, and loss. A discussion of *Love Poems* would be incomplete without mentioning what may be the only truly affirmative poem of the lot, "In Celebration of My Uterus." In a 1966 letter to Robert Bly, Sexton describes the occasion of this poem: "Day before yesterday they were going to give me a hysterectomy but yesterday I want to some big deal specialist in Boston and I can keep it. So saved is a part of the soul of the woman who lives in me. I thought today that I would write a poem 'In Celebration of My Uterus' but . . . you wouldn't like it (too extreme)" (*L,* 302). Whether or not the poem is too extreme for a male audience, it joyfully celebrates femaleness and shows, for once, a lively disregard for the approval, or disapproval, of external male authority. "Sweet weight, / in celebration of the woman I am" is the poem's refrain; the poem celebrates "the soul of the woman I am / and . . . the central creature and its delight." "I sing for you," declares the speaker. "I dare to live" (*LP,* 12).

The *Love Poems,* then, are fierce, intense, angry, joyful, and self-assured. They are indeed love poems with a difference, exploring love's violence as well as love's joy, and offering such topics as physical sex, masturbation, and adultery. Clearly, as Maxine Kumin observes, "Women poets in particular owe a debt to Anne Sexton, who broke new ground, shattered taboos, and endured a barrage of attacks along the way because of the flamboyance of her subject matter, which, twenty years later, seems far less daring. . . . Today, the remonstrances seem almost quaint."[10]

A Woman Who Writes

It should be said, at this point, that the available evidence indicates that Anne Sexton did not consider herself a feminist; she did not, that is, claim for herself a public position supporting women's issues or advocating women's rights, either as an individual or as the member of an organization. There is, to be sure, some evidence in her writing of subtle but noteworthy change in her attitudes toward herself as a woman and toward other women. Nevertheless, it would probably be inaccurate to claim her as a consciously feminist writer. The rationale we may offer for viewing her in that light is to apply to her work that famous slogan of the 1960s: the personal is political. According to that dictum, all personal experiences, even the most trivial, are a result of the dynamics of and the struggle for power.

Anne Sexton was a suburban housewife and for most of her life claimed to be relatively comfortable with that role. Before she began seriously writing poetry in 1958 at the age of twenty-eight, she had a husband of eight years, two children, and a house in Newton Lower Falls, Massachusetts. She was, as she observed in a 1968 interview, "trying my damnedest to lead a conventional life, for that was how I was brought up, and it was what my husband wanted of me."[11] In a 1959 letter to Carolyn Kizer she wrote:

My two children keep interrupting my chain of thought for a cookie, girl scout variety. I have two girls, age 5½ and 3½, and a good husband who is not the least a poet, and very much a business man—but all in all a happy marriage in the suburbs. I have only been writing for a little over a year. But have really put great energy into it and would be no one at all without my new tight little world of poet friends. I am kind of a secret beatnik hiding in the suburbs in my square house on a dull street. (*L*, 70–71).

Even though she may have thought of herself as a "secret beatnik," this suburban housewife of the late 1950s subscribed in conventional ways to the prevailing attitudes of a male-dominated culture. In 1958, while a student in Robert Lowell's graduate writing seminar at Boston University, Sexton wrote in a letter to W. D. Snodgrass of her "secret fear" that Lowell would consider her a "reincarnation of Edna St. Vincent" Millay and expressed her "fear of writing as a woman writes. I wish I were a man—I would rather write the way a man writes" (*L*, 40). In a 1959 letter to Carolyn Kizer, Sexton related a conversation she had had with Robert Lowell about Kizer's poem "A Muse of Water." "It seems," wrote Sexton, "a careful poem to me, no rape or danger and still not the usual weakness displayed by the female poet. He agreed" (L, 69).

It would have been marvelously convenient and enlightening for later feminist critics if Sexton had specified what she meant, in these early letters, by "writing as a woman writes" and by "the usual weakness displayed by the female poet." What we can see in these and other letters is Sexton's ambivalence toward her work and her role; she considered herself at once a happy suburban housewife, a "secret beatnik," and a woman writer who feared writing like a woman; she found a certain female weakness in writing of "rape or danger." Apparently she felt, perhaps as a result of encouragement by her male mentors, that any honest or direct expression of her female nature was socially and artistically unacceptable, something to be done furtively and well out of sight. Although she was driven to write her kind of poetry, she feared that it would find no acceptance in the world she knew; as she wrote in a 1959 letter, "The stuff I write is so controversial. NO ONE WILL LIKE IT. . . . The whole trouble being that my writing has guts, but I do not" (L, 68).

Such pronouncements, offered up in Sexton's letters and interviews and realized in her poems, render her work of great significance to any reader interested in the attitudes, impulses, strategies, and accommodations of the modern woman writer. As feminist critic Jane McCabe puts it, "Although I would not suggest that Anne Sexton is a feminist poet, I think that her poetry catches the feminist's eye and ear in special ways."[12] In many ways, Sexton is the last prefeminist poet; she wrote her early confessional work in what was probably the final decade of this century in which a woman could write without being fully aware of feminist concerns. Love Poems, her fourth volume, was published in 1969 and accepted in 1968, the same year Mary Ellmann's pioneering Thinking About Women appeared. Observes feminist critic Annette Kolodny:

Had anyone had the prescience, in 1969, to pose the question of defining a "feminist" literary criticism, she might have been told, in the wake of Mary Ellmann's Thinking About Women, that it involved exposing the sexual stereotyping of women in both our literature and our literary criticism. . . . What could not have been anticipated in 1969, however, was the catalyzing force of an ideology that, for many of us, helped to bridge the gap between the world as we found it and the world as we wanted it to be.[13]

Sexton's insecurities and domestic ambivalence are exactly the sorts of issues on which feminist criticism focused; "exposing the sexual stereotyping of women" is precisely what her poems accomplish.

In exclaiming that "my writing has guts, but I do not," Sexton expressed clearly the kind of culturally imposed insecurity that women have long felt and that feminist writers are now, through recognition, trying to explode. As feminist critic Elaine Showalter points out, "Women writers have always been . . . susceptible . . . to the aesthetic standards and values of the male tradition, and to male approval and validation."[14] Deference to these values and a continuous quest for this "approval and validation" are principal characteristics of Sexton's early work.

In "The Double Image" (*TB*) the speaker addresses her daughter: "Today my small child, Joyce, / love your self's self where it lives. / There is no special God to refer to." (*TB*, 54). Sexton knows that this is the best advice she can give her daughter, yet it is advice that she cannot believe in for herself. In her early poems she constantly refers to other gods, almost always men, and in doing so continually seeks to validate herself in terms of male authority figures. We have already noted the observation of Sexton's friend, Maxine Kumin, that "in Sexton's poetry the reader can find the poet again and again identifying herself through her relationship with the male Other."[15] In Sexton's first four volumes of poetry, then, we find the poems' speaker seeking childlike approval from her male psychiatrist ("What large children we are / here. All over I grow most tall / in the best ward" [*TB*, 4]) or, childlike and lost, asking directions of a male stranger ("Wait Mister. Which way is home?" [*TB*, 8]), or looking for understanding from a disapproving male mentor (in "For John, Who Begs Me Not to Enquire Further" [*TB*,, 51–52]), or proclaiming that she "lay there like an unconscious woman" before being awakened by her lover's touch ("The Touch" [*LP*, 1–2]). Whether the male figure be doctor, father, husband, lover, or someone else, the speaker expresses submission and deference.

A feeling of powerlessness is one product of habitual submission and deference, and feminist theory has drawn our attention to the possibility of female madness and suicide as the threatened result. Much has been written about female madness, death, and suicide in literature as the only way for a female character situated in such a submissive and deferential position to achieve power and self-expression. A number of Anne Sexton's *Love Poems* explore the destructive result of female submission. Ruinous anger and hate explode in such poems as "The Break" and "Again and Again and Again"; the result of such strong emotion is death or paralysis. Many of Sylvia Plath's *Ariel* poems evince similar themes. The fictional case histories of other writers abound as well, from the mad narrator of Charlotte Perkins Gilman's "The Yellow Wallpaper" to Kate Chopin's suicidal Edna Pontellier, Edith Wharton's Lily Bart, and Sylvia Plath's Esther Greenwood, to name only a few. As Adrienne Rich points out, "If you deviate from a situation which is described to you as normal, you start feeling abnormal." This is "the situation of the American middle-class woman who is expected to spend her life full-time on child care."[16] Angry and frustrated at being relegated to an outsider status, closed off from the sources of power, women, says Rich, respond with "revolutionary violence. Obviously we're not talking about smashing the dishes, beating one's children. Women have done that for centuries. And we've turned our anger even more often into self-destructiveness,"[17] to the point, one should add, where women completely sublimate the anger and cease feeling it, or anything, at all.

Anne Sexton, who commented on the poet–suburban housewife duality in her own existence, who said that she had always been afraid, both in her poetry and in her life, to express anger,[18] who wrote "I had a rather violent fight with my [male] . . . psychiatrist . . . and went into the mental institution for a while" (L, 144), would appear to be the prototypical male-dominated, powerless, silently angry, self-destructive, mid-twentieth-century woman. But are we on firm enough ground to reach such a conclusion? In a discussion of such personal poetry, the distinction between poet and poem-speaker blurs and often disappears. Clearly it is the text to which we must apply our primary focus rather than the poet herself; we can never know with certainty what Sexton's demons were. There are poems, however, especially in the volume *Love Poems,* that demonstrate Sexton's cognizance of the destructive effects of anger turned inward. "The Break," for example, gives us simultaneously the speaker's experience of destructively suppressed anger and the poet's creative use of that anger. In creating a distance between speaker and poet, Sexton here and elsewhere effectively dramatizes the female dilemma of which Adrienne Rich speaks.

The madness and the suicidal impulses realized in Sexton's poetry are, therefore, one aspect of her work that "catches the feminist's eye and ear"; another closely related aspect is the poet-speaker's relation to male authority figures. Sexton realizes these themes in some of her best poems, for her best early poems are her most confessional ones in which she dares to write about various aspects of herself, exploring her role as a wife, a mother, a daughter, and an artist. Even if she dares not be completely, sanely open, rhetorically dismissing herself as "a poet or a crazy writer" (*L,* 160) in order to speak frankly, she does speak. And it is our opportunity as readers to look behind the mask.

Another theme of interest to feminists in Sexton's poetry is her relationship with her mother, and her relationship as a mother with her own daughters. In "The Double Image" (*TB*), a poem addressed both to mother and to daughters, the speaker and her mother are "the double woman who stares / at herself"; the mother is "my mocking mirror, my overthrown / love, my first image" (*TB,* 60). The speaker is uneasy about her female identity; to her daughter she says:

> I, who was never quite sure
> about being a girl, needed another
> life, another image to remind me.
> And this was my worst guilt; you could not cure
> nor soothe it. I made you to find me.
>
> (*TB,* 61)

The speaker of "Housewife" (*PO*) concludes that "a woman *is* her mother. That's the main thing" (*PO,* 48). Such a realization, according to Elaine Showalter, moves beyond "scenarios of compromise, madness, and death" to signal the advent of "a new women's writing, which explores the will to change" by repudiating the "rejection of the mother that daughters have learned under patriarchy": "Hating one's mother was the feminist enlightenment of the fifties and sixties, but it is only a metaphor for hating oneself. Female literature of the 1970s goes beyond matrophobia to a courageously sustained quest for the mother."[19] Sexton shows both impulses. In "Christmas Eve" (*LD*) she speaks to her mother, Mary Gray Sexton:

> I saw you as you were.
> Then I thought of your body
> as one thinks of murder. . . .

Then I said Mary—
Mary, Mary, forgive me.
                    (LD, 55)

Here, Sexton's speaker moves beyond matrophobia and self-hate to acceptance of herself as daughter and as mother.
    A further question of interest to feminists that Sexton herself has raised has to do with language. What does she signify by expressing her "fear of writing as a woman writes"? It strikes one that Sexton may have had in mind her voice, more than her themes, by this reference. What she may have meant by "the usual weakness displayed by the female poet" may refer to the obvious, familiar, and sexist criticism often made of women's voices. Terms like *shrill, shriek, screech,* and *bitchy* are reserved principally for description of the way women speak, negative, critical terms used by men or by women unaware of linguistic sexist bias. And Sexton has indicated her efforts to rid her poetry of just these sorts of sounds. "Although I have many 'poet-friends,'" she writes in a 1959 letter, "they are so used to my extra-flamboyant stuff that they have missed reminding me . . . to flatten it down" (L, 55). "I've been trying a new tone," Sexton writes in another letter of the same year. "I don't want my next book to be as boomy as the Bedlam one. A little more restraint and never a false shriek" (L, 94). "I don't think L. I. Ferry really a good poem of mine," she writes two years later—"too sentimental. But perhaps I'm wrong. Perhaps I ought to allow my female heart more room. . . . but I'm going to harden up soon I promise myself . . . stop all the emoting around and get down to facts and objects" (L, 127).
    Anne Sexton is here doing violence to herself by denying two aspects of her linguistic style. First, she realizes that she writes powerfully and flamboyantly in spite of her instinct, imposed by traditional male values, that she ought to behave in stereotypically "feminine," passive ways. She remains conflicted on this point, for at the same time that she thinks that she ought to write with more restraint (and "stop emoting around"), her genuine (better, one might say) inclinations won't permit it. The poet's socialized self, then, strives to suppress her innate impulses. Furthermore, when Sexton criticizes her work as "too sentimental," she expresses a different sort of denial. Instead of wishing her tone to be more stereotypically feminine by moderating the false shrieks, she expresses the suspicion that she sounds *too* feminine. To resolve this dichotomy (I don't sound at all like a woman should sound—I sound too much like a woman), she suggests the elimination

of feeling altogether ("get down to facts and objects"), or at least achieving the appearance of having done so. Such a dilemma has notable precedent; as Alicia Ostriker points out,

> throughout most of her history, the woman writer has had to state her self-definitions in code form, disguising passion as piety, rebellion as obedience. Dickinson's "Tell all the Truth but tell it slant" speaks for writers who in every century have been inhibited both by economic dependence and by the knowledge that the true *writer* signifies assertion while the true *woman* signifies submission[20]

To be sure, there is clear evidence of the expression of slanted truth in Sexton, what Ostriker calls "revisionist mythmaking": "hit-and-run attacks on familiar images [of gender stereotypes embodied in myth] and the social and literary conventions supporting them."[21] The "two male Ph.D.'s" of "Venus and the Ark" (*TB*), who are painstakingly, pretentiously thorough in bringing male and female animal species to populate Venus, forget to include human women and end by "crying alone / for sense, for the troubling lack / of something they ought to do" (*TB, 20*). The speaker of "Cripples and Other Stories" (*LD*) dares momentarily to damn the authority of her psychiatrist-father:

> *Each time I give lectures*
> *or gather in the grants*
> *you send me off to boarding school*
> *in training pants.*
>
> God damn it, father-doctor.
> I'm really thirty-six.
>
> (*LD, 80*)

And the speaker also damns, in anger, the Nazi-lover of "Loving the Killer" and "Eighteen Days without You" (*LP*).

We also find in Sexton's work the sort of inactivity that is the product of the feminine–nonfeminine conflict we have noted. Images of passivity pervade these superficially flamboyant poems, a passivity that, suggests Ostriker, results from Sexton's perception that "the hypocrisies of civilized rationality are powerless to destroy what is destructive in the world and in ourselves. . . . Wherever we find images of compelling dread, there we also find images of muteness, blindness, paralysis, the condition of being manipulated."[22] Examples abound.

Listen to the mad, lost, institutionalized speaker of "Music Swims
Back to Me":

> It was the strangled cold of
> November;
> even the stars were strapped in the sky
> and that moon too bright
> forking through the bars to stick me
> with a singing in the head.
> I have forgotten all the rest.
>
> (TB, 8)

The speaker of "Wanting to Die" (LD) opens with these lines: "Since
you ask, most days I cannot remember. / I walk in my clothing, unmarked by that voyage" (LD, 58). In "The Break" (LP) the speaker's
broken body is one corpse, and her spirit is "the other corpse, the
fractured heart" (LP, 25).

All this evidence, however, points more to the subtle, slant, revisionist use of imagery and tone than to any particularly female use of
language itself. The linguistic question is a difficult one, one that a
number of feminist critics have addressed in various ways but that
remains unsolved. Mary Ellmann, for example, builds an interesting
case in support of her contention that since male writing is assertive
and female writing undercuts solemn assertion by means of amusement
or hostility, "the *sensation* of authority remains . . . the only test . . .
by which one can distinguish between male and female prose."[23] Alicia
Ostriker, as we have seen, emphasizes the subversive nature of female
writing: "If male poets write large, thoughtful poems while women
poets write petite, emotional poems," modern "book-length mythological poems by women [such as H.D.'s *Helen in Egypt,* Susan Griffin's
Woman and Nature: The Roaring Inside Her, Anne Sexton's *Transformations*] challenge not only our culture's concepts of gender but also its
concepts of reality."[24] And it is not only in poetry that much modern
women's writing realizes its subversive intent; "the gaudy and abrasive
colloquialism of Alta, Atwood, Plath, and Sexton, for example, simultaneously modernizes what is ancient and reduces the verbal glow
that we are trained to associate with mythic material. . . . With
women poets we look at, or into, but not up at, sacred things; we
unlearn submission."[25] Most theories that seek to identify sex differ-
ences in language do, in fact, grow from the premise that men's linguistic usages are products of the biological, cultural, and social power

and authority with which men have traditionally been invested, and that women's language somehow reflects their historical role of outsider, either confirming or subverting feminine stereotypes (which are, according to Mary Ellmann, "Formlessness, Passivity, Instability, Confinement, Piety, Materiality, Spirituality, Irrationality, Complacency, and Shrew/Witch"[26]).

Such theories are appealing; the female reader is delighted to hear, in Sexton's poetry, a refreshingly subversive colloquialism in such lines as:

> O little Icarus,
> you chewed on a cloud, you bit the sun
> and came tumbling down, head first,
> not into the sea, but hard
> on the hard packed gravel.
> You fell on your eye. You fell on your chin.
> What a shiner!
>
> (*LD, 67*)

Or, as we have seen in "The Break," the poet thoroughly, colloquially undercuts the speaker's emotional appeal to mythic authority: "I cried, 'Oh Jesus, help me! Oh Jesus Christ!' / and the nurse replied, 'Wrong name. My name / is Barbara'" (*LP, 23*).

But any linguistic theory that refers to historical sexual stereotyping runs the risk either of perpetuating those stereotypes or of creating new ones, a result clearly to be avoided. Furthermore, it cannot be said that the colloquial use of language is gender marked. Jane McCabe's observation is accurate:

although women and men do not and will never share the same kind of body, they do share the same language. Of course, we all use language according to the occasion; we talk differently to the motor vehicle clerk than we do to our lovers. Public talk has a different cadence than private talk. But women cannot claim to have introduced a personal, colloquial language into poetry. Perhaps they use it more naturally now because they are more thoroughly used to it, but it cannot be said to have been invented by women as a new approach to poetry. Wordsworth, after all, wanted in 1800 . . . "to imitate . . . [and] adopt the very language of men." And we think of Whitman or Williams or Ginsberg or Lowell or a dozen other male poets.[27]

It is certain that the quality of looking "at, or into, but not up at sacred things," of "unlearn[ing] submission" does mark much female

writing, but since such a subversive tendency does not mark all or only
female writing, one finds it difficult to elevate that principle, attractive
though it may be, to the status of a general rule.

Subversion and irreverence are, however, qualities that mark Anne
Sexton's poetry. Her confessional poems are nearly always flamboyant,
irreverent, and subversive. Perhaps their very defiance is a product of
the poet's own ambivalence, since Sexton's colloquialisms undercut her
own timidity while at the same time challenging male authority. In a
1965 interview, Patricia Marx asked Sexton, "What is your feeling
about the 'feminine mystique'? One is always hearing of the problems
of modern woman. Do you think it's any worse now?" Sexton's reply
is instructive and revealing in its diffidence: "Maybe modern woman
is more conscious now, more thinking. I can't tell. Sometimes I feel
like another creature, hardly a woman. . . . I can't be a modern
woman. I'm a Victorian teenager—at heart" (L, 78).

This "other creature" appears in several of Sexton's early poems.
Alienated from her female self, this "secret beatnik hiding in the suburbs," this "boomy," flamboyant poet characterizes her true self as a
witch. Witches (always female, of course) are by nature alienated, different, shunned by society. More important, a witch possesses magic
powers. And Sexton is one of "Her Kind":

> I have gone out, a possessed witch,
> haunting the black air, braver at night;
> dreaming evil, I have done my hitch
> over the plain houses, light by light:
> lonely thing, twelve-fingered, out of mind.
> A woman like that is not a woman, quite.
> I have been her kind.
>
> (TB, 21)

This witch may appear an ordinary woman in daytime, but she lives
on the border of sanity and normalcy, going out into the night world
to pursue her true imaginative vision, transforming the ordinary domestic scene into something mad and nightmarish: "I have found the
warm caves in the woods, / filled them with skillets, carvings, shelves,
/ . . . / A woman like that is misunderstood. / I have been her kind"
(TB, 21). In "The Black Art" Sexton refers again to witchery:

> A woman who writes feels too much,
> those trances and portents!

> As if cycles and children and islands
> weren't enough; as if mourners and gossips
> and vegetables were never enough.
> She thinks she can warn the stars.
> A writer is essentially a spy.
> Dear love, I am that girl.
>
> (*PO*, 65)

Poetry is the witch's magic, and "trances and portents" are her tools: "A woman who writes feels too much."

Simultaneously driven and afraid to write as a woman writes, the witch-poet-speaker of *Love Poems* becomes one of "her kind" as a matter of survival. She speaks, from the border of night, of dreams and nightmares; celebrating touch, she strives to achieve "a rebirth of a sense of self."[28] These passionate, defiant, subversive love poems evince not so much joy as euphoria, not so much tenderness as submission. For this witch, imagination obviates the chance for ordinary domestic existence; for this poet, anger is both creative fire and destruction; for this woman, love is both life and death.

Anne Sexton did grow in the direction of feminism. In an interview just months before her death in 1974, Sexton and Maxine Kumin discussed with Elaine Showalter their long friendship. After Kumin observed that "We're [Kumin and Sexton] very autonomous people, but it *is* a nurturing relationship," Showalter asked: "What difference would it have made if there had been a women's movement?" Kumin replied: "We would have felt a lot less secretive." Added Sexton: "Yes, we would have felt legitimate."[29]

Chapter Six
Transformations: Fairy Tales Revisited

The seventeen poems in *Transformations,* Anne Sexton's fifth volume of poetry, were written in about one year, between the winter of 1969–70 and November 1970, when Sexton submitted the volume to Houghton Mifflin. Published in 1971 *Transformations* received general critical acclaim, despite its publisher's initial reluctance to accept it; as Linda Gray Sexton and Lois Ames observe, "Houghton Mifflin did not take well to the dark ribaldry of [Anne Sexton's] book, and told her so. . . . Undaunted by subtle pressure from Houghton Mifflin not to publish her book, Anne hinted that she might take her work elsewhere. Ultimately, *Transformations* was to sell more hard-bound copies than any other Sexton book" (*L,* 359).

Markedly different from Sexton's earlier work, these poems seemed at first to Sexton not a conscious departure but "a kind of dalliance" (*L,* 363). Reacquainted with the familiar Grimm fairy tales by her daughter Linda's interest in them, Sexton began to write her own versions. As Maxine Kumin points out, "The book more or less evolved; she had no thought of a collection at first, and I must immodestly state that I urged and bullied her to go on after the first few poems to think in terms of a whole book of them."[1] Sexton's method of selecting which tales to "transform" in a poem was spontaneous and instinctive; she chose the ones she liked because they suggested to her a special or particular meaning. As she commented in a 1973 interview, "Sometimes my daughter would suggest 'read this or that, try this one' . . . and if I got, as I was reading it, some unconscious message that I had something to say, what I had fun with were the prefatory things, . . . that's where . . . I expressed whatever it evoked in me—and it had to evoke something in me or I couldn't do it."[2]

Fairy-Tale Subjects

Indeed, fairy tales, which are part of the childhood experience of most of us, suggest a multiplicity of both subconscious and plain messages to readers of any age. Developed within the Western European oral tradition, recorded and overlaid with nineteenth-century didacticism, these tales express the underlying values of Western culture. As the scholar and translator Jack Zipes points out in the introduction to his 1987 translation of the Grimm tales, the Grimm brothers "made major changes while editing the tales," changes that "underline morals in keeping with the Protestant ethic and a patriarchal notion of sex roles."[3]

From these tales, then, which project a mixture of entertainment, folk wisdom, and Western morality, we remember the beautiful and beleaguered heroines, the evil and cackling witches, the leering and threatening wolves and monsters, the gentle and helpful doves and fish and ants, the powerful kings, and the incredibly handsome princes. The stories are vivid and exciting. Beautiful Cinderella (we remember the colorful illustrations), kept in bondage and made to do all the dirty housework by her very selfish and clumsy stepmother and stepsisters, finds release through the magical intercession of several white birds, the persistent search of a handsome, love-smitten prince, and the essential coincidence of a small, dainty foot. Snow White, whose very name is purity, is finally discovered by her prince, too, with whom we are certain she will live happily ever after. Her preliminary tribulations are caused by a jealous stepmother whose maddeningly honest mirror continues to proclaim Snow White "a thousand times more fair"; she supports herself, before the prince's advent (and before she eats an apple, which of course causes a great deal of trouble) by keeping a tidy little house for the seven cute little dwarfs. The witch, always a female, appears variously and often in fairy tales; she seems most interested in ruining the innocent by burning them, or by imprisoning them, or by magically creating an unwelcome change in their identity.

Though we probably don't realize it when we are children, we are being mentally and imaginatively programmed as we are delighted and terrified. A mature reader can plainly see in these tales the patriarchal bias of a male-oriented social view. Ambitious women are witches, ugly and scheming, wielding over other women and men alike a magical, evil power of transformation, or at least wielding some kind of power. Good women are quiet, domestic, and submissive; they take care of children and/or home while their men go out and "work." Strangely, housework is drudgery for some heroines, like Cinderella, and her reward is escape. But we do not think that revolutionary thought at the time; it is her discovery by the prince that captures our attention. And surely, there will be no housework in her future. And so, like Cinderella, sometimes in these fairy tales if the heroine has not yet become a wife, if she is very lucky and very beautiful (the first depends on the second), and of course if she is virginally pure, her charming prince may come along, discover that the shoe fits, free her from the tower, or awaken her with a kiss. (She has, of course, been only sleeping in all her previous life without the prince.) What happens to her then we are never told, except that the beautiful princess and handsome prince live happily ever after. That is perhaps what we mean when, as adults, we use the term "fairy tales."

Though this fairy-tale world may be peopled with demure princesses and adventuresome men, however, it is also a world of nightmare and terror, where heroines and heroes must pass through a period of testing before triumphing over the witch, finding their way out of the forest, or breaking the evil spell. Although we must recognize a tendency in these tales to advocate the maintenance of a sexist status quo, such a structure alone cannot account for the fairy tales' ageless appeal to children and to adults alike. Child psychologist Bruno Bettelheim argues that fairy tales, by enchanting, terrifying, and delighting children, help them to "cope with the psychological problems of growing up and integrating their personalities." By experiencing the fairy-tale world, which "simplifies all situations," and in which "characters are typical rather than unique," children face and solve moral, psychological, ethical, and emotional conflicts and learn to master by themselves "the problem which has made the story meaningful . . . in the first place."[4]

Such anxieties and fears as separation from parents, oedipal conflicts, sibling rivalry, sexual awakening, and parental rejection are given both shape and resolution in these tales. Hansel and Gretel survive in the threatening forest without their deserting parents; Gretel burns the witch and frees her brother; Snow White and Cinderella are saved both by males and by their own efforts from their jealous stepmothers and sisters; Rapunzel provides with her own body the means of escaping from the witch to her prince. It is therefore "uninformed," contends Bettelheim, to see the happily-ever-after fairy-tale ending as "unrealistic wish-fulfillment," for such an ending assures the child of the desirability of separating from parents to form new relationships. "If we try to escape separation anxiety and death anxiety by desperately keeping our grasp on our parents, we will only be cruelly forced out, like Hansel and Gretel."[5] As psychoanalyst William Mark Dean points out,

> fairy tales express universal states of regression which all children experience when faced with the traumata and conflicts of growing up. Children can identify with the heroines and heroes of fairy tales and vicariously struggle through their ordeals. Most importantly they learn that there are ways out of these dilemmas, that with perseverance and courage, the challenges and conflicts of growing up can be overcome.[6]

These stories, then, evoke a multitude of responses in us that are likely to vary depending upon the age, experience, and predilections of the reader. The "unconscious messages" that they evoked in Anne Sexton appear consistent with the thematic concerns of her previous poetry: guilt, love, anger, and madness; uneasy relationships between parents and children; ambivalence over women's roles; imaginative identification of poet with witch; anxiety and fear over sexual awakening, parental rejection, or oedipal conflicts; and the torment and joy of passion. Such themes are precisely those that Bettelheim designates as typical fairy-tale subjects.

Structure: "an enlarged paper clip"

If Sexton's themes in *Transformations* are congruous with fairy-tale concerns, her method in these poems is indigenous to the fairy-tale mode as well. Each poem follows a prologue-body form, except for the first poem in the series, "The Gold Key," which serves as a general prologue to the whole volume (and which is itself also a "transformation" of a very short Grimm tale called "The Golden Key"). The remaining sixteen poems begin with a prologue of one or more stanzas, indented to emphasize the prefatory nature of the section and to clarify its boundaries. Here, Sexton introduces the context that she has chosen for the tale, providing a thematic focus for the rest of the poem. Sexton's retelling of the tale follows; in this section of each poem we find a story that resembles the Grimm version but that Sexton has reshaped. "Oh, yes," she comments in an interview, "I embellished [the Grimm tale], oh, indeed, it wasn't that way."[7] For example, here is part of the prologue of "Rumpelstiltskin":

> Inside many of us
> is a small old man
> who wants to get out.
> ....
> He is a monster of despair.
> He is all decay.
> He speaks up as tiny as an earphone
> with Truman's asexual voice:
> I am your dwarf.
> I am the enemy within.
> I am the boss of your dreams.
> ....
> See. . . .
> ....
> It is your Doppelgänger
> trying to get out.
> Beware . . . Beware . . .

Then the tale begins:

> There once was a miller
> with a daughter as lovely as a grape.[8]

The style is campy and humorous (dark and otherwise) as the speaker retells and reinvents the Grimm stories, offering witty embellishments along the way. Such an approach coincides neatly with the original fairy-tale mode, for in order to dramatize their meanings clearly and effectively, fairy tales offer us cartoon characters involved in complex situations that have been reduced to bare essentials. So Sexton announces precisely this approach in "The Gold Key"; this is, she writes, a "book of odd tales / which transform the Brothers Grimm.

> ....
> As if an enlarged paper clip
> ....
> could be a piece of sculpture.
> (And it could.)
>   (T, 2)

This volume is to be a pop-art creation, true to the cartoon nature of fairy-tale character and situation; it will have illustrations, as do all respectable fairy-tale books. Writes Sexton in a 1970 letter, anticipating the artwork of Barbara Swan, "I'd like [these poems] to be well-illustrated—a real zap of a production even if they aren't the old Sexton style" (*L,* 361).

Thus, while illustrations designate and simplify theme and character, language and imagery underscore the poems' quality of caricature. Snow White is introduced in offhand and slangy language as a kind of pop-art poster, "a lovely number: / cheeks as fragile as cigarette paper"; when revived by the dwarfs from her first encounter with her wicked stepmother, she is "as full of life as soda pop" (*T,* 3, 7). When the heroine of "Rumpelstiltskin" is unable to spin straw into gold, she weeps "of course, huge aquamarine tears" (*T,* 18). The parson in "The Little Peasant," discovered hiding in the miller's closet, stands "rigid for a moment, / as real as a soup can" (*T,* 30). Rapunzel's song pierces the prince's heart "like a valentine" (*T,* 40). Huntsmen disappear into Iron Hans's forest "like soap bubbles" (*T,* 45). One-Eye's eye is "like a great blue aggie" (*T,* 61). After the witch's supper, Hansel and Gretel sleep, "z's buzzing from their mouths like flies" (*T,* 103).

Shortly before Sexton submitted the completed *Transformations* for publication, she wrote a letter in which she offered her assessment of her new volume. Her comments show her view of these poems both in themselves and as they relate to her previous work:

> I realize that the "Transformations" are a departure from my usual style. . . . I wrote them because I had to . . . because I wanted to . . . because it made me happy. I would like my readers to see this side of me, and it is not in every case the lighter side. Some of the poems are grim. In fact I don't know how to typify them except to agree that I have made them very contemporary. It would further be a lie to say that they weren't about me, because they are just as much about me as my other poetry. (*L,* 362)

The tales that evoked an "unconscious message" in Sexton are precisely those to which she felt a subliminal connection; these poems are therefore "just as much about [her] as [her] other poetry." Sigmund Freud theorizes that some individuals may make "fairy tales into screen memories," so that the fairy tales themselves come to symbolize submerged feelings and conflicts, actually "tak[ing] the place of memories of their own childhood."[9] Moreover, the creative writer, suggests Freud, is likely to be, at some instinctive, subconscious level, in especially close touch with the meaning of fairy tales and dreams, for "there can be no doubt that the connections between our typical dreams and fairy tales and the material of other kinds of creative writing are neither few nor accidental. It sometimes happens that the sharp eye of a creative writer has an analytic realization of the process of transformation of which he is habitually no more than the tool."[10] It is perhaps this process to which Sexton refers in "The Gold Key" when she asks: "Do you remember when you / were read to as a child? / . . . have you forgotten? / Forgotten the ten P.M. dreams / where the wicked king / went up in smoke?" (T, 1).

Anne Sexton's "transformations," then, are just as much about the poet herself as her earlier poetry. They are Grimm fairy tales recalled, recast, and reshaped by Sexton; the poet's personal stamp is evident in the very selection of tales to "transform," in the prologues that she provides for each poem-tale, and in the breezy, offhand comments and observations interspersed through each poem. In noting that the *Transformations* poems are "very contemporary," Sexton no doubt points both to her thematic adaptation of the tales for her own creative use and to the related "enlarged paper clip," pop-art quality that we have noted. These poems are also both, and often simultaneously, humorous and "grim" (pun intended?). They are inventive, surprising, and witty; they exemplify revisionist mythmaking at its best.

"A Different Language"

The most striking feature of these poems, and the characteristic that makes them most dramatically Sexton's own, is the sound of the speaker's voice. When we read a fairy tale, or when we remember hearing fairy tales in our childhood, we hear immediately a disembodied, omniscient third-person speaker. "Once upon a time" does not attempt to make either narrator or tale sound individual or "real"; in fact, the attempt is just the opposite. In terms of reality, intensity, and immediacy, the fairy tale is the most distanced of any kind of narrative, and purposely so. By inviting the reader to listen to a little tale of something that might have happened a long, long time ago in make-believe land, the fairy-tale narrator clears the way for offering to the widest possible audience a story that entertains while offering a cautionary or didactic message and manages to accomplish this purpose without offending anyone.

Sexton's transformations, on the other hand, are spoken by a very real first-person narrator who reminds us constantly, with prologues and frequent interpolations, that mythic materials are being shaped for specific use. In a voice that demands our attention, this narrator is sarcastic, sympathetic, and funny; she warns, or draws conclusions, or makes connections that are entirely her own. Listen, for example, to the opening of "Little Red Cap" in Grimm:

Once upon a time there was a sweet little maiden. Whoever laid eyes upon her could not help but love her. But it was her grandmother who loved her most. She could never give the child enough. One time she made her a present, a small, red velvet cap, and since it was so becoming and the maiden insisted on always wearing it, she was called Little Red Cap.[11]

Now hear the way Sexton begins the story of "Red Riding Hood" in *Transformations:*

> In the beginning
> there was just little Red Riding Hood,
> so called because her grandmother
> made her a red cape and she was never without it.
> It was her Linus blanket, besides
> it was red, as red as the Swiss flag,
> yes it was red, as red as chicken blood.
> But more than she loved her riding hood
> she loved her grandmother who lived
> far from the city in the big wood.
>
> (*T*, 76)

This story, says the speaker to the audience, may be cast in a "once upon a time" mode in your memory and imagination, but I am going to make it new for you, for me, for this specific moment. "In the beginning" there may have been "just little Red Riding Hood," but I am taking that tale and discovering in it my own personal and contemporary meanings.

And this speaker reminds us continually of her presence; her voice is persistent and ubiquitous. As Sexton admits in a 1970 letter in which she asks Kurt Vonnegut to write an introduction to her new volume:

I've taken Grimms' Fairy Tales and "Transformed" them into something all of my own. . . . I do something very modern to them. . . . They are small, funny and horrifying. Without quite meaning to I have joined the black humorists. I don't know if you know my other work, but humor was never a very prominent feature . . . terror, deformity, madness and torture were my bag. But this little universe of Grimm is not that far away. (L, 367)

The poet has indeed taken these tales, which perpetuate patriarchal and sexist values, which advocate traditional moral behavior, which facilitate ethical, psychological, and emotional growth, which help us to overcome the anxieties and conflicts of childhood and to achieve an integrated identity, and has done "something very modern to them" in precisely those ways she mentions. The "universe of Grimm" is certainly not very far from the universe of Sexton, and in combining the two, this poet has indeed created a language of her own.

We hear this language, the rhythm and sound of this unique voice, in all the *Transformations* poems. "Snow White" can serve as an example. In the Grimm tale, Snow White's mother dies shortly after giving birth to her beautiful daughter. The new stepmother is "beautiful but proud and haughty, and she [can] not tolerate anyone else who might rival her beauty."[12] Until Snow White is seven, the stepmother-queen's magic mirror assures the queen that she herself is fairest in the realm, but then the mirror begins to proclaim Snow White by far the fairest. The queen cannot bear this situation; "like weeds, the envy and arrogance grew so dense in her heart that she no longer had any peace, day or night." In an attempt to get rid of Snow White, the queen enlists a huntsman to kill her stepdaughter and bring her lungs and liver to the queen, but the huntsman, amazed at Snow White's beauty, instead warns Snow White of her danger and brings to the queen the organs of a wild boar, which the queen eats. Snow White escapes into the forest ("Wild beasts darted by her at times, but they did not harm her"), finds the seven dwarfs' cottage, and agrees to keep house for the dwarfs (who are also impressed by her beauty) in exchange for their protection. The evil queen, meanwhile, discovers from her mirror that Snow White has survived ("As long as Snow White was the fairest in the realm, the queen's envy would leave her no peace"), and tries three times to eliminate her competition, each time by visiting the dwarfs' cottage in disguise and gaining access to Snow White with "pretty wares." Twice the dwarfs arrive home in time to save Snow White, first by untying a tight staylace that has nearly suffocated the beautiful girl, second by removing from her hair a poisoned comb. The third time, however, the queen entices Snow White to eat a poisoned apple. The

dwarfs, unable to revive her, place her in a glass coffin which a passing
prince, much later, sees; he falls in love with the beautiful, motionless
girl, and takes and then drops the coffin so that the apple flies out of
Snow White's throat, thereby reviving her. The evil queen, invited to
the wedding of Snow White and the prince, discovers once again from
her mirror that Snow White lives and surpasses her in beauty. Arriving
for the wedding, she finds that "iron slippers had already been heated
over a fire, and they were brought over to her with tongs. Finally, she
had to put on the red-hot slippers and dance until she fell down dead."
    The language Sexton uses to "transform" this tale is the most con-
spicuous feature of this poem. Here is the first stanza and prologue of
"Snow White and the Seven Dwarfs":

> No matter what life you lead
> the virgin is a lovely number:
> cheeks as fragile as cigarette paper,
> arms and legs made of Limoges,
> lips like Vin Du Rhône,
> rolling her china-blue doll eyes
> open and shut.
> Open to say,
> Good Day Mama,
> and shut for the thrust
> of the unicorn.
> She is unsoiled.
> She is as white as a bonefish.
>
> (*T*, 3)

The cadences are apparently effortless, clear and fluent; the diction is
slightly slangy, confidential, and irreverent. Metaphor and adverb contribute to the breezy, "contemporary" sound. There is also, as Christopher Lehmann-Haupt points out in a 1971 review of *Transformations*,
"the surprise of odd juxtapositioning: similes that deflate romance,
humor as black as ebony."[13] Nearly every line of this first stanza uses
simile or metaphor to develop theme and tone: "the virgin is a lovely
number," "cheeks as fragile as cigarette paper, / arms and legs made of
Limoges," and so forth. Line lengths also express meaning; the three-
word lines sound mechanical, doll-like. By all these means, Sexton
deflates characters' pretensions, undercuts most expectations held by
readers of Grimm, and rebuilds in their place her own view of things.
Later in the poem, when the wicked queen first visits Snow White and

sells her a staylace, she fastens it "as tight as an Ace bandage, / so tight that Snow White swooned. / She lay on the floor, a plucked daisy." When the dwarfs undo the stay, "she revived miraculously. / She was as full of life as soda pop" (*T*, 7).

Words and phrases are carefully crafted; the contrast between the older, appropriately fairy-tale usage of "swooned" and the slangy words surrounding it is humorous and offers subtle demonstration that Sexton is subverting mythic materials for her own use. With this linguistic technique in mind, listen to the poem's second stanza, which follows the prologue:

> Once there was a lovely virgin
> called Snow White.
> Say she was thirteen.
> Her stepmother,
> a beauty in her own right,
> though eaten, of course, by age,
> would hear of no beauty surpassing her own.
> Beauty is a simple passion,
> but, oh my friends, in the end
> you will dance the fire dance in iron shoes.
> The stepmother had a mirror to which she referred—
> something like the weather forecast—
> a mirror that proclaimed
> the one beauty of the land.
> She would ask,
> Looking glass upon the wall,
> who is fairest of us all?
> And the mirror would reply,
> You are fairest of us all.
> Pride pumped in her like poison.
>
> (*T*, 5)

Grimm to Sexton: A Magic Mirror

Clearly, then, Sexton's use of language is one of the principal means by which she "transforms" fairy tales into modern poems. Through language the poem's speaker rebuilds the original Grimm materials, reconstituting them into something all her own. Furthermore, what the poet achieves in these poems through language she also accomplishes with content. The analogy of a fun-house mirror is apt (and recalls the queen's magic mirror in "Snow White"): like a distorting mirror that enlarges and collapses parts of the original image reflected in it, both amusing and frightening the viewer, Sexton's *Transformations* distort the original Grimm tales, amplifying and magnifying some details, contracting and eliminating others. These poems are in several ways like an "enlarged paper clip" sculpture, both in language and in the content to which that language gives shape.

To continue with the example of "Snow White," the original Grimm version concerns, as we have seen, an innocent girl beset by the jealousy of her evil stepmother, saved by a hunter, by dwarfs, and by a prince, nearly destroyed by her own vanity and by a poisoned apple, and ultimately delivered from her troubles. Bruno Bettelheim discusses the emotional and psychological structure of this story, pointing out the ways in which the tale helps a child subliminally work through complex and threatening problems and achieve an integrated identity. "Snow White," he writes, "deals essentially with the oedipal conflicts between mother and daughter; with childhood; and finally with adolescence, placing major emphasis on what constitutes a good childhood, and what is needed to grow out of it."[14] It is narcissism that undoes the queen and almost undoes Snow White; the queen represents the jealous mother, envious of her daughter's budding sexuality, whose desire to claim Snow White's attractiveness for herself is symbolized by her eating of what she thinks are Snow White's lungs and liver. Snow White's own narcissism causes her to succumb to the queen's evil blandishments; she is nearly destroyed but is ultimately saved by others.

Among those "rescuing male figures," says Bettelheim, are the hunter (a protective father-figure who sides secretly with the daughter but is too weak to stand up to the mother-queen) and the dwarfs (substitute fathers with whom she lives in peace but who, because they are not true relatives but represent only wish-fulfillment, are ultimately unable to protect her). The dwarfs (miners, who dig into the earth) represent as well "males who are stunted in their development" and as such demonstrate along with Snow White "childhood before puberty, a period during which all forms of sexuality are relatively dormant." Snow White's encounters with the queen dramatize her movement into adolescence, showing conflict and unsuccessful attempts to escape back into "a conflict-free latency period" (represented by the dwarfs' cottage), together with the temptation of vanity as Snow White three times lets the queen into the house. Says Bettelheim, "Since it is Snow

White's own vanity which seduces her into letting herself be laced, she and the vain stepmother have much in common." After Snow White eats the poisoned apple, which stands, says Bettelheim, both for love and for sex (recollecting the apples of Aphrodite and Eden), the child in her dies and she is eventually reborn a woman from the glass coffin. But "before the 'happy' life can begin, the evil and destructive aspects of our personality must be brought under our control"; thus, the queen must die. "Untrammeled sexual jealousy, which tries to ruin others, destroys itself—as symbolized not only by the fiery red shoes but by death from dancing in them."[15]

All these materials are present in Anne Sexton's transformations of "Snow White," but Sexton's magic mirror elevates Snow White's vanity to a position that moves beyond Grimm and Bettelheim, developing Snow White into someone who promises to follow in her stepmother's shoes, a sort of junior queen. In Sexton's "Snow White and the Seven Dwarfs," as in Grimm, the queen is narcissistic and envious, and Snow White is prepubescent, a "dumb bunny," with "china-blue doll eyes" that "open and shut." Unlike Grimm's, however, Sexton's forest through which Snow White passes on the way to the dwarfs' cottage is full of sexual threat: there is a wolf with "his tongue lolling out like a worm"; there are birds that "[call] out lewdly," and there are "snakes hung down in loops" (T, 6). Sexton also emphasizes the phallic nature of Snow White's environment during her stay with the dwarfs: the dwarfs themselves are "little hot dogs" (T, 6), and the poisoned comb that Snow White buys from the queen is "a curved eight-inch scorpion" (T, 8). Furthermore, if as Bettelheim says the eating of food represents in fairy tales the eater's desire to "acquire the powers of characteristics of what one eats,"[16] Sexton demonstrates Snow White's sexual urges by having her eat the dwarfs' "seven chicken livers," as the poem has previously shown the queen's will to claim Snow White's beauty by eating her lungs and liver. In Grimm, Snow White eats only the dwarfs' more innocuous vegetables (variety unspecified) and bread.

Thus in Sexton's "Snow White," as in many other poems of *Transformations,* sexual themes are magnified, and the fairy-tale promise of finding an emotionally mature, psychologically integrated, happy life remains unfulfilled. The heroine of Sexton's tale fails to work her way successfully through the complex problems of growing up and, becoming her mother, remains caught in a nightmarish world. At the end of the poem, the queen, clearly a figure of evil and destructive sexual jealousy, "danced until she was dead, / a subterranean figure, / her tongue flicking in and out / like a gas jet." But her destruction does not represent the lowering of the final barrier to Snow White's happy maturity, for "meanwhile Snow White held court, / rolling her china-blue doll eyes open and shut / and sometimes referring to her mirror / as women do" (*T*, 9). Sexton's Snow White remains naïve; she is a child who still has "china-blue doll eyes" that "open and shut," a reference that echoes the poem's prologue and suggests that Snow White still shuts those eyes "for the thrust of the unicorn." Yet she is corrupt as well; since she now "refer[s] to her mirror," she has become in all ways the new queen. And this behavior is, says the poem's last line, not isolated but typical; it is something that "women do."

Witches, Women, Wives

Anne Sexton appropriately begins "The Gold Key" with these words: "The speaker in this case / is a middle-aged witch, me—" *T*, 1). Sexton's identification of herself as witch evokes New England traditions of witchcraft and is clear in such earlier poems as "Her Kind" (*TB*) and "The Black Art" (*PO*); in those poems, and in references in many others, the poet-writer-witch characterizes herself as different, misunderstood, and possessed, as one who transforms the ordinary domestic scene into something weird and nightmarish, who pays for her imaginative powers with her sanity or even with her life but who bravely affirms her power nonetheless. She is subversive, creative, and shunned. This witch-creator shapes the *Transformations* poems; particularly in the prologues, the speaker frequently calls attention to herself. In "Iron Hans," for example, she declares: "I am mother of the insane. / Let me give you my children" (*T*, 43); one of those "children" is "a woman talking, / purging herself with rhymes" (*T*, 44). The prologue of "Red Riding Hood" offers a list of "deceivers," among whose number the speaker twice lists herself: "And I. I too. / Quite collected at cocktail parties, / meanwhile in my head / I'm undergoing open-heart surgery. / . . . And I. I too again. / I built a summer house on Cape Ann. / . . . and this too was / a deception—nothing haunts a new house" (*T*, 75). The speaker of "The Frog Prince" states, "My guilts are what we catalogue" (*T*, 93). The process outlined by Freud, in which fairy tales serve as the means of transforming subconscious materials into conscious ones, seems clearly at work here.[17]

In *Transformations* Sexton's imagination produces outcast, evil, and powerful witches, daughter-women who both love and hate their mothers, fathers, and lovers but who come to perpetuate maternal transgressions in any case, and wives who are scheming, miserable, numb, or lifeless. Many of the tales Sexton chooses to transform from Grimm focus, in the Grimm version, on the plight of a disenfranchised heroine, a young girl mistreated or abandoned, most often by a selfish or manipulative mother-figure. In the Grimm tales, the wicked mother (usually a stepmother) is punished while the heroine emerges happy, triumphant, and married, thus offering a positive didactic model for the child-reader.

No such outcome awaits the heroine of Sexton's transformations. Snow White survives the jealous queen's attacks and finds her prince, but her forever-after will not be happy since she has incorporated the queen's vanity into her own character. Cinderella finds her prince, too, but the poem's speaker makes it clear that her happily-ever-after is an illusion. Like Snow White, Cinderella (and her prince as well) is a lifeless doll:

> Cinderella and the prince
> lived, they say, happily ever after,
> like two dolls in a museum case
> never bothered by diapers or dust,
> never arguing over the timing of an egg,
> never telling the same story twice,
> never getting a middle-aged spread,
> their darling smiles pasted on for eternity.
> Regular Bobbsey Twins.
> That story.
>
> (T, 56–57)

Daily reality is no fairy tale, suggests this sardonic conclusion. The prologue to "Cinderella" offers examples of people who become suddenly rich, such as "the charwoman / who is on the bus when it cracks up / and collects enough from the insurance. / From mops to Bonwit Teller. / That story" (T, 53–54). But for them as for Cinderella, the fairy-tale promise of wealth and automatic happiness is a delusion.

Marriage is less than blissful in most of Sexton's transformations, since most heroines marry their "rescuing male figures"; in "The Maiden without Hands," the king "marries a cripple / out of admiration" (T, 81). And in "The Twelve Dancing Princesses" the marriage of the oldest princess to the soldier who has reported the princesses' nightly escapades to the king may be a reward for the soldier, but it represents the end of fun and dancing for the princesses:

> He had won. The dancing shoes would dance
> no more. The princesses were torn from
> their night life like a baby from its pacifier.
> Because he was old he picked the eldest.
> At the wedding the princesses averted their eyes
> and sagged like old sweatshirts.
> Now the runaways would run no more and never
> again would their hair be tangled into diamonds,
> never again their shoes worn down to a laugh,
>
> . . .
>
> (*T*, 92)

In "The Frog Prince," too, marriage offers no happy ending for the princess. The poem seems to come to us from the borders of sanity; in the prologue the speaker chants:

> I write for you.
> I entertain.
> But frogs come out
> of the sky like rain.
>
> . . . .
>
> Frog has no nerves.
> Frog is as old as a cockroach.
> Frog is my father's genitals.
> (*T*, 93–94)

Obviously phallic, this father-male-frog, who frightens and repulses the princess in both the Grimm and the Sexton versions of the tale, imprisons her, in the Sexton poem, after becoming her prince-husband:

> He hired a night watchman
> so that no one could enter the chamber
> and he had the well
> boarded over so that
> never again would she lose her ball,
> that moon, that Krishna hair,
> that blind poppy, that innocent globe,
> that madonna womb.
> (*T*, 99)

As "The Frog Prince" uses imagery, among other poetic devices, to objectify the terror that the princess feels, many other transformations employ imagery of violence to link love with torment, anger, and death. The theme so evident in *Love Poems* of lover as killer is again present in *Transformations;* Sexton recapitulates it often here through references to World War II horrors. "The Frog Prince" is addressed to "Frau Doktor, / Mama Brundig" (*T,* 93). That Hansel and Gretel's mother does not love them is clear from the plot line and reinforced by diction; her plot to get rid of them is "the final solution" (*T,* 102). The evil witch, shoved into the oven by Gretel, "turned as red / as the Jap flag" (*T,* 105). Even Gretel turns from victim to victimizer; "Ja, Fräulein," she says to the witch, "show me how it can be done" (*T,* 104).

Other poems focus on mother-daughter atrocities in other ways. The Sexton transformation of "One-Eye, Two-Eyes, Three-Eyes" stresses the psychotic and defensive tendency of mothers to bestow inordinate amounts of love upon freakish and crippled children, and concludes (as in "Snow White") with Two-Eyes repeating the maternal behavior that had caused her so much trouble. One-Eye and Three-Eyes, now "beggars, . . . were magical":

> They were to become her children,
> her charmed cripples, her hybrids—
> oh mother-eye, oh mother-eye, crush me in.
> So they took root in her heart
> with their religious hunger.
>
> (*T,* 65)

In "The Wonderful Musician" the fox is another daughter-figure, "a womanly sort" (*T,* 68) who tries unsuccessfully to kill the musician for deceiving her; in the end, the musician is "saved by his gift / like many of us— / little Eichmanns, / little mothers— / I'd say" (*T,* 71). The sins of the mothers are visited upon the daughters in these and in other *Transformations* poems; this is a prominent theme in Sexton's earlier poetry as well. A daughter is never free from the destructive mother, even if she goes off to live in a castle. Either the mother becomes internalized in the daughter, or marriage offers no escape, or both. There are no fairy-tale endings.

"Rapunzel" also explores the complicated mother-daughter relationship, but with a surprising twist. In the Grimm tale, Rapunzel is abandoned by her real mother, who prefers eating lettuce to keeping her first-born child, is imprisoned by her second mother, the witch called "Mother Gothel," and ultimately finds happiness with her prince, "who escorted her back to his kingdom, where he was received with joy, and they lived happily and contentedly for a long time thereafter."[18] Sexton transforms this tale into Mother Gothel's story, introducing a theme that concerns love between women (as we have seen in such earlier poems as "Song for a Lady," *LP*). "A woman who loves a woman is forever young," begins the prologue of "Rapunzel"; "the mentor / and the student / feed off each other" (*T*, 35). In Sexton's "Rapunzel," Mother Gothel is the woman desperately (and futilely) trying to retain her youth through loving a younger woman, and Rapunzel is very much like the "dumb bunny" Snow White, both needing and accepting indiscriminately the advances first of Mother Gothel and then of the prince. This mother-daughter relationship is, however, apparently sexual; in the tower where Mother Gothel keeps and often visits her lovely prisoner, "Mother Gothel cried: / Hold me, my young dear, hold me, / and thus they played mother-me-do" (*T*, 40). The prince complicates this oedipal relationship; he is described in phallic terms (a "beast" with "muscles in his arms / like a bag of snakes," a "prickly plant" with "moss on his legs" [*T*, 41]) and, blinded "by thorns" in his leap from Mother Gothel in the tower, he wanders "for years," "blind as Oedipus" (*T*, 41). Rapunzel eventually resolves this dilemma by making the heterosexual choice, leaving her mother and going off with her prince-father, "proving that mother-me-do / can be outgrown, . . . / A rose must have a stem" (*T*, 42). Yet the poem's closing stanza focuses wistfully and sympathetically on the abandoned Mother Gothel:

> As for Mother Gothel,
> her heart shrank to the size of a pin,
> never again to say: Hold me, my young dear,
> hold me,
> and only as she dreamt of the yellow hair
> did moonlight sift into her mouth.
>
> (*T*, 42)

Many other *Transformations* poems present overtly oedipal motifs. "Iron Hans" draws this conclusion: "He who kills his father / and thrice wins his mother / undoes the spell" (*T*, 50). In "Briar Rose (Sleeping

Beauty)" the princess awakens from her long sleep "crying: / Daddy!
Daddy!" (*T*, 110). Here Sleeping Beauty, whom Bruno Bettelheim
calls "the incarnation of perfect femininity,"[19] is transformed into Daddy's girl. "Papa" speaks these words to her in Sexton's poem's prologue:
"Come be my snooky / and I will give you a root" (*T*, 107). And the
princess's long sleep in the Sexton poem represents not the "time of
quiet growth and preparation" to which Bettelheim refers, from which
she will awaken into sexual maturity,[20] but rather a recurring nightmare in which she is joined with her father:

> Daddy?
> That's another kind of prison.
> It's not the prince at all,
> but my father
> drunkenly bent over my bed,
> circling the abyss like a shark,
> my father thick upon me
> like some sleeping jellyfish.
>   (*T*, 112)

There should be no surprise, then, in Sexton's remark that these
poems are not for children; she quite definitely asserts that "none of
them are children's stories."[21] The speaker's "peers" who "draw near"
as the "middle-aged witch" begins her tale are themselves middle-
aged, or near it. "Alice" is "fifty-six," "Samuel" is "twenty-two," and
we readers (however old we are) are part of that audience as well. The
group meets for this story-telling session not to be lulled to sleep but
to "have the answers" (*T*, 1,2).

In search of those answers, the spinner of these modern fairy tales
examines in her magic mirror both her own and the fairy-tale characters' experience of the joy and torment of love, parent-child relationships, personal anguish and suffering, and emotional breakdown;
Sexton's new twist in this volume is that fairy-tale characters are sometimes elevated to a position equally as important as the speaker's own.
Yet as in a dream, all characters and events are projections of the speaker's psyche, and therefore, as in the confessional poem, all poetic materials point to the author-speaker herself. There is an intimacy of
revelation in the poems of *Transformations* similar to that of the confessional poem. And further, as in the confessional poem the poet's voice
is always present in her "transformations," judging, commenting, ed-
itorializing. In a 1970 letter to Stanley Kunitz, Sexton writes,

It strikes me funny that you say it is my sacred confession to be confessional. I don't see *Transformations* as confessional but perhaps it is indeed. At one time I hated being called confessional and denied it, but mea culpa. Now I say that I'm the *only* confessional poet. No matter how hard you work at it, your own voice shows through. (*L*, 372)

In *Transformations* Sexton uses fairy-tale materials in multiple ways, adapting plots for her own creative purpose and devising meanings that are at once consonant with the original tales and uniquely her own. Most of the characters fail to emerge whole and truly transformed from their period of trial but remain caught in their nightmares for eternity. The quiet, domestic, submissive fairy-tale heroines become, in Sexton's transformations, mindless, vapid dolls like Snow White or Cinderella. The happy future of these and other heroines is really a kind of living death; the princess of "The White Snake" and her new husband

> played house, little charmers,
> exceptionally well.
> So, of course,
> they were placed in a box
> and painted identically blue
> and thus passed their days
> living happily ever after—
> a kind of coffin,
> a kind of blue funk.
> Is it not?
>
> (*T*, 15)

Through sarcastic language and allusion, these *Transformations* poems tell us that marriage is, for the women, either complete self-denial, or imprisonment, or drudgery, or some kind of consolation prize. "Ever after" is not the successful achievement of a mature, integrated personality but rather unrelieved monotony, dehumanized captivity, or madness. The fairy-tale promise of happiness and domestic joy remains unfulfilled and forever out of reach.

Sexton has commented that the *Transformations* "end up being as wholly personal as my most intimate poems, in a different language, a different rhythm, but coming strangely, for all their story sound, from as deep a place" (*L*, 367). Certainly the painful themes of Sexton's more obviously confessional mode either are openly expressed in her "transformations" or lurk just beneath the surface. Yet that surface compels attention. The "different language, . . . different rhythm" is comic, droll, facetious, and brilliant; it is what Sexton calls "a dark, dark laughter" (*L,* 365). We laugh our way through this book even while we are telling ourselves that we shouldn't be laughing; we chuckle in delight at Sexton's gallows humor, at her asides and quips, in spite of ourselves. These poems are, for all their desperate, bitter, nightmarish content, funny. As we have heard, Sexton admits that she was happy while writing them. She no doubt derived as much pleasure from composing these frightening, witty, pop-art poems as we experience in reading them.

Chapter Seven
The Book of Folly: Fire and Ice

After completing work on her *Transformations* poems in 1970, Anne Sexton turned to the composition of *The Book of Folly.* Most of the poems collected in this, her sixth published volume, were written from early 1971 to 1972, though Sexton wrote a few of them ("The Fire-bombers," "The Assassin," "Going Gone," and possibly others) in 1968–70. Houghton Mifflin published *The Book of Folly* on 9 November, 1972, Sexton's forty-fourth birthday.

These *Book of Folly* poems are, as Sexton described them, often "surreal" and "unconscious" (*L,* 361). They evince a return to a more or less direct handling of Sexton's familiar themes of madness, memory, longing, guilt, loss, and oedipal confusion, yet also a decided departure from earlier expressions of these subjects. Reading this sixth volume, one receives the impression of greater urgency and desperation; the voices we hear in the poems of *The Book of Folly* are both more diverse and more confident than the voice of Sexton's earlier confessional poems. Here we find a variety of speakers, as we have not in previous volumes. As before, we hear Sexton herself, though this Sexton-voice is newly charged; we also hear a number of character-speakers, such as a one-legged man, an assassin, and religious figures. There is at once a greater daring in these poems and a bold, even reckless abandonment of the Anne Sexton persona so evident in the first four volumes. In *The Book of Folly* Sexton seems truly transformed, unconstrained by her mundane self, so that she appears to become the images she creates.

After studying these poems, one is peculiarly reminded of a short poem by Robert Frost, whose work is generally so unlike Sexton's. In "Fire and Ice" Frost's theme so objectifies Sexton's concerns, attitudes, postures, and subjects in *The Book of Folly* that one cannot help thinking how appropriate an epigraph "Fire and Ice" might have been for this volume:

> Some say the world will end in fire,
> Some say in ice.

> From what I've tasted of desire
> I hold with those who favor fire.
> But if it had to perish twice,
> I think I know enough of hate
> To say that for destruction ice
> Is also great
> And would suffice.[1]

These *Book of Folly* texts concern not only obvious subject matter but also language, voice, and structural realization. Whether they are about the fire of passion or the ice of hate and death, they speak of destruction. And in these poems, appropriate colors predominate: they are red and white and black.

"The Ambition Bird"

The volume's opening poem, "The Ambition Bird," typifies Sexton's new voice and attitude and her thematic departure. Here the poet-speaker is plagued by "insomnia at 3:15 A.M."; "the business of words keeps me awake."[2] There have been references in the poems of earlier volumes to Sexton's habit of writing late at night; in the prologue to "The Twelve Dancing Princesses," for example, the poet refers to herself as "the drunken poet / (a genius by daylight) / who places long-distance [death] calls / at three A.M." (*T,* 88). In "The Ambition Bird," the speaker has become transformed even from the *Transformations* poem, no longer so clearly Sexton herself but rather disembodied nerves and energy driven to work late, both needing and hating the drive. Echoing the words of Saul Bellow's Henderson (perhaps consciously, since Sexton derived the title and epigraph of *Live or Die* from Bellow's *Herzog*), the speaker becomes one with the Ambition Bird, chanting "He wants, I want" (*BF,* 4). "It has," says the speaker in the poem's first line, "come to this" (*BF,* 3): the Bird is the ambitious, driven part of herself, at war with the other part of herself who "would like a simple life" (*BF,* 3) but who knows there is no real chance of pursuing that course. Even though at 3:15 A.M. she is "drinking cocoa, / that warm brown mama" (*BF,* 3), she expresses in the subjunctive her whimsical hope of finding haven in that safe place: "Dear God, wouldn't it be / good enough just to drink cocoa?" (*BF,* 4)

The Ambition Bird is, then, at once part of the speaker's self and the Other; the bird is "he" as distinguished from "I," yet "all night"

his "dark wings / . . . [flop] in my heart" (*BF*, 3). As we have seen in
Sexton's *Love Poems* and elsewhere, there has been a persistent tendency
of the Anne Sexton persona to identify herself by contrast with a male
Other, usually by placing herself in a position of subservience or powerlessness in relation to this male authority figure of lover, or husband,
or doctor, or father. In *The Book of Folly* the speaker's relationship with
the Other is both extended and internalized. The kinds of male Others
who have peopled earlier poems remain in, for example, "The Doctor
of the Heart," "The Wifebeater," "Going Gone," and "The Death of
the Fathers." In "The One-Legged Man," however, we can observe an
innovation in treating this motif. The speaking voice of this poem is
not undisguised Sexton but rather the voice of the title character, a
man searching for his other leg, which is both "it" and a wife: "I keep
thinking that what I need / to do is buy my leg back. / . . . / I want
to write it letters" (*BF*, 16,17). Here the Sexton theme of wife-woman
as subservient, dehumanized "it" is dramatized in a new way that both
shows Sexton's tendency in this volume to shed her familiar persona
and reminds us of one of Sylvia Plath's *Ariel* voices: "It can sew, it can
cook, / It can talk, talk, talk."[3]

"The Other" reveals yet another new approach to this theme. Here
the speaker is Sexton, but the male Other loses all independent identity. Recalling the doppelgänger of "Rumpelstiltskin" in *Transformations,* this "Other," although described in the poem in male terms,
transcends sexual distinction while remaining the male enemy; it is
that contrary part of the speaker's self that torments her and that has
the potential to destroy. It is "Mr. Doppelgänger. My enemy. My lover.
/ When truth comes spilling out like peas / it hangs up the phone"
(*BF*, 30). In "The Ambition Bird," this tendency is announced; this
"he" is both an alien and an inseparable part of the speaker. The "I"
who would like "to just drink cocoa" is female ("mama"), yet the bird
persists; "he wants, I want." Like most of the earlier male authority
figures, and like the "Other," this bird is driving the speaker toward
death: the poems that he impels her to create go into "my immortality
box"; they are "my lay-away plan, / my coffin" (*BF*, 3).

The images of this poem, like the bird himself, appear to be beyond
the poet's conscious control; they seem, unlike the images of earlier
poems, spontaneous and unrehearsed. This Bird "wants to be
dropped," to flame, "to fly," "to pierce" (*BF*, 3–4). In Sexton's earlier
"To a Friend Whose Work Has Come to Triumph," Icarus "casually /
. . . glances up and is caught, wondrously tunneling / into that hot

eye" *PO*, 8). For Icarus, flying is a joyful triumph far more important than its consequences; the answer to the speaker's rhetorical question ("Who cares that he fell back to the sea?" [*PO*, 8]) is clear. What matters is not that Icarus falls but that he flies. In "The Ambition Bird" it remains most important to fly, yet diction and context complicate the action's atmosphere. This bird, this doppelgänger, is both a joy and an affliction. The Ambition Bird obviates for the speaker the possibility of "a simple life," yet his action, similar to Icarus', is rendered in terms that are wondrous and even more impulsive: "He wants to . . . / . . . bolt for the sun like a diamond" (*BF*, 4).

In "The Gold Key" of *Transformations* "the boy [the male self-other] has found a gold key / and he is looking for what it will open. / . . . / It opens this book of odd tales" *T*, 2). There is a similar key in "The Ambition Bird," but here the Bird is not looking for the key—he *is* the key. "He wants to be pressed out like a key / so he can unlock the Magi" (*BF*, 4). It is "the Magi" of the imagination that Sexton unlocks in this poem and in this volume.

Another action of the Ambition Bird also typifies the poems of this volume. This Bird "wants to take leave among strangers / passing out bits of his heart like hors d'oeuvres" (*BF*, 4). There are many strangers to whom *The Book of Folly* passes out bits of heart; chief among them are we, the poems' audience. But there are other strangers within the poems, all of them men, to whom the speaker bares her unprotected heart: doctors, a wifebeater ("chewing little red pieces of my heart" [*BF*, 13]), an assassin, Jesus. As in earlier poems, the speaker leaves herself vulnerable by offering her heart; here, however, there is no regret. She sees the folly of pursuing such a course but forges ahead. While it may be both foolish and costly to "bolt for the sun like a diamond" and "unlock the Magi," that is what this Ambition Bird must do.

"The Doctor of the Heart"

Since the new, daring speaker of these *Book of Folly* poems is plainly evident in "The Doctor of the Heart," a useful way to dramatize Sexton's transformed persona is to examine this poem and to compare it with earlier "Doctor" poems. "You, Doctor Martin" (*TB*), "Cripples and Other Stories" (*LD*), and "The Doctor of the Heart" offer similar dramatic postures; in each, a speaker who is plainly the poet herself addresses her psychiatrist. The similarity of situation ends there, however, for *The Book of Folly* speaker bears little resemblance to her sisters in tone, in cadence, or in the imagery by which she defines her plight. In both "You, Doctor Martin" and "Cripples and Other Stories," the speaker projects various attitudes of respect, admiration, and caring for her doctor. She adopts a position of subservience, assuming the role of a child who hopes for and expects wise guidance from the authority figure, and any anger is directed as much at herself as at the doctor and is short-lived. "Of course, I love you," she says to Doctor Martin; "you lean above the plastic sky, / god of our block, prince of all the foxes" (*TB*, 3). This persona is a diffident woman who speaks in juvenile cadences: "What large children we are / here. All over I grow most tall / in the best ward" (*TB*, 4). The structure through which this persona communicates is carefully patterned into seven-line stanzas with regular end rhyme and diagonal left margins; the tone is calm, evincing the disjunction in time between the experience of the speaker-character and the speaker-poet's actual writing of the poem. In "Cripples and Other Stories," where the personae of character and poet appear fused, we hear an even more childlike voice speaking in nursery-rhyme form. Here, doctor and father are melded into a single authority figure, and the subservient speaker is both daughter and patient: "you rock me in your arms / and whisper my nickname" (*LD*, 80). Although this persona verbalizes anger at her position ("God damn it, father-doctor. / I'm really thirty-six" [*LD*, 80]), such feelings are generally suppressed; in the last stanza, the speaker remains a child-woman: "Father, I'm thirty-six, / yet I lie here in your crib" (*LD*, 82).

In "The Doctor of the Heart" diffidence and subservience are gone and the poem's tone and rhythms are new. Cadences are clipped; the poem comprises short sentences formed into two-line stanzas with no end rhyme. The speaker's voice is hard, angry, and accusatory. The doctor here is no "prince," no "god," no gentle father; the spelling of his name reveals, in the poem's opening line, that he is an authoritarian victimizer: "Take away your knowledge, Doktor. / It doesn't butter me up" (*BF*, 5). The persona of this poem is rude, reckless, and unafraid of anger. She may have found safety in adopting childlike postures in earlier poems, but here she has developed a purer, more courageous self-expression. This "doktor" may treat her like a child, but she is an angry woman who has discovered that the "doktor" is powerless to help her: "You say my heart is sick unto. / You ought to have more respect!" (*BF*, 5). He has mistreated her heart, and she now rejects him together with her hope for cure.

Reading this poem, one has the feeling that Sexton is becoming her images rather than merely creating them. As critic Estella Lauter has observed, "In *The Book of Folly* [Sexton] often gives up the distance that simile often allows and steps into dramatic relationship with elements that previously would have been related only to each other."[4] Although there are a few similes in "The Doctor of the Heart," there is no distance: "Give me the Phi Beta key you always twirl / and I will make a gold crown for my molar" (*BF*, 5).

We also hear in this poem (as in other *Book of Folly* poems) the distinct sound of one of Sylvia Plath's *Ariel* personae. The rhythm, tone, and imagery of "The Doctor of the Heart" bear a remarkable similarity to many of Plath's late poems, and the severe, sarcastic, desperate voice of Sexton's "Doctor of the Heart" brings to mind a poem like Plath's "Lady Lazarus." Listen first to the close of Sexton's poem:

> Is there such a device for my heart?
> I have only a gimmick called magic fingers.
>
> Let me dilate like a bad debt.
> Here is a sponge. I can squeeze it myself.
>
> O heart, tobacco red heart,
> beat like a rock guitar.
>
> . . . .
> Herr Doktor! I'll no longer die
>
> to spite you, you wallowing
> seasick grounded man.
>
> (*BF*, 6)

And then to the end of Plath's "Lady Lazarus":

> there is a charge
> For the hearing of my heart—
> It really goes.
>
> And there is a charge, a very large charge,
> For a word or a touch
> Or a bit of blood

Or a piece of my hair or my clothes.
So, so, Herr Doktor.
So, Herr Enemy.

. . . .

Out of the ash
I rise with my red hair
And I eat men like air.[5]

Sexton's poem, chronologically the later of the two, is thematically reinforced and amplified by Plath's. Each persona is grim, desperate, and free; each has literally reconstructed herself, piece by piece. Each offers a defiant verbal gesture which says to the "doktor" and to everyone, go away. Leave me alone. I mean to take care of myself. Further, each presents a red, fiery resurrection of the speaker, newly bold and contemptuous.

New Voices, New Postures

Other poems of *The Book of Folly* require attention for their new treatment of familiar themes. For example, the poet's guilt over her mother's death, examined in such earlier poems as "The Double Image" (*TB*), "The Operation" (*PO*), and "Christmas Eve" (*LD*), reappears here in "Dreaming the Breasts," where the mother's breasts symbolize both life-giving milk and death-dealing cancer: "Mother, / . . . I ate you up. / . . . / In the end they cut off your breasts. / . . . I took them . . . / and planted them" (*BF*, 26–27). Here, however, the speaker has distanced and transformed guilt into metaphor; the breasts that gave the daughter life and brought the mother death are "planted" now, and from them sprout dreams: "so that your great bells, / those dear white ponies, / can go galloping, galloping, / wherever you are" (*BF*, 27). Sexton's guilt over her Nana's madness ("Elizabeth Gone" and "Some Foreign Letters" in *TB;* "Walking in Paris" in *LD*) reappears as well; the refrain "Did I make you go insane?" (*BF*, 22–23) punctuates "Anna Who Was Mad." In "The Hex" the speaker is "still the criminal"; the "Nana-hex" of guilt destroys pleasure: "Every time I get happy / the Nana-hex comes through." But here, the speaker's self is both double and newly bold, as in "The Other": "Yes!" declares the speaker-crimi-

nal, only my guilty self is culpable. "Take me to the station house. /
But book my double" *BF,* 24–25).

In "The Death of the Fathers," which J. D. McClatchy calls "the
book's centering six-poem sequence,"[6] we hear again the new, daring,
urgent voice of this volume and see the poet's method of blending
memory and guilt with imagination to create experience. The first
three poems of "The Death of the Fathers" present, in chronological
frames, the speaker's recollection of time she spent with her father,
imagistically recalling and evaluating key incidents of her sexual and
emotional development. She is fifteen in "Oysters," the first poem,
eating oysters with her father at the Union Oyster House. This occasion signifies for the speaker "the death of childhood," the loss of innocence. As the child overcomes her fear "to eat this father-food," the
woman-speaker clarifies through imagery and diction the meaning of
this sexual ritual:

> It was a soft medicine
> that came from the sea into my mouth,
> moist and plump.
> I swallowed.
> ....
> and the child was defeated.
> The woman won.
>
>   (*BF,* 41)

Oedipal sexual fantasy is extended in "How We Danced," the second
poem. Here, where the speaker-daughter is nineteen and dancing with
her father on "the night of my cousin's wedding," daughter and father
become imaginatively transformed into the nuptial pair: "and we
danced, Father, we orbited. / We moved like angels washing themselves. We moved like two birds on fire":

> . . . the serpent spoke as you held me close.
> The serpent, that mocker, woke up and pressed against me
> like a great god and we bent together
> like two lonely swans.
>
>   (*BF,* 42–43)

The third poem, "The Boat," offers a marvelous imagistic extension of
this oedipal relationship. In this re-created experience the daughter is
seven, riding in her father's mahogany speedboat "out past Cuckold's

Light," her mother safely distant in the bow. In this fantasy the speeding boat becomes an analogue for sexual consummation and for the
nearly simultaneous destruction of the daughter's innocence as rhythms
and diction express meaning:

> It is bumpy and we are going too fast.
> The waves are boulders that we ride upon.
> ....
> Now the waves are higher;
> they are round buildings.
> We start to go through them
> and the boat shudders.
> Father is going faster.
> I am wet.
> ....
> Give me a sign,
> cries Father,
> and the sky breaks over us.
>
> (*BF*, 44–45)

This apocalyptic event leads into the next three poems, which recount and reflect upon the meaning of the sequence's title, "The Death
of the Fathers." Forced from innocence into adulthood, the speaker
recalls in the fourth poem, "Santa," the loss of belief. Here the father
who wore a Santa Claus suit, who "used to buzz me on the neck" with
his white beard, "is dead," and that death is both literal and figurative:

> The year I ceased to believe in you
> is the year you were drunk.
> My boozy red man,
> ....
> I cried and ran from the room
> and you said, "Well, thank God that's over!"
> ....
> . . . you fade out of sight
> like a lost signalman
> wagging his lantern
> for the train that comes no more.
>
> (*BF*, 46–47)

The loss of belief in "Santa" is exacerbated by the loss of the last ves-
tiges of innocent trust in the next poem, ironically entitled "Friends."

Here, the father both literally and figuratively gone, the daughter is revulsed by the furtive and clumsy sexual advances of one of her mother's friends: "and his tongue, my God, his tongue, like a red worm and when he kissed / it crawled right in" (*BF,* 48–49). The sixth and last poem in the sequence extends the question that ends "Friends": "He was a stranger, Father. / Oh God, / he was a stranger, / was he not?" In "Begat" the speaker, expressing the common childhood fear that one's parents aren't really one's parents at all, recollects the motifs of the earlier poems (the oysters, the boat ride, the lecherous friend), but finds that memory is inadequate to provide framing materials for her mature, lonely condition. Now forty-two, she both loves her father as she once did and feels betrayed by his permanent departure: "Oh Father, Father-sorrow, / where has time brought us?" (*BF,* 50). Yet the poem sequence comes full circle as the speaker makes a conscious decision to reject the father who appeared to threaten and abandon her, choosing the father of her childhood. In "How We Danced," father and daughter were "two lonely swans"; they were "like two birds on fire." Here, in the closing lines of "The Death of the Fathers," the speaker remembers "those times he ate my heart in half," yet concludes, "Red. Red. Father, you are blood red. / Father, / we are two birds on fire" (*BF,* 53).

These fiery birds appear to inhabit some unearthly place, as Sexton appears to have abandoned the persona so consistent and familiar in her earlier poems. Estella Lauter sees the world of Sexton's later volumes as "an archetypal chamber, a non-human world where angels speak and humans are at the mercy of their signs." In the poetry of Sexton's last four years, observes Lauter, "Sexton's choice of masks and her multipartite poetic forms show her courage. Whereas in her earlier work the *persona* 'Anne' bore the closest possible resemblance to herself, in her last books Sexton adopts the masks of taboo figures . . . and God-figures (Jesus and Mary, among others) as a deliberate means of understanding experiences that lie beyond her own."[7] We have seen this tendency in Sexton's imaginative identification with a variety of "Others" in her poems and in her adoption of identifiable personae; we see it as well, together with the tendency toward the "surreal" and "unconscious" (*L,* 361) in the poem sequence that ends *The Book of Folly,* "The Jesus Papers."

Sexton observed that *The Book of Folly* has "got a little hangover from the voice of *Transformations* with some poems called 'The Jesus Papers,' which are called either 'blasphemous' or 'devout'—it's probably blasphemous, I would say" (*L*, 154). Whether blasphemous or not, this poem sequence evinces a new and daring sort of devotion. Although we do hear the irreverent, witty, campy cadences of *Transformations* in "The Jesus Papers," we realize that this language is being put to very serious use. As in *Transformations*, the linguistic contrast between archaic style and diction and modern, offhand, sometimes slangy usage offers clear demonstration that Sexton is adapting mythic materials for her own purposes. The poems of "The Jesus Papers" are at once humorous and earnest, and with *Transformations*, they exemplify revisionist mythmaking at its best.

Indeed, although the witty, irreverent voice of *Transformations* does lead us through "The Jesus Papers," this *Book of Folly* sequence reveals several new developments that are evident as well in other poems of the volume. In earlier poems, as we have seen, Sexton has chosen to create imaginative identification of herself in subservient relationship to a male authority figure; in this volume, however, she either rejects that figure entirely or incorporates him into her fictive personality. In some of "The Jesus Papers," as in other *Book of Folly* poems, she speaks with his voice. There are multiple speakers in these nine poems. In two of them ("Jesus Suckles" and "Jesus Dies"), Jesus himself speaks. Six others ("Jesus Awake," "Jesus Asleep," "Jesus Raises Up the Harlot," "Jesus Cooks," "Jesus Summons Forth," and "Jesus Unborn") are narrated by a voice similar to the one we have heard in the fairy-tale sections of the *Transformations* poems, a storytelling Sexton who makes humorous interjections and imposes contemporary language upon traditional and ancient subjects. The last poem of the sequence, an epilogue ("The Author of the Jesus Papers Speaks"), resembles the prologue to each of the *Transformations* poems, where the poet speaks directly to the audience, offering an evaluative frame for the rest of the work.

Appropriately, Sexton begins her sequence with a poem reminiscent of "Dreaming the Breasts," where mother's breasts are "your great bells, those dear white ponies" (*BF*, 27). In "Jesus Suckles" (*BF*, 93) Jesus speaks to Mary, moving through the stages of infant development. The newborn Jesus of the first stanza suckles, grows, and expresses symbiotic, oedipal attachment ("I'm a jelly-baby and you're my wife"). The child of the second stanza already perceives himself as separate from the mother ("No. No. / All lies. / I am small / and you hold me.") In the third stanza, where the child has grown to manhood, a single image designates the sexual and commercial realities of power

in Jesus's society as in ours: "No. No. / All lies. / I am a truck. I run
everything. / I own you."

The following seven poems amplify, in chronological order, significant moments in Jesus' life. In the six of them where narrative perspective changes from Jesus' first-person voice to a more general
Sexton-narrator's third-person viewpoint, we hear the breezy, contemporary language evident in *Transformations* to achieve a similar effect.
"Jesus Cooks" can serve as an example:

> Jesus saw the multitudes were hungry
> and He said, Oh Lord,
> send down a short-order cook.
> And the Lord said, Abracadabra.
> Jesus took the fish,
> a slim green baby,
> in His right hand and said, Oh Lord,
> and the Lord said,
> Work on the sly
> opening boxes of sardine cans.
> And He did.
> Fisherman, fisherman,
> you make it look easy.
> And lo, there were many fish.
> Next Jesus held up a loaf
> and said, Oh Lord,
> and the Lord instructed Him
> like an assembly-line baker man,
> a Pied Piper of yeast,
> and lo, there were many.
> Jesus passed among the people
> in a chef's hat
> and they kissed His spoons and forks
> and ate well from invisible dishes.
>   (*BF,* 98)

One is reminded of Sexton's comment, "My transformations of the
Brothers Grimm are full of food images but what could be more directly food than cooking the kids and finally the wicked lady. Smack
in the oven like a roast lamb" (*L,* 352–53). "Jesus Cooks" is arranged
around food images. (Would a male poet conceptualize Jesus or Grimm
in this way?) Other connections with *Transformations* are evident as
well: there is magic here ("Abracadabra") and reference to fairy tales

(Pied Piper). Furthermore, the language affords both linkage to *Transformations* and the development of theme and tone. The most striking feature of this poem is the juxtaposing throughout of modern and informal with traditional biblical phrasing, such as "send down a short-order cook . . . And lo, there were many fish." Through language Sexton achieves humor (but not blasphemy), reconstructing biblical materials into something all her own. In this poem as in the others, Sexton engages seriously with New Testament materials; her lack of reverence is one measure of that seriousness. There is no posture of servility here, as there has been in earlier poems.

The concluding poem and epilogue, "The Author of the Jesus Papers Speaks," recounts a dream that emphasizes both this new posture and this serious engagement. Sexton's shunning of spurious reverence is justified here by God's words: "God spoke to me and said: / People say only good things about Christmas. / If they want to say something bad, / they whisper." (*BF*, 105). Yet Sexton's struggle with God, evident in the poems of earlier volumes and predominant in the poems of volumes to follow, is not resolved in "The Jesus Papers." Here, the dream-cow gives not white milk to the "author" but blood. "The Author of the Jesus Papers" who "speaks" appears to be both Sexton and God, and her/his concluding words indicate both victory and danger: "we must all eat sacrifices. / We must all eat beautiful women" (*BF*, 105).

In "The Jesus Papers," then, we hear a variety of speakers whose voices are at once more diverse and more confident than those that speak from earlier poems. Here, Jesus represents the ultimate extension of the male "Other" motif; this male has become a totally separate character. With the abandonment of the posture of diffidence and subservience in relation to authoritative males ("The Jesus Papers," "The Doctor of the Heart"), Sexton can herself adopt the position of the male authority figure and step out into a new landscape. This speaker is rude, reckless, and unafraid of danger. This speaker, as both Sexton and Jesus, is the ultimate giver of self, "passing out bits of his heart like hors d'oeuvres," the ultimate confessional poet.

Colors of Fire and Ice

Throughout *The Book of Folly*, then, red is the heart-color, the color of blood, the color of fire and passion. Barbara Swan, the illustrator of *Transformations*, *The Book of Folly*, and *The Death Notebooks*, has noted that in designing the cover for *The Book of Folly*, "I . . . said the border should be red, a bloody red. As I read the poems, . . . the color red seemed to me pervasive."[8] And indeed it is pervasive. For example, in "The Wifebeater," the "wifebeater"-"childbeater," who has victimized both speaker and daughter, who has been a lover but is now "the enemy with a heart of lies," is "chewing little red pieces of my heart" (*BF*, 13, 14). This enemy has metamorphosed from lover to misogynist; "Tonight all the red dogs lie down in fear / and the wife and daughter knit into each other / until they are killed" (*BF*, 14). In "The Assassin" the female speaker prepares to kill "this man, . . . my evil and my apple," with "a blood bolt" (*BF*, 18). In "The Red Shoes" the speaker recalls the dance of untamed passion in "Snow White" ("but, oh my friend, in the end / you will dance the fire dance in iron shoes" *T*, 5); wearing "red shoes," "all those girls . . . did . . . the death dance" (*BF*, 28, 29). In "The Death of the Fathers," as we have seen, a sexually menacing male visitor with "red fingers" has a "tongue, / like a red worm"; in her father's arms, the speaker's mother is "red, red . . . blood red"; the speaker's father, her forbidden oedipal love, is red Santa, "my boozy red man." "Red. Red. Father, you are blood red," the speaker exclaims. "Father, / we are two birds on fire" (*BF*, 47, 49, 53).

In these poems red is the color of all kinds of passion: anger, hate, love, fear. It is the color of sexual feeling and obsessive emotion, paradoxically both desired and loathed, at once forbidden, experienced, and renounced. It is also the color of life, however repugnant and destructive. Like all fires, the redness in these poems destroys the material that feeds it. As Robert Frost writes, "From what I've tasted of desire / I hold with those who favor fire." "The world" of these *Book of Folly* poems "will end in fire" (*CP*, 268).

Black in these poems emphasizes the destructive, aberrant quality of red. The murdering wife-beater forces the complicity of his female victim: "With a tongue like a razor he will kiss, / the mother, the child, / and we three will color the stars black" (*BF*, 13). In "Angels of Blizzards and Blackouts," black connotes both absence and dismissal from life: "O Angel of the blizzard and blackout, Madam white face, / take me back to that red mouth" (*BF*, 61). Red is life and passion. It is also destruction, and it is that meaning that black shares.

If red and black, the colors of destructive passion, pervade *The Book of Folly*, white, the color of blankness and death, is equally as pervasive.

Many poems of this volume link these images to describe and amplify the commonality of destruction. In "The Death of the Fathers," for instance, the speaker's father, either absent from home ("You had sunk like a cat in the snow" [*BF*, 49]) or literally dead, who represents for the speaker a death of spirit, is Santa Claus; the speaker has "applied rouge to your cheeks / and Chalk White to your eyebrows" (*BF*, 47). "Father, / you died once," says the speaker, "salted down at fifty-nine, / packed down like a big snow angel" (*BF*, 52). In "The Silence," where images of death show life gone awry, white imagery predominates over red and black: "My room is whitewashed, / . . . whiter than chicken bones / bleaching in the moonlight" (*BF*, 32). Here, the speaker's creativity is an action that resists the deadening effect of her environment, yet it will surely claim her. Although her "dark" hair "has been burnt in the white fire," she is "filling up the room / with the words from my pen. / Words leak out of it like a miscarriage" (*BF*, 32). As Estella Lauter points out, Sexton "refuses to put herself at a safe distance from what she sees or feels";[9] she is *in* this silence, and "the silence is death":

> It comes each day with its shock
> to sit on my shoulder, a white bird,
> and peck at the black eyes
> and the vibrating red muscle
> of my mouth.
>
> (*BF*, 33)

Surely this poem demonstrates the lack of distancing we have noticed in this volume; Sexton's "imaginative risk" is plain.

The poem "Oh" is built entirely around multiple images of whiteness that expand and diversify the speaker's association of snow with death. Snowflakes here are "paper spots," "little white lesions" that wound all that they touch. A ghostly old woman, who had been "combing / out her long white wraith hair," is dead, "embalmed," and "nothing / issues from her but her last word— / 'Oh.' Surprised by death." This is an environment that the speaker wishes to join, shedding her consciousness and her "madness"; "I would lie outside in a room of wool and let the snow cover me" (*BF*, 7). One is reminded of the white snow and hospital imagery of Sylvia Plath's "Tulips," where the speaker says, "And I have no face, I have wanted to efface myself."[10] The wish for effacement pervades "Oh" as well; "Oh" becomes the last word, first of the old woman (the speaker's avatar), then of the speaker herself, and finally of God:

> "Oh," He says.
> I see the child in me writing, "Oh."
> Oh, my dear, not why.
>
> (*BF*, 8)

This echo of Plath has another dimension. Sexton's closing line in "Oh" ("Oh, my dear, not why") recalls the third stanza of her earlier poem "Wanting to Die": "But suicides have a special language. / Like carpenters they want to know *which tools*. / They never ask *why build*" (*LD*, 58). Sexton quoted the whole of "Wanting to Die" in "The Barfly Ought to Sing," the reminiscence of Plath that she wrote for Charles Newman's special Plath number of the *Tri-Quarterly*. Immediately following the poem in "The Barfly Ought to Sing," Sexton emphasized the poem's third stanza, recalling her meetings with Plath at Boston's Ritz Hotel bar:

And balanced there we did meet and never asking *why build*—only asking *which tools*. This was our fascination. I neither could nor would give you reasons why either of us wanted *to build*. It is not my place to tell you Sylvia's why nor my desire to tell you mine. But I do say, come picture us exactly at our fragmented meetings, consumed at our passions and at our infections.[11]

These two poets, says Sexton, were "consumed" by their "passions," and their passions to create and to write, "to build," were "infections." Even though these infections were fatal, the two poets were interested not in analyzing the forces that drove them to pursue their deadly craft but in finding the tools to pursue it. In "Oh," where Sexton is "surprised by death," the passion to create remains the infection she describes in "The Barfly Ought to Sing"; one of death's manifestations in "Oh" is "little white lesions."

Creative passion, then, is bonded to suicide and to death. Unexamined, this passion must eventually consume its host. So experienced and described, this passion appears to be consonant with the imagery of red in *The Book of Folly*. Yet in "Oh," the poem that invites the linkage to Sexton's "The Barfly Ought to Sing," the predominating color is white. We must, then, admit a final dimension to the meaning of white in this volume. White is the deathly color of absence, blankness, emptiness, and effacement. It is also the color of destructive passion; remember the "white fire" of "The Silence" (*BF, 32*). Fittingly, one of the "Angels of the Love Affair" combines these properties; she is a "fire woman" of "the fierce solar energy" and of "ice" (*BF, 57*). The sun of this volume burns both red and white, and as we have seen in earlier Sexton poems ("The Sun," for example, in *Live or Die*), it kills. We are reminded once again of the Robert Frost poem: "Some say the world will end in fire, / Some say in ice." Either the "fire" of "desire" or the "ice" of "hate" is sufficient to destroy. In these poems of Sexton, the fire is red and black, the ice is white, and both burn with annihilating power. Yet the poetry will survive this destruction. As Sexton concludes "Sweeney,"

> Surely the words will continue, for that's
> what's left that's true.
>
> (*BF*, 10)

Chapter Eight
The Death Notebooks: "not to die, not to die"

Anne Sexton conceived *The Death Notebooks* as a different sort of volume from her others. In 1970, when she was forty-two, Sexton imagined a poetry collection that would be her life's work. She had just completed her fifth volume, *Transformations,* and had begun writing the poems to be published two years later in her sixth volume, *The Book of Folly.* But *The Death Notebooks* would be, she wrote, "the book of poems that I shall work on all my life" (*L,* 368). What length of time Sexton meant by "all my life" is unclear; she did, however, intend to "work on the *Death Notebooks* until I die" (*L,* 363). And in a 1971 letter she expressed her sense of urgency: "the 'blazing hurry' is that I'm so God damned sure I'm going to die soon. I know it's silly, but it's a conviction" (*L,* 374).

The Death Notebooks, then, is unique among Sexton's volumes of poetry both in conception and in effect. Sexton intended *The Death Notebooks* as a collection of meditations on death; she planned to work on these poems concurrently with her work on other, future volumes, and she meant to publish *The Death Notebooks* posthumously. As it turned out, Sexton actually spent about as much time on this volume's composition as she had spent creating earlier volumes, submitting the completed manuscript in January 1973 for publication in February 1974. In a 1973 interview Sexton discussed her original as well as her changed plans: "I had this crazy idea I'd publish [*The Death Notebooks*] posthumously, . . . not that I was going to kill myself and bring out this book, but I thought, wouldn't it be *nice,* you know, after I was dead if there were a statement about death?"[1]

Published about seven and one-half months before Anne Sexton's death, the sixteen poems and poem-sequences of *The Death Notebooks* do make the statement the poet intended. But many of these poems make, as well, a very rich statement about something else. As she began work on this volume in 1970, Anne Sexton noted that these "poems will be very Sexton . . . intense, personal, perhaps religious in places" (*L,* 363). When she submitted the manuscript to her agent in January 1973, Sexton wrote, "I am sure that here and there in this book is the beginning of a 'new life'" (*L,* 392).

In this volume we find an Anne Sexton who is both familiar and new. A motif threaded through Sexton's poetry and letters is her hunger, sharp and unsated. "O my hunger! My hunger!" is the refrain of Sexton's early "Flee on Your Donkey" (*LD*). In a 1973 letter, she acknowledges her "immense . . . hunger for love" (*L,* 396), and she comments in a July 1974 letter that "I can only acquiesce numbly when you say you feel 'such a deep hunger in myself'" (*L,* 419). It may be that in *The Death Notebooks,* along with "the beginning of a 'new life,'" Sexton finds in the religion of which she writes some relief from that hunger.

For these poems look both backward and forward. Some of them reflect upon Sexton's previous confrontations with death, seeking peace and self-understanding through memory. Others anticipate death, seeking contexts through which to comprehend its inevitability. But the overriding impression of this volume is that Sexton has at last reached a new frontier of belief that may at least begin to satisfy her hunger. "There is no special God to refer to," says the speaker of Sexton's early poetry ("The Double Image," *TB*). "I imitate / a memory of belief / that I do not own" ("The Division of Parts," *TB*). "I detest my sins and I try to believe / in the Cross. . . . / . . . / But I can't. Need is not quite belief" ("With Mercy For the Greedy," *PO*). Here, in *The Death Notebooks,* Sexton fulfills the need and achieves the belief that she has so long sought.

"Making a Living"

For this volume's epigraph, Sexton chose a quotation from Hemingway: "Look, you con man, make a living out of your death." Sexton is at once the con person (trying to trick herself and her audience, to swindle them into believing in her various postures), the convict (guilt being a persistent theme in her poetry), and the *con*fessional writer. Here she is making a living out of her death by writing poems (doing what she does to make money) about death. And she is also making life out of death by creating words that will last and by moving, by means of those words, beyond defeat to praise and affirmation.

The volume's first three poems offer a tripartite introduction. The first, "Gods," sketches the search of "Mrs. Sexton" for "the gods," recounting that though she looked for them in all the world, she found them finally "back [in] her own house" (*DN*, 1, 2). Even in this opening poem, God and death are fused by implication; the story reminds one, in a reverse way, of the familiar story of the man who fled his home to avoid death, only to meet him in his new location.

"Making a Living," the volume's second poem, which derives its title from the volume's epigraph, offers more detail. The poem's controlling metaphor is the biblical story of Jonah; consistent with her practice throughout this volume, Sexton turns these biblical materials entirely to her own use. "Jonah made his living / inside the belly. / Mine comes from the exact same place" (*DN*, 3). The poems by which I make my living, Sexton seems to say, come straight from the belly. Their genesis is feeling and guts. In this poem, Jonah is stripped of all worldly connections; his money, his pictures of his father and mother, his clothing are all actually and symbolically "washed away." "This is my death, / Jonah said out loud, / and it will profit me to understand it. / I will make a mental note of each detail" (*DN*, 3–4). Like Jonah, this is Sexton's task in this volume. And like Jonah as well, who at the poem's close undergoes a sort of second baptism, being "vomited . . . back out into the sea," Sexton will make a living by writing poems of her mental notes, becoming in the process a sort of Christ figure who suffers in the telling but who also achieves redemption by means of it: "Then he told the news media / the strange details of his death / and they hammered him up in the marketplace / and sold him and sold him and sold him. / My death the same" (*DN*, 4).

In this connection it is relevant to note Sexton's comments in a 1968 interview about one context in which readers might view her confessional poetry. "Perhaps your critics, in time to come," said interviewer Barbara Kevles, "will associate the suffering in your confessional poetry with the kind of sufferers you take on in your religious poetry." "You've summed it up perfectly," replied Sexton. "That ragged Christ, that sufferer, performed the greatest act of confession, and I mean with his body. And I try to do that with words."[2]

The volume's third poem, "For Mr. Death Who Stands with His Door Open," amplifies the closing motif of "Making a Living" by enumerating (and publishing) some of "the strange details of [her] death." The poem's first six and a half stanzas recall various avatars of death in the poet's past: "Time grows dim. Time that was so long / grows short

. . . / . . . / Mr. Death, you actor, you have many masks" (*DN*, 5).
Then, in its last four lines, the poem, turning to the present, offers
what might well serve as another epigraph to the volume: "But when
it comes to my death let it be slow, / let it be pantomime, this last
peep show, / so that I may squat at the edge trying on / my black
necessary trousseau" (*DN*, 6).

　The Death Notebooks are indeed a sort of "last peep show" of Sexton's
"trying on / [her] black necessary trousseau." Sexton creates a companion metaphor in "The Death Baby," where she, with her friend "Max,"
has "made a pact / . . . To build our death like carpenters" (*DN*, 14–
15). And like Jonah, in these poems Sexton will take various approaches to understanding her death and assume various voices, both
past and present, in order to profit by the understanding. Some poems,
reminiscent of earlier ones, reflect upon past guilts and failures.
Among these are the weaker entries in the volume; such poems as
"Faustus and I," "Grandfather, Your Wound," "Baby Picture," "Praying on a 707," "Clothes," and "God's Backside" seem sometimes man-
nered, sentimental, prolix, derivative. Other poems, however, break
new ground.

　One hint of the "new life" Sexton communicates through this volume comes in the poem "Rats Live on No Evil Star." The poem's sub-
title tells us that this is "a palindrome seen on the side of a barn in
Ireland" (*DN*, 18), and the editors of Anne Sexton's *Letters* observe that
she "had repeatedly told family members and friends that she wanted
[that palindrome] carved on her gravestone. The words . . . gave her
a peculiar kind of hope" (*L*, 423). The poem spins a fantastic tale of
the creation: first Adam is created, then Eve, then from Eve in "an
unnatural act" an ugly rat who "died before its time" and was placed
on a "STAR":

> Now all us cursed ones falling out after
> with our evil mouths and our worried eyes
> die before our time
> but do not go to some heaven, some hell
> but are put on the RAT'S STAR
> which is as wide as Asia
> and as happy as a barbershop quartet.
> We are put there beside the three thieves
> for the lowest of us all
> deserve to smile in eternity.
>
> 　　　　　　　　　　　　(*DN*, 19)

Sexton clearly refers here to herself: she may feel "cursed" because she has so far failed to achieve redemption; she expects to "die before [her] time"; and the "evil mouth" may be the one that confesses intimate, shocking things, or that speaks blasphemous words. The slang meaning of "rat" may enter into this meaning; this poet has been one who turns informer, who squeals both on herself and on those closest to her. Yet this rat heaven, this Rat's Star, is a happy place where Anne forms a "barbershop quartet" with "the three thieves" (perhaps the two who were crucified with Christ and the one, Barabbas, who was freed). As we have seen in "Making a Living," the experience both of the thieves and of Christ parallels the confessional poet's. In this poem, then, death is a desirable end, for it is not an end at all. The title palindrome itself carries major thematic weight; in a palindrome, which can be read the same way both forward and backward, the end is the beginning.

Sunrise

The three poem-sequences of *The Death Notebooks* offer further evidence that death is at once an end, a beginning, and a satiation of hunger. In the fifteen-poem sequence called "The Furies" expressions of anger, loss, yearning, and deprivation alternate in images of burial, affirmation, and rebirth. Titled after the mythological avenging deities whose retributive energies form a sort of background motif through the sequence, this poem moves from bereavement to hope. In the first poem, "The Fury of Beautiful Bones," the speaker, near death, remembers and relinquishes passion and love. Her lover's "bones / . . . are the tough / ones that get broken and reset"; she is, by contrast, "me of the death rattle" (*DN, 27*). Having taken leave of her physical, passionate body in the first poem, the speaker in the second, surreal poem, "The Fury of Hating Eyes," expresses her desire to shed destructive emotional baggage, represented here by the "hating eyes" of father, mother, lover, martyrs, and herself. There is no baptismal rebirth in this poem, as there was for a character similarly situated in "Making a Living." Here there is only the urge expressed in the opening line: "I would like to bury . . ." (*DN, 29*).

The third poem in the sequence, "The Fury of Guitars and Sopranos," introduces a new theme. In this fantasy, which anticipates death as both life and love, a nurturing, beautiful dream-mother sings:

> This singing
> is a kind of dying,
> a kind of birth,
> ....
> I have a dream-mother
> ....
> She sang for my thirst,
> mysterious songs of God
> ....
> [and] ate into my heart
> violent and religious.
>
> (DN, 31–32)

This dream-fulfillment, which is both dying and birth, proposes at last a way to satisfy hunger. The speaker's heart has always been "violent and religious," but the dream-mother's singing finally offers nourishment. The following two poems offer apocalyptic analogues of this new discovery. "The Fury of Earth" expresses, through images of fire with typical Sexton variations, an apocalyptic vision of the end of time:

> The day of fire is coming, the thrush
> will fly ablaze . . .
> ....
> . . . the houses
> . . . will in their tides
> of fire be a becoming and an ending, a red fan.
> What then, man . . .
> ....
> of the New Jerusalem?
> You will have to polish up the stars
> with Bab-o and find a new God
>
> (DN, 33)

And in "The Fury of Jewels and Coal," a poem reminiscent of Sylvia Plath's "The Colossus," the buried Jesus rises, completing and extending the burial imagery of "The Fury of Hating Eyes."

The sixth through fourteenth poems of this sequence retreat from this apocalyptic vision, musing both on various modes of salvation and on human suffering and weakness (mostly the speaker's), only occasionally glimpsing the fiery New Jerusalem. In "The Fury of Cooks," the kitchen is a metaphor for love, nourishment, and acceptance, from which the speaker is excluded. "The Fury of Cocks" is a nursery rhyme that (as the title suggests) offers a hymn to sexual passion: "She is the house. / He is the steeple. / When they fuck they are God" (*DN*, 37). In the surreal "The Fury of Abandonment" the speaker again perceives herself to be abandoned by God, love, and/or dream-mother; her abandonment is symbolized by her hands having been cut off so that she cannot touch, love, or use the phone to call for help. A childlike speaker returns in "The Fury of Overshoes," where we hear a plaintive yearning for maturity and social acceptance. In "The Fury of Rainstorms," the speaker perceives that it is within her power to shed exclusion and abandonment from life and to enter the kitchen: "Depression is boring, I think, / and I would do better to make / some soup and light up the cave" (*DN*, 43). "The Fury of Flowers and Worms" extends the familiar *Live or Die* theme, counterbalancing the urge to live and love (pick daisies) against the inexorable claim of death (burial, worms); "The Fury of God's Good-bye" and "The Fury of Sundays" offer vignettes in which the speaker is both deprived of and ignorant of God. "The Fury of Sunsets," a slight poem, offers transition to the sequence's finale: "Why am I here?" (*DN*, 49) asks the speaker.

"The Fury of Sunrises," the fifteenth, closing, and most successful poem of the sequence, fulfills the promise of rebirth. The poem opens with an emergence, at dawn, from "darkness / as black as your eyelid." One is reminded of Sylvia Plath's "Ariel," another poem that begins with the speaker's emergence from darkness and ends in a new day of apocalyptic triumph. As the world becomes light at sunrise, Sexton's poem offers a joyous hymn to the senses: smell, hearing, touch, sight, taste. In a world filled with color ("yellow, blue at the tops of trees, / more God, more God everywhere") and with love, breakfast becomes a "sacrament" of brightness and morning. This is, in fact, the apocalyptic day prefigured in "The Fury of Earth"; now,

> . . . the day commencing,
> not to die, not to die,
> as in the last day breaking,
>
> . . . .
> After the death,
> after the black of black,
> this lightness—
> not to die, not to die—
> that God begot.
>
> (*DN*, 51)

Such a joyous, uncompromising, unalloyed affirmation is new in Sexton. We remember Sexton's comment, while discussing Sylvia Plath in a 1968 interview, that "suicide is, after all, the opposite of the poem."[3] And indeed, Sexton's poems do live on, surviving the death of their composer. But now we have evidence that the composer herself may have come to regard her death as a passage into life.

Another poem-sequence in this volume achieves affirmation through the ironic use of the Eliotic mode in which personality is extinguished. Sexton's title, "Hurry Up Please It's Time," the famous refrain of "A Game of Chess," the second section of T. S. Eliot's *The Waste Land,* points thematically to Eliot's poem, and verbal and structural echoes abound. As the wasteland dwellers live in a world blighted by a curse where there is no love, no faith, and no hope, so do the various characters of Sexton's poem. But Sexton moves beyond Eliot's theme as stated by the Sybil in his epigraph: "I want to die."

As in Eliot's "A Game of Chess," Sexton's poem offers scenes of life from a contemporary waste land from which meaning and value have gone. Sexton's poem is built on the questions of the opening lines: "What is death, I ask. / What is life, you ask" (*DN,* 62). The poem proceeds through a series of juxtaposed images, voices, and lines that reveal potency and impotency (with stress on the latter), and through which the "overwhelming question" (to use Prufrock's words) of the first two lines insistently returns (but is never restated). Sexton borrows Eliot's principles of unity: imagery, refrain, and repeated concepts, connected by psychological association. In this context, it is interesting to note Sexton's observation in a 1974 letter: "Raising of the Unconscious . . . is a rather fancy title and yet quite accurate for the type of work I have been trying to do. That does not mean one forgets form and plot and what makes a good line, and how to end—It means that I have [tried] to . . . [bring] up strange juxtapositions" (*L,* 411–12).

"Hurry Up Please It's Time," then, juxtaposes the monologues, voices, and preoccupations of several characters. One principal speaker is Ms. Dog, possibly a descendant of Eliot's *Waste Land* dog, who threatens to dig up the corpse from the frosty garden, and whose activity underscores both the attempt to bury memory and the failure of faith in resurrection and thus in ultimacy of life. Ms. Dog's speech reveals a character who is tough, bawdy, slangy, defiant, utterly secular, and ultimately empty:

> You've got it made if
> you take the wafer,

take some wine,
take some bucks,

. . . .
la de dah.

. . . .
Who's that at the podium
in black and white
blurting into the mike?
Ms. Dog.
Is she spilling her guts?
You bet.

. . . .
I am sorrowful in November . . .

. . . .
Who's thinking those things?
Ms. Dog! She's out fighting the dollars.

                                   (*DN*, 64–65)

In Ms. Dog's monologues we hear snatches of songs ("Toot, toot, tootsy
don't cry. / Toot, toot, tootsy goodbye" *DN*, 65), fragments of nursery
rhymes ("Hi-ho the derry-o, / we all fall down" *DN*, 67), and frequent
interjections of "la de dah."

Another principal speaker is Anne. Anne's voice is childlike, calmer,
and less brittle than Ms. Dog's, yet its lifeless cadences show that Anne
too suffers from spiritual vacuity. Facts are her anchor to reality:

Today is November 14th, 1972.
I live in Weston, Mass., Middlesex County,
U.S.A., and it rains steadily
in the pond . . .

. . . .
The pond is waiting for December and its Novocain.

                                   (*DN*, 63)

Verbal clues identify Anne with Ms. Dog:

Anne says:
This is the rainy season.
I am sorrowful in November.
The kettle is whistling.
I must butter the toast.
And give it jam too.
My kitchen is a heart.

                                   (*DN*, 65–66)

This kitchen imagery recalls the "Fury of Cooks" section of "The Furies," where the speaker's abandonment and deprivation of love is realized in her banishment from a kitchen ruled by a woman named Helen, who refuses to let her in. In "Hurry Up Please It's Time," however, Anne is not closed out from life but is part of it: "My kitchen is a heart. / I must feed it oxygen once in a while" (*DN*, 66). Only her drained tones reveal her spiritual emptiness.

Three times between sections of Anne and Ms. Dog are juxtaposed dialogues between Anne and an Interrogator, brief sections that advance theme by presenting straightforward commentary. In the first dialogue Anne offers limited affirmation from her spiritual exhaustion:

> Interrogator:
> What can you say of your last seven days?
>
> Anne:
> They were tired.
>
> Interrogator:
> One day is enough to perfect a man.
>
> Anne:
> I watered and fed the plant.
> (*DN*, 63)

In the second dialogue, simple Anne affirms her faith in resurrection, childishly combining Lazarus with Santa Claus:

> Interrogator:
> What goes up the chimney?
>
> Anne:
> Fat Lazarus in his red suit.
> (*DN*, 68)

The third dialogue offers another merging of Anne with Ms. Dog:

> Ms. Dog stands on the shore
> and the sea keeps rocking in
> and she wants to talk to God.
>
> Interrogator:
> Why talk to God?

> Anne:
> It's better than playing bridge.
>   (*DN*, 71)

Here, reference to *The Waste Land* recalls, perhaps, both Madame So-
sostris's vulgar, empty fortune-telling through her tarot cards and the
arbitrary meaning of the chess game. If these games in Eliot's poem
objectify life's meaninglessness, Anne's response in the Sexton poem
signifies her inclination to shun such empty activity and move through
the waste land toward a locus of meaning and value that is God. Also,
since Anne and Ms. Dog join in this impulse and speak with one voice
to the end of the poem, their newly integrated personality serves as a
further sign of hope. Additionally, the Interrogator herself may be a
God-figure, offering subtle direction throughout the poem to this affirmative end.

Furthermore, the refrain "Forgive us, Father, for we know not"
punctuates the poem. "Us" may denote Anne and Ms. Dog as well as
humans in general; in any case, the sentence is a clear variation of
Christ's words as, from the cross, he forgave his accusers and murder-
ers: "Father, forgive them; for they know not what they do" (Luke
23:34).

There is clear evidence, then, that Sexton in "Hurry Up Please It's
Time" quotes Eliot's poem for a dual purpose, both to stress the wasteland quality of contemporary life and to offer a solution. Sexton's title,
while echoing Eliot's great refrain of ultimate human frivolity, points
as well to the approach of an event of ultimate meaning. The collage
of monologue, dialogue, literary and biblical reference, and refrain offers juxtapositions that may indeed at first appear strange but that gain
energy and meaning through the poem. "You better get straight with
the Maker," says Ms. Dog, "cuz it's a coming, it's a coming! / . . . /
There's power in the Lord, baby" (*DN*, 66–67). Here is how the poem
ends:

> And one other thing:
> to consider the lilies of the field.
> Of course earth is a stranger,
> we pull at its arms
> and still it won't speak.
> . . . .
> It is only known that they are here to worship,
> to worship the terror of the rain,

> the mud and all its people,
> the body itself,
>
> ....
> But more than that,
> to worship the question itself
> though the buildings burn
> and the big people topple over in a faint.
> Bring a flashlight, Ms. Dog,
> and look in every corner of the brain
> and ask and ask and ask
> until the kingdom,
> however queer,
> will come.
>
> (*DN*, 73–74)

Surely such a carefully wrought affirmation is new in Anne Sexton's poetry.

The final poem-sequence of *The Death Notebooks*, "O Ye Tongues," is also its finest and most affirmative. Anne Sexton called "O Ye Tongues" not only "a major poem" (*L*, 379) but also "my last prayer" (*L*, 410). The poems that constitute "O Ye Tongues" are "a series of psalms," which, together with the poems of "The Furies," "are praise."[4]

We should note at the outset that Sexton, in composing this poem, had to have been aware of *Jubilate Agno (Rejoice in the Lamb)* by the eighteenth-century poet Christopher Smart. As Sexton draws ironically on materials from *The Waste Land* in "Hurry Up Please It's Time," in "O Ye Tongues" she echoes verbal, structural, and thematic materials of *Jubilate Agno*. Anne Sexton and Christopher Smart had much in common: they were both poets; both drank excessively and spent time in mental institutions; both had two daughters. And the great, un-realized love of Christopher Smart's life was a woman named Anne, who appears as "Anne Hope," her real and thematically significant married name, in his poem. Smart wrote *Jubilate Agno* in a madhouse; Sexton, in an interview, described the commonality of religious and mad visions:

I have visions—sometimes ritualized visions—that come to me of God, or of Christ, or of the Saints, and I feel that I can touch them almost . . . that they are part of me. It's the same "Everything that has been shall be again." It's reincarnation, speaking with another voice . . . or else with the Devil. If you want to know the truth, the leaves talk to me every June.[5]

Perhaps Smart's work provided for Sexton the affirmation, if not the epiphany, that she had been seeking. Surely Christopher's existence and companionship facilitated Anne's writing of this "praise" poem, as the poem itself tells us.

Curiously, the words of scholar William Force Stead, writing in 1939 of *Jubilate Agno,* aptly describe "O Ye Tongues" as well:

This is a curiosity, an extraordinary document. . . . Bewildering at the first glance, it contains much that is intelligent and beautiful, which I believe will reward the reader who makes an allowance for absurdities and examines the obscurities. . . . this [is a] strange composition, written by that Cambridge prodigal, Christopher Smart, while confined in a madhouse. . . . There is plenty of rubbish, there are frequent intrusions of the meaningless and grotesque; yet amid all this, one is continually coming upon a revealing phrase which tells us what the poet had been thinking, reading, praying for, enduring and suffering. There are bright little thumbnail sketches, whimsical fancies, and here and there some bold gigantic images. There are fragments of wide and curious learning, with signs of a hundred friendships and of more than one love affair.[6]

The theme of *Jubilate Agno,* says Stead, is "the bringing together of the whole of creation in praise of the creator."[7] That is also the theme of "O Ye Tongues."

"O Ye Tongues" comprises ten poems, each called a "psalm." The psalms are written in alternating, paired "Let" and "For" sections; all or most poetic lines in the first, third, fifth, seventh, and ninth psalms begin with the word "Let," and all or most poetic lines in the second, fourth, sixth, eighth, and tenth psalms begin with the word "For." *Jubilate Agno* also observes a "Let" and "For" structure, although not in regularly alternating sections. Smart's precise intention in this matter remains unclear, since *Jubilate Agno* is a fragment discovered, in random order, after the poet's death. Scholars suggest that Smart may have "intended the *Jubilate* to be a first step toward the reformation of the Anglican liturgy"; since "the title and peroration of *Jubilate Agno* are so closely parallel to portions of the Order for Morning Prayer and the Psalter[,] the poem was intended as a responsive reading."[8] Or he may have written "in a form which he had reason to believe resembled the original compositions of the sacred poets," especially the Hebrew poets.[9] In any case, whether meant to be read antiphonally or alternately, the "Let" and "For" sections of *Jubilate Agno* differ in effect. As Sophia B. Blaydes points out, "The poem relies upon antithesis for its effect, i.e., the *Let* verses establish some idea through a name, an object, or an idea, and then Smart responds with an appropriate, if not conventional, idea in the *For* section," where his personal attitudes also appear. "Through such a technique Smart intended to write a praise of God."[10]

Through a similar technique, Anne Sexton has written her praise. Sexton's "First Psalm," a "Let" section, offers the poet's unique version of Genesis, in which God, sun, earth, darkness, light, water, stars, land, vegetation, seasons, and man are created. The opening verse, "Let there be a God as large as a sunlamp to laugh his heat / at you" (*DN*, 77), while echoing Smart's frequent reference to the sun (no doubt a pun on "son") as divinity ("For the Sun's at work to make me a garment. . . ."[11]), also exemplifies Sexton's practice throughout the poem of mixing sacred and profane materials: "Let God share his Hoodsie" (*DN*, 77). This sunlamp image is recapitulated in the poem's closing verse. The "Second Psalm," a "For" section, offers a sort of personal confession:

> For I pray that John F. Kennedy will forgive me for stealing his free-from-the-Senate Manila envelope.
>
> For I pray that my honorary degree from Tufts is not making John Holmes stick out his tongue from the brackish grave in Medford.
> . . . .
> For she prays that she will not cringe at the death hole.
>
> For I pray that God will digest me.
>
> (*DN*, 80–81)

Consistent with a psalm of praise, the tone of this poem is supplicatory, self-assured, and, above all, joyful. And the joy is multifaceted. It is located in the perception of several speakers; we note that the "I" is sometimes clearly Sexton herself, sometimes Anne and Christopher combined, and sometimes an outside speaker who refers to Anne in the third person.

In the "Third Psalm," which recounts a sort of rebirth in enumerating the creatures released from Noah's Ark, we first meet the characters "Anne and Christopher" who "kneel" and "give praise" and "rejoice" (*DN*, 82–83). The paired "Fourth Psalm" explains the genesis of these twins and introduces a thematic image:

For Anne and Christopher were born in my head as I howled
at the grave of the roses, the ninety-four rose crèches of my
bedroom.

For Christopher, my imaginary brother, my twin . . .

For I became a *we* and this imaginary *we* became a kind
company. . . .

For I was in a boundary of wool and painted boards. Where
are we Christopher? Jail, he said.

For the room itself was a box. Four thick walls of roses. . . .
. . . .
For birth was a disease and Christopher and I invented the
cure.

For we swallow magic and deliver Anne.

                                                          (*DN*, 84–86)

Anne Sexton finds kinship with Christopher Smart through Smart's
love of *his* Anne and through Sexton's discovery of their kindred spirits
in his poem; with Christopher, Anne is no longer alone; together they
can find the cure for birth. Christopher is invented, born to Anne in
bedlam, where there are roses on the walls. This rose-covered "bedroom" is Anne's prison. It is her physical and imaginative body, the
source both of trouble and salvation from and through which she will
find release.
    The following two psalms develop this theme. Anne and Christo-
pher are together, and Christopher's love helps her to endure her confinement. In the "Fifth Psalm":

Come forth with a cockroach large enough to be Franz Kafka
(may he rest in peace though locked in his room). Surely all
who are locked in boxes of different sizes should have their
hands held. Trains and planes should not be locked. One should
be allowed to fly out of them and into the Lord's mouth. The
Lord is my shepherd, He will swallow me. The Lord is my
shepherd, He will allow me back out.

                                                          (*DN*, 88)

In the "Sixth Psalm":

> For America is a lady rocking on her porch in an unpainted house
> on an unused road but Anne does not see it.
> . . . .
> Anne does not see it. Anne is locked in. . . .
> . . . Anne hides inside folding and unfolding rose
> after rose. She has no one. She has Christopher.
>
> (*DN*, 89–90)

The "Seventh Psalm" presents a joyous choral anticipation of the poem's final sections; the verbs "rejoice" and "give praise" predominate. The "Eighth Psalm," then, offers images of fertility, birth, and new life. Rose-covered walls are left behind; "she has come through the voyage fit and her room carries / the little people" (*DN*, 93). Anne and Christopher have given birth, and "the baby lives. The mother will die and when she does / Christopher will go with her. Christopher who stabbed his / kisses and cried up to make two out of one" (*DN*, 95).

The ninth and tenth psalms are paired as well. In the "Ninth Psalm," all the earth praises God ("the chipmunk," "the airplane," "the Good Fairy," and so on), and here, praise is linked with ascension. As Smart mentioned Jacob's Ladder in *Jubilate Agno* ("For Jacob's Ladder are the steps of the Earth graduated / hence to Paradise [*sic*] and thence to the throne of God"[12]), so Sexton also brings it into her poem: "Let the chipmunk praise the Lord as he bounds up Jacob's Ladder" (*DN*, 96). As the dreaming Jacob, seeing the ladder reaching to heaven, heard God tell him that his progeny would prosper and be blessed and that God would always be with him (Gen. 28:12–22), so Anne is similarly chosen and blessed. The closing "Tenth Psalm" offers images of release and triumph: "For I am not locked up" (*DN*, 98). Anne, Christopher, and their child (who, we assume, is love personified and who, according to God's promise to Jacob, will multiply and prosper) grow and walk, and then

> a light is clicked on by gentle fingers.
>
> For death comes to friends, to parents, to sisters. Death comes
> With its bagful of pain yet they do not curse the key they were
> given to hold.

> For they open each door and it gives them a new day at the
> yellow window.
>
> (DN, 98–99)

Death is life, here. It is the light of a new day as well as the apocalyptic light of sunrise we have seen in the concluding poem of "The
Furies." It is the light, prefigured in this poem's opening line, of "God
as large as a sunlamp." "For," writes Christopher Smart in *Jubilate
Agno*, "the approaches of Death are by illumination."[13] One critic calls
Jubilate Agno a "bright celestial vision."[14] "O Ye Tongues" offers a vision no less bright. Through her own searching, through the discovery
of her spiritual twin Christopher, Anne Sexton has reached a conclusion
toward which her poetry has been tending, an affirmation to nourish
her "violent and religious heart" (*L*, 366). Need has become belief, the
confessional mask has dropped, revealing Anne, and this rat indeed
lives on "no evil star." Anne and Christopher

> . . . hung up a picture of a rat and the rat smiled and
> held out his hand.
>
> For the rat was blessed on that mountain. He was given a white
> bath.
>
> For the milk in the skies sank down upon them and tucked
> them in.
>
> For God did not forsake them but put the blood angel to look
> after them until such time as they would enter their star.
>
> . . . .
> For God was as large as a sunlamp and laughed his heat at us
> and therefore we did not cringe at the death hole.
>
> (DN, 99–100)

Chapter Nine
Last Volumes, Last Poems

The Awful Rowing Toward God: "In Search of an Answer"

The Awful Rowing toward God is the last volume of poetry that Anne Sexton planned, prepared, and submitted to the publisher. A consideration of the poems in this volume, then, is essential to a study of Sexton's work, even though most of the poems are interesting chiefly because they are there. By Sexton's own admission, the poetry in *The Awful Rowing toward God* is "raw" and "unworked" (*L,* 390). By contrast, one remembers some of Sexton's comments about the composition of her earlier work: "I really prefer dramatic situations to anything else," she wrote while composing her first volume, *To Bedlam and Part Way Back.* "I prefer people in a situation . . . , and then, in the end, find the thought" (*L,* 61). "I am given to excess," she wrote in 1962; "I have found that I can control it best in a poem" (*L,* 144). Indeed, control of informed emotion is one of the great strengths of Sexton's poetry, for such control renders emotion even more powerful. Creation of a dramatic situation by which to realize theme is another strength of many of Sexton's best poems. Such strengths are largely absent from *The Awful Rowing toward God.*

Anne Sexton wrote the poems of this, her eighth volume, in January 1973 and submitted the volume to Houghton Mifflin in February 1974, seven months before her death. She had composed all the poems, as she revealed in a 1973 interview, "in two and a half weeks," the "poems coming five, six, seven or whatever . . . a day."[1] The volume was published in February 1975, four months after her death. Linda Gray Sexton and Lois Ames, editors of Sexton's *Letters,* provide further enlightening information about the composition of these poems:

On the file folder of first drafts for *The Awful Rowing toward God* in the Boston University archive, [Anne] noted that "these poems were started 1/10th/73 and finished 1/30th/73 (with two days out for despair, and three days out in a mental hospital). I explain this so you will understand they are raw, un-worked poems, all first drafts, written in a frenzy of despair and hope. To get out the *meaning* was the primary thing—while I had it, while the muse was with me. I apologize for the inadequate words. As I said in one of the poems, 'I fly like an eagle, but with the wings of a wren.' (1/31/73)"

The published poems in *The Awful Rowing toward God* differ little from those early first drafts. (*L*, 390–91)

"Words" is the *Awful Rowing toward God* poem that the editors quote in this note. As other lines of the poem suggest, Sexton's creative in-stinct remained keen, yet the urge to express content had perhaps over-come the need to hone her craft: "Be careful of words, / even the miraculous ones. / . . . / . . . they can be both daisies and bruises. / . . . / . . . I am in love with words. / . . . / Yet often they fail me" (*AR*, 71). Sexton's observation that these *Awful Rowing toward God* poems were written in a "frenzy" becomes the title of another poem in the volume, a poem that also reveals both the poet's method and her approach. "Frenzy" opens with these lines: "I am, each day, / typing out the God / my typewriter believes in. / Very quick. Very intense" (*AR*, 76).

In these poems, Sexton is surely "typing out the God / [her] type-writer believes in." The editors of her *Letters* suggest that Sexton "had succeeded in creating her own private God—perhaps He would never leave her" (*L*, 390). Perhaps, indeed, her search for a God she could believe in was motivated in part by her need for constant love; however, the evidence of Sexton's finest religious poetry, largely collected in *The Death Notebooks*, reveals Sexton's search as profound and at least imag-inatively fulfilling. "The Godmonger" begins with these words: "With all my questions, / all the nihilistic words in my head, / I went in search of an answer, / I went in search of the other world" (*AR*, 62). This is the search chronicled in *The Death Notebooks*. And although that search seems completed in that volume, it continues in *The Awful Row-ing toward God*.

It is primarily an inner search that *The Awful Rowing toward God* verbalizes, an examination of both intellect and emotion. These poems take the form of intense musings about life, about death, and about the poet's relationship with her God. Here there are no fully realized dramatic situations, as in earlier poems; instead, these poems seem rather to be Sexton's own, undisguised thoughts and responses, re-corded as they occurred. The hunger that threads through Sexton's earlier work is clearly evident here, still sharp and still unsated. "I am

torn in two," writes Sexton in "The Civil War," "but I will conquer
myself. / . . . / I will pry out the broken / pieces of God in me. / . . .
/ I will put Him together again" (*AR*, 3). As she writes in "The
Children,"

> the place I live in
> is a kind of maze
> and I keep seeking
> the exit or the home.
>
> ....
>
> [to] find the real McCoy
> in the private holiness
> of my hands.
>
> (*AR*, 6)

In these poems God is to be found within, in the poet's own hands,
and the pain of unbelief is caused by the poet's own skepticism. "I have
tried prayer," Sexton writes in "The Poet of Ignorance," "but as I pray
the crab grips harder / and the pain enlarges." In fact, she discovers,
"the crab was my ignorance of God" (*AR*, 29). In this connection the
defiant, secular Ms. Dog of "Hurry Up Please It's Time" (*DN*) reappears here briefly, in "Is It True?" Still spiritually vacuous, the Ms.
Dog of *The Awful Rowing toward God* is now labeled "evil":

> When I tell the priest I am evil
> he asks for a definition of the word.
>
> ....
>
> Evil is maybe lying to God.
> Or better, lying to love.
>
> ....
>
> Ms. Dog,
> Why is you evil?
> It climbed into me.
> It didn't mean to.
>
> (*AR*, 49, 50)

Yet this manifestation of Ms. Dog seems a theological precursor to the
Ms. Dog of "Hurry Up Please It's Time," since her dilemma is unre-
solved and her pain unrelieved:

> I have,
> for some time,

called myself
Ms. Dog.
Why?
Because I am almost animal
and yet the animal I lost most—
that animal is near to God,
but lost from Him.

                                                    (AR, 55)

The search for God, then, must also assume another direction, still
within the speaker's consciousness but moving away from pain and evil
in an upward direction. Sexton may remain the witch, a familiar and
thematically central guise throughout her poetry: "Yes," she writes in
"The Witch's Life," "It is the witch's life, / climbing the primordial
climb" (AR, 12). But she must struggle toward God, either by crawling, as she does in "The Sickness unto Death" ("I . . . wanted to crawl
toward God / . . . / [He] put his mouth to mine / and gave me his
air" (AR, 41)) or by climbing. One must disregard danger, writes Sexton in "Riding the Elevator into the Sky," "if you're climbing out of
yourself. / If you're going to smash into the sky" (AR, 17). For this
poem's celestial elevator may possibly reach God: "Floor six thousand:
/ the stars, / skeletons on fire, / . . . / And a key, / . . . / that opens
something— / . . . / up there" (AR, 18).

As in *The Death Notebooks,* "the exit" and "the home" that Sexton
seeks (in "The Children" [AR, 6]) are finally the same place, the apocalyptic discovery of which must be both death and rebirth. "The stars,"
writes Sexton in "The Earth Falls Down," "are pears / that no one can
reach, / even for a wedding. / Perhaps for a death" (AR, 14). If evil
and ignorance have separated her from the discovery of God, they can
be shed in death, specifically, in "The Wall," by dying "before it is
time." "Take off the wall," Sexton writes in this poem, "the wall / that
separates you from God." "In nature . . . / all is change, . . . / all
disappear. Only to be reborn" (AR, 47, 46). The poem "Welcome
Morning" recalls the sacramental breakfast imagery of "The Fury of
Sunrises" (DN); here, "There is joy / in all: / . . . / for this is God,
this laughter of the morning" (AR, 58, 59). And Sexton concludes
"Jesus, the Actor, Plays the Holy Ghost" with this stanza:

                    Oh, Mary,
                    Gentle Mother,
                    open the door and let me in.

....

> I have been born many times, . . .
> but let me be born again
> into something true.
>
> (*AR*, 61)

This is the search Sexton records in *The Awful Rowing toward God,* the search for God, for understanding, and for figurative and perhaps actual rebirth. The quite successful framing and title poems of the volume establish and reinforce that thematic emphasis. Entitled "Rowing" and "The Rowing Endeth," the volume's opening and closing poems might well be considered parts of a single poem, the first part introducing the search, and the second part affirming its conclusion.

"Rowing" offers a sort of biographical summary ("A story, a story!" [*AR*, 1]) in which Sexton, from birth to the present time, becomes a figurative boat-rower searching for an island called God. Although this island has always been there, the poet, even while compelled to row, has been ignorant of her destination: "God was there like an island I had not rowed to, / still ignorant of Him, my arms and legs worked, / and I grew, I grew" (*AR*, 1). In this poem, arrival at the destination is only promised, yet the poet anticipates her arrival as both release and fulfillment. "I know that that island will not be perfect, / . . . / but there will be a door / and I will open it" (*AR*, 2). In this place, "I will get rid of the rat inside of me" (remember the rat of the Irish palindrome and the *Death Notebooks* poem), "the gnawing pestilent rat. / God will take it with his two hands / and embrace it" (*AR*, 2).

As the speaker anticipates relief and perhaps even transfiguration, we must take note of another aspect of this journey and of this island. There is evidence here of Anne's emotional and physical submission to the male Other who has defined her search throughout her poetic journey, and against whose dominating influence she has fought. As Diana Hume George observes,

I find it poignant to discover that the "island of God" may have been the island of childhood where she summered, and where, as her editors remind us in the *Letters,* "Anne's happy memories centered." I also confess that I find it beautiful; I contemplate that simplicity, that perfect circle of sought-after comfort, one that brings the middle-aged poet back to the finest moments of a troubled and unhappy past. Perhaps anyone's idea of heaven is some such journey into the past.[2]

"The Rowing Endeth," as its title implies, describes that journey's end. Here, the speaker, blistered and salt-caked from her long journey, is "mooring my rowboat / at the dock of the island called God" (*AR*, 85). And this God, though he may be created out of Sexton's own need as the intervening poems suggest, is also a Christian God: "This dock is made in the shape of a fish" (*AR*, 85). The poem joyfully and successfully adopts a metaphor from the game of poker; God and Sexton are the players, and God, with five aces (one wild card) wins over the speaker's royal straight flush. Such an outcome, however, means that both God and Sexton are winners at this cosmic game; as Sexton commented in an interview conducted three and one-half months before her death, "Here he [God] is laughing: he is slumped over me laughing, and I'm laughing. He didn't beat me; we both won!"[3] The speaker has done her best to win; a royal straight flush is ordinarily an unbeatable combination. But God, with his wild card, has prevailed. And they laugh together,

> such laughter that He doubles right over me
> laughing a Rejoice-Chorus at our two triumphs.
> Then I laugh, the fishy dock laughs
> the sea laughs. The Island laughs.
> The Absurd laughs.
>
> Dearest dealer,
> I with my royal straight flush,
> love you so for your wild card,
> that untamable, eternal, gut-driven *ha-ha*
> and lucky love.
>
> (*AR*, 86)

For one of the epigraphs to this volume, Sexton offered this: "Sören Kierkegaard says, 'But above all do not make yourself important by doubting'" (*AR*, vi). In "The Rowing Endeth," pain, evil, questioning, and doubt are joyfully abandoned in this "Rejoice-Chorus." Yet there is ambiguity in this outcome, since the speaker is, however joyfully, beaten by God. And God is the ultimate male Other who leans over her in a dominant (even sexually dominant) posture.

45 *Mercy Street:* A Strange Hegira

45 *Mercy Street*, published by Houghton Mifflin in 1976, is the volume on which Anne Sexton was working at the time of her death. She

had begun to compose the poems of this ninth volume while writing the poems of *The Death Notebooks* and *The Awful Rowing toward God;* according to Linda Gray Sexton and Lois Ames, "Between June of 1972 and October 1974, she had written three new books: *The Death Notebooks, The Awful Rowing toward God,* and *45 Mercy Street*" (*L,* 390). After submitting *The Awful Rowing toward God* in February 1974 for publication, then, Sexton turned to complete the planning for this new volume. By Sexton's own account, her new volume's working title was *The Life Notebooks:* "As of yesterday," she wrote in January 1973,

I started a new book, entitled *The Life Notebooks* [later retitled *45 Mercy Street*], which indeed [it] could be called, because with the clear realization of death, one gets . . . less concerned with getting the house-cleaning done. . . . I ought to be able to write by now, and it seems to me at this point I ought to know how to live. That is, I ought to be able to dig a trench in my soul and find something there. . . . this book will come out in the winter of 1974. (*L,* 392)

By February 1974, however, when Sexton submitted *The Awful Rowing toward God* for publication, she wrote to her agent that "another book [*45 Mercy Street*] slowly being filled, but I feel it must be quite delayed because part of it is too personal to publish for some time" (*L,* 403). In a June 1974 letter, Sexton wrote, "I actually have finished another book but am glad to have the time to reform the poems, rewrite and delete. I have it in mind to call it *45 Mercy Street.* . . . I absolutely cannot call it *The Life Notebooks* because I think I have yet to write that book" (*L,* 416). And a July 1974 letter refers to the "1976 (probably) publication" of *45 Mercy Street,* "which is a kind of jumble of a book but does deal with my divorce and a deep love affair that ended in disaster" (*L,* 419–20). Sexton committed suicide on 4 October 1974. Her daughter Linda Gray Sexton, whom Anne had appointed as her literary executor on Linda's twenty-first birthday in July 1974, finished preparing the volume and submitted it for publication.

In an editor's note, Linda Gray Sexton comments that "the manuscript [of *45 Mercy Street*] has been edited but changes are few."[4] The changes involve the arrangement of the poems ("the new arrangement allows the poems to build to a clear progression of thought and emotion," since Anne "had not yet arrived at a final arrangement"), the interpretation of some words ("I have struggled to decipher her handwriting"), and the deletion of an indeterminate number of poems ("omitted . . . because of their intensely personal content, and the pain their publication would bring to individuals still living") (*45M*, vii–viii).

One can only guess at what direction *The Life Notebooks*, which remained unwritten, might have taken. Based on the evidence of the apocalyptic, life-in-death theme explored in *The Death Notebooks* and to a lesser extent in *The Awful Rowing toward God*, one might surmise that at one point, near the end of her life, Anne Sexton may have felt inclined to affirm and to explore in more elaborate detail the vision of such poems as "The Furies," "Hurry Up Please It's Time," "O Ye Tongues," and "The Rowing Endeth." Perhaps this is at least partly what Sexton meant by "know[ing] how to live" (*L*, 392). In any case, as Sexton herself observed, *45 Mercy Street* is not that book.

What *45 Mercy Street* is, perhaps surprisingly, is a volume that recalls and extends the poetry of Sexton's early confessional mode in combination with the free-associative dream-structures of her later work. Linda Gray Sexton points out that this volume "charts Anne Sexton's poetic growth and the events of her life from 1971 through 1974" (*45M*, vii). Presenting a variety of subjects and often a variety of modes, these poems show more evidence of care and revision than do the poems of the previous volume, and since Linda Gray Sexton assures us that "each line appears exactly as she wrote it" (*45M*, viii), we can assume that the care evident here is Anne Sexton's own. Only sometimes "raw" or "unworked . . . drafts," the poems of *45 Mercy Street* contribute positively to Anne Sexton's oeuvre and to our appreciation of it.

The volume is divided into four sections that do, as Linda Gray Sexton observes, "build to a clear progression of thought and emotion" (*45M*, vii). The first section is entitled "Beginning the Hegira"; a hegira is, as Linda Gray Sexton tells us she learned from Lois Ames, "a journey or trip especially when undertaken as a means of escaping from an undesirable or dangerous environment; or, as a means of arriving at a highly desirable destination" (*45M*, 1). Yet if, as that definition suggests, we look here for evidence of the abandoned *Life Notebooks*, we do so in vain. An undesirable environment appears rather to surround and preoccupy the speaker of this section's twelve poems, which deal with such subjects as the death or near-death of children, John F. Kennedy's assassination, and child abuse.

The first and title poem, "45 Mercy Street," offers a dreamscape, "my real dream" (*45M*, 3) of the speaker's journey through memory in an unsuccessful search for mercy and redemption. Objectified by an address that the speaker cannot find, the speaker's elusive goal shifts through familiar materials (mother, grandmother, great-grandmother, Nana, married Anne); finally, the disillusioned speaker declares that "this is no dream / just my oily life" (*45M*, 5). The mood of the poem's conclusion is one of frustration and anger: "who wants to own the past / that went out on a dead ship / and left me only with paper?" (*45M*, 5). The speaker is indeed left with her poetry, but this seems like a consolation prize: "I pull the dream off / and slam into the cement wall / of the clumsy calendar / I live in, / my life, / and its hauled up / notebooks" (*45M*, 6).

The volume's second poem, "Talking to Sheep," offers a confessional manifesto such as we have not seen since the early volumes, but with a new, bitter twist. Like "45 Mercy Street," "Talking to Sheep" is largely retrospective both in its reference to subjects about which Sexton has written confessional poems (mother, father, great-aunt) and in the speaker's damning assessment of the way her confessions have been received and have demeaned her. "My life / has appeared unclothed in court, / detail by detail" (*45M*, 7), she begins. "I was shamed at the verdict / . . . / But nevertheless I went on / . . . / confessing, confessing" (*45M*, 7). Even now her confessional poems, "the latrine of my details," is an apparently unpleasant "compulsion," "my fate":

> Now,
> in my middle age,
> I'm well aware
> I keep making statues
> of my acts, carving them with my sleep—
> or if it is not my life I depict
> then someone's close enough to wear my nose—
> (*45M*, 7–8)

The fifth poem of this section, "Food," recapitulates another familiar theme: the poet's unsated hunger. Here, again, the speaker's vocation seems to win last prize. The poem offers an extended image where the speaker experiences a series of rejections in her unsuccessful attempt to suckle like a baby: "I want mother's milk." "I need food / and you walk away reading the paper" (*45M*, 13). This is the rejection at the poem's center: "I am hungry and you give me / a dictionary to decipher" (*45M*, 13).

The volume's second section, called "Bestiary U.S.A.," has for its epigraph "(I look at the strangeness in them and the naturalness they cannot help, in order to find some virtue in the beast in me)" (*45M*, 25). This section comprises eighteen poems, each titled for a beast. As the epigraph suggests, each poem offers an extended metaphor that makes a thematic connection between certain traits held in common by the beast of the title and the human speaker. In "Bat," for example, a complex relationship is established; the bat's skin's reminding the speaker of her own skin moves into an oblique reference to their common nocturnal witchery and resolves with a comment on the shared fate of the ugly, outcast bat-witch-speaker:

> I flew at night, too. . . .
> . . . .
> If you had caught me with your flashlight
> you would have seen a pink corpse with wings,
> . . . .
> That's why the dogs of your house sniff me.
> They know I'm something to be caught
> somewhere in the cemetery hanging upside down
> like a misshapen udder.
>
> (*45M*, 27)

These are well-constructed, carefully crafted poems. Yet the metaphorical realizations reveal a speaker who imagines herself as outcast, misunderstood, rejected, repulsive, barren, dead. In "Hog," for instance, the speaker, waiting for death like the fat "brown bacon machine" (*45M*, 28), also experiences a "little death" each night. The "Hornet" threatens the speaker with its "red-hot needle," its "nest of knives" (*45M*, 31); the "Snail" is eaten; the "Lobster" is cooked. In "Seal," the speaker-poet, like the seal, craves a new environment where she can fly: "Lord, let me see Jesus before it's all over, / crawling up some mountain, reckless and outrageous, / calling out poems / as he lets out his blood" (*45M*, 40). The "Gull" represents lost innocence for the speaker: "Oh Gull of my childhood, / . . . take me back, / . . . teach me to laugh / and cry again that way that was the good bargain / of youth" (*45M*, 45). Yet such a wish is futile. This poem repeats the theme, by now becoming quite familiar in this volume, of the speaker's surviving reluctantly in a dead world with only her art for company. In "Gull," the sun is "a dead fruit / and all that flies today / is crooked and vain and has been cut from a book" (*45M*, 45).

The volume's third section, "The Divorce Papers," contains seventeen poems about divorce and about love. As Linda Gray Sexton and Lois Ames tell us, "In February of 1973 Anne asked Kayo for a divorce. . . . against the advice of her psychiatrist and many of her friends, she began legal proceedings. Kayo contested the divorce until its bitter end in November, convinced that Anne was acting precipitously" (*L*, 389). These poems reveal a speaker who is lost, confused, ambivalent, and troubled by her dreams. "Where It Was Back Then" recounts a dream of reconciliation: "Husband, / last night I dreamt / they cut off your hands and feet. / . . . / Now we are both incomplete." The speaker washes these hands and feet "in magical waters" and places "each one / where it belonged on you. / 'A miracle,' you said and we laughed / the laugh of the well-to-do" (*45M*, 49). The title ("Back Then") suggests, however, that the possibility to achieve such wholeness is past. Indeed, "Bayonet" recalls a dream of violent aggression, in which the speaker considers possible uses for the bayonet she holds ("for the earth of your stomach," "to cut the daylight into you / and let out your buried heartland" (*45M*, 59). "The Stand-Ins" offers a dream of victimization and shunned salvation; in this dream, the speaker-victim (wearing a "Yellow Star") is cooked in an oven by a "killer" wearing a swastika, but at death ("when it is ready for serving") the speaker has a vision of Jesus on the cross, saying, "This is the start. / This is the end. / This is a light. / This is a start" (*45M*, 73). The speaker awakens, however, brusquely though tentatively rejecting the profound meaning of this dream: "Oh well, / it doesn't belong to me, / if a cigar can be a cigar / then a dream can be a dream. / Right? / Right?" (*45M*, 74).

Other poems of "The Divorce Papers" trace the speaker's ambivalence about this divorce, revealing conflicting emotion both within and between poems. Poems like "The Wedlock," "Landscape Winter," "Despair," "Divorce," and "Waking Alone" show the speaker's perception of her failed marriage. Some of these poems achieve this result through images of coldness ("we lie / like two frozen paintings in a field of poppies" [*45M*, 51]); "Snow, . . . / my rock outside my word-window, / . . . / . . . soon, soon I'd better run out / while there is time" (*45M*, 52–53). Others ("When the Glass of My Body Broke," "The Break Away"), clearly developing a love-lost theme, are addressed to an unnamed lover, sometimes clearly Sexton's husband. (But we remember also the brief reference in Sexton's *Letters* to a "deep love affair that ended in disaster" [*L*, 420]). In "Divorce" and "Waking Alone," guilt, fear, confusion, and love intermingle. In "Divorce," for example, the speaker says that "I have killed our lives together, / . . .

/ I have killed all the good things, / but they are too stubborn for me."
Memory revives love: "I loved you then, so wise from the shower, / and
I loved you many other times / and I have been, for months, trying to
drown it, / to push it under" (45M, 55). "Waking Alone" is a love
poem framed with hate and fear:

> husband, husband,
> I lust for your smile,
> ....
> and your chin, ever Nazi, ever stubborn
> ....
> I love you the way the oboe plays.
> I love you the way skinny dipping makes a body feel.
> I love you the way a ripe artichoke tastes.
> Yet I fear you,
> as one in the desert fears the sun.
>
> (45M, 57)

Still other poems present a speaker who seeks death as a response to
rejection or loss. In "The Love Plant" the speaker poisons herself.
"The Red Dance" recalls the *Transformations* poem "Snow White and
the Seven Dwarfs": "but, oh my friends, in the end / you will dance
the fire dance in iron shoes" *T*, 5). Here, in the 45 *Mercy Street* poem,
the "girl"-protagonist, wearing a red dress, "danced and danced and
danced. / It was a death dance" (45M, 79); at the poem's close, she
drowns. "Killing the Love" reverses the title and the thematic thrust
of the *Love Poems* poem "Loving the Killer." In the earlier poem, the
speaker loves her husband even though (or perhaps because) he is a
killer of animals, and by extension of her. Here in the 45 *Mercy Street*
poem, the speaker herself is the killer; "alone with the dead," she kills
all that she loves, including her husband ("I am the love killer" 45M,
77). And she plans her own death as well: "When a life is over, / the
one you were living for, / where do you go? / . . . / I'll dance in the
city. / . . . / And there'll be no scream / from the lady in the red dress
/ . . . / as the cars go by" (45M, 78).

The fourth section of 45 *Mercy Street*, "Eating the Leftovers," contains twelve quite good poems that continue and conclude the themes,
so consistently pervading this volume, of loss and death. "Divorce, Thy
Name is Woman" extends the "Divorce Papers" theme, although here
the speaker melds "Daddy" and husband together, divorcing them
both. Also as in the "Divorce Papers" section, several poems of "Eating

the Leftovers" imagine the speaker's death. "The Consecrating Mother" creates an extended image of the sea as a sacramental woman to be joined and, in a kind of love-death, "entered like kneeling your way into church, / descending into that ascension, / though she be slick as olive oil" (*45M*, 113); "at night when you enter her / you shine like a neon soprano" (*45M*, 114). In the short, concluding stanza, the speaker asserts: "I am that clumsy human / on the shore / loving you, coming, coming, / going, . . ." (*45M*, 114). If death is a kind of sexual inverse consecration in "The Consecrating Mother," it offers clear escape for "Annie" from Daddy (and husband) in "'Daddy' War-bucks." And in "Leaves That Talk," the leaves "[call] out their death wish: / 'Anne, Anne, Come to us.' / to die of course" (*45M*, 94).

Death in these poems is surely not conceptualized as a new begin-ning, except in occasional tentative or ironic ways. In "The Big Boots of Pain," the speaker's whole painful life is projected as an accretion of teaspoonfuls of pain, building from "the pain that begins in the crib" (*45M*, 103) and becoming finally so overwhelming that "Somehow DECEASED keeps getting / stamped in red over the word HOPE" (*45M*, 104). "One learns not to blab about all this," says the speaker in a wry aside, "except to yourself or to the typewriter keys / who tell no one until they get brave / and crawl off onto the printed page" (*45M*, 104). This poem concludes with a humorous statement of lim-ited hope, though diction and rhythm continue to project despair:

> Well,
> one gets out of bed
> and the planets don't always hiss
> or muck up the day, each day.
> As for the pain and its multiplying teaspoon,
> perhaps it is a medicine
> that will cure the soul
> of its greed for love
> next Thursday.
>
> (*45M*, 105)

Such typical Sexton humor, with its no-nonsense voice and its comic, absurd treatment of a very serious subject, also pervades "The Passion of the Mad Rabbit." This poem offers an absurd, comical, and intricate subversion of the crucifixion story; the speaker, "Mr. Rabbit," is cru-cified but doesn't die, and so is burned, singing, among his colored Easter eggs:

Fire lit, I tossed the eggs to them, *Hallelujah* I sang
to the eggs,
....
My blood came to a boil as I looked down the throat of
madness,
but singing yellow egg, blue egg, pink egg, red egg, green
egg,
Hallelujah, to each hard-boiled-colored egg.

In place of the Lord,
I whispered,
a fool has risen.

(45M, 91)

Finally, there is "Cigarettes and Whiskey and Wild, Wild Women"
(where humor is implied, in the song from which this poem derives
its title, in the line that follows the title: "They'll drive you crazy,
they'll drive you insane"). This is the first poem of "Eating the Leftovers" and perhaps the thematically central poem of the volume. Here
is its second and final stanza:

Now that I have written many words,
and let out so many loves, for so many,
and been altogether what I always was—
a woman of excess, of zeal and greed,
I find the effort useless.
Do I not look in the mirror,
these days,
and see a drunken rat avert her eyes?
Do I not feel the hunger so acutely
that I would rather die than look
into its face?
I kneel once more,
in case mercy should come
in the nick of time.

(45M, 89)

It is abundantly clear why Anne Sexton renamed this volume, re-
serving the title *The Life Notebooks* for a later date that never came.
There is only scanty evidence in *45 Mercy Street* that Sexton "[knew]
how to live," as she observed in an optimistic moment in early 1973,
that she could "dig a trench in [her] soul and find something there"

(*L,* 392). What she found there, if the poems of this volume can be said to offer sufficient evidence, was pain, loss, hunger, and emotional exhaustion, from which no one or nothing could deliver her: not another human being, not God, and not her art. The poems do indeed "build to a clear progression of thought and emotion" (*45M,* vii), as Linda Gray Sexton observes, yet the final structure is hardly the one promised by "hegira," the title of the volume's opening section. These poems appear to document not a journey to escape a dangerous environment but a journey to catalogue the dangers. And if this journey succeeds in reaching a highly desirable destination, it is death with its obliteration of consciousness and pain that is desired, rather than the joyful rebirth prefigured in *The Death Notebooks.* This volume begins "the hegira" with "45 Mercy Street," where mercy is an elusive dream. It ends, thematically, with the speaker "kneel[ing] once more, / in case mercy should come / in the nick of time." After reading this volume, one senses that the odds for that to happen are not very good.

Words for Dr. Y. and "Last Poems"

Words for Dr. Y., published posthumously in 1978, is the tenth and last volume of Anne Sexton's work to be published. It is also, as Linda Gray Sexton tells us in an editor's note, "the first collection of Anne Sexton's poetry from which her editorial guidance was totally absent."[5] Its contents are poems and stories that were found among her papers after her death, possibly including the "untitled binder of new poems" to which Linda Gray Sexton refers in the editor's note to *45 Mercy Street* (*45M,* vii). The poems of *Words for Dr. Y.* are arranged by order of composition and dated when possible; they span the years from 1960 to 1971. "Last Poems" is the concluding section of *The Complete Poems.* These six poems which Sexton wrote in the seven months before her death had been previously uncollected; they are dated as well, from March 24, 1974 to September 27, 1974. *Words for Dr. Y.* comprises four sections, chronologically ordered. Linda Gray Sexton tells us that the first section, "Letters to Dr. Y.," "written from 1960 to 1970, was originally a series of poems Anne wanted to include in her sixth volume, *The Book Of Folly.* When friends and editors convinced her it did not belong there, she specifically reserved it for publication after her death. As far as I know, this is the only time she ever set work aside for such a purpose" (*WD,* v).

"Letters to Dr. Y." contains twenty-three poems, all untitled. Because they are untitled, and because they are chronologically arranged and dated, they take the form of journal entries presented as one long poem: records of meetings with the psychiatrist Dr. Y., responses to sessions, examinations of subjects discussed in or occasioned by therapy, notes addressed directly to Dr. Y., recollected dialogues with the doctor. These poems catalogue the peaks of a ten-year history of fears, desires, failures, psychoses, and triumphs.

The therapy itself is the theme of several poems; often it is represented, as well it might be, as a digging: "I begin again, Dr. Y., / this neverland journal, / full of my own sense of filth. / Why else keep a journal, if not / to examine your own filth?" WD, 8). Perceiving her task and her worth in this way, the speaker often becomes the child, being toilet-trained, trying to please her parent. As we have seen in many of Sexton's poems in *The Book of Folly* and elsewhere, the psychiatrist is the male Other who holds power over her and whom she tries to please. In another poem of this sequence, she writes: "But brown eyes where Father Inc. waits, / that little Freud shoveling dirt in the cellar, / that Mr. Man, Mr. Cellar Man, brown as / old blood" (WD, 16).

Several poems of this section record dialogues with Dr. Y. In one, in a refrain between stanzas, the doctor repeats, with the voice of the superego: "*And where is the order?*" (WD, 5–6). In another poem, Dr. Y. begins by asking "*What do the voices say?*" (WD, 20) The speaker answers, in the specific images of six stanzas, that her voices well up from her past and cover her present with paralysis and death. In another dialogue, the doctor asks questions based on statements and answers just offered by the speaker:

> *Have the leaves always talked? Even when you were young?*
> you ask.
>
> When I was five I played under pines.
> Pines that were stiff and sturdy.
> State of Maine pines . . .
> ....
> *The leaves tell you to die?* you ask.
> Yes.
>
> (WD, 30)

Throughout this section of the volume, death is a persistent theme, heralded by the close of the first poem:

> Bravo, I cry,
> swallowing the pills,
> the do die pills.
> Listen ducky,
> death is as close to pleasure
> as a toothpick.
> To die whole,
> riddled with nothing   ,
> but desire for it,
> is like breakfast
> after love.
>
> (*WD*, 4)

The reference to breakfast here recalls the sacramental morning imagery of "The Fury of Sunrises" (*DN*), suggesting again the familiar linkage of death with new life. In other poems of this "Letters to Dr. Y." sequence, death takes different forms: death calls for the speaker in the surreal, nightmarish shape of a murderous "My Lai soldier" (*WD*, 27); it also appears as a man, a razor, a whip (*WD*, 20–21).

Other familiar themes appear here as well; one short entry states that "this loneliness is just an exile from God" (*WD*, 10), and in another, where the mocking speaker declares that "God is only mocked by believers!" God turns away: "And God was bored. / He turned on his side like an opium eater / and slept" (*WD*, 17–18). Here and elsewhere, God and Dr. Y. merge into a composite male-Other authority figure: "Your hand is the outrageous redeemer" (*WD*, 32), says the speaker to both of them. Evil and guilt appear here as well, as one might expect. The poet weaves evil into the practice of her craft: "None of them [John, Maxine, George] has / the sense of evil that I have, / evil that jaw breaker, / that word wife" (*WD*, 7). Here and in another poem, evil is given the name of "wife," indicating deep self-loathing in the very formation of this linguistic identification. Thus, in the other entry, although "I am no longer at war with sin,"

> the old sense of evil remains,
> evil that wife.
> Evil who leaves me here,
> most days,
> dead broke.
>
> . . . .
> She is my other face. . . .
>
> (*WD*, 23)

Also among these entries, however, is interspersed affirmation and hope. One poem, free-associating on the pleasure of "the word warm," concludes: "In the beginning, / summer is a sense / of this earth, / or of yourself" (*WD*, 9). Another very short entry declares that "I begin to see. Today I am not all wood" (*WD*, 33). The closing poem of the sequence emphasizes this positive note, for it is a hymn to happiness:

> I am happy today with the sheets of life.
> . . . .
> I hung out the bedsheets and watched them
> slap and lift like gulls.
> When they were dry I unfastened them
> and buried my head in them.
> All the oxygen of the world was in them.
> . . . .
> So this is happiness,
> that journeyman.
>
> (*WD*, 34)

Clearly, Dr. Y. has helped the poet to know "that journeyman," for another poem in "Letters to Dr. Y." concludes with this couplet: "I am in a delight with you, Music Man. / Your name is Dr. Y. My name is Anne" (*WD*, 22).

The volume's second section, entitled "Poems 1971–1973," contains poems written between July and July of those years. Linda Gray Sexton comments cryptically in the editor's note that Sexton "had no chance to incorporate these [poems] into a book or place them with magazines" (*WD*, v). From their dates, we can ascertain that these nine poems were composed during the time that Sexton was writing the poems published in *The Death Notebooks, The Awful Rowing toward God,* and *45 Mercy Street.* Clearly, Sexton chose not to include these nine in any of those volumes, for reasons we cannot know. They are, in fact, "raw" and "unworked" poems, much like those of *The Awful Rowing toward God* (*L,* 390), yet they are fiercer. There is the suggestion in them ("To Like, To Love") of homosexual love, but we have seen that in earlier poems. There is in these poems an echo of the old, jaunty, angry voice ("The Surgeon," "Buying the Whore"). Some poems are Plath-like; some are prolix. Perhaps Sexton was saving these poems to rework for a later volume. Or perhaps she had simply discarded them.

The volume's third section is called "Scorpio, Bad Spider, Die: The Horoscope Poems (1971)." This series of poems, Linda Gray Sexton tells us, was one about which Anne Sexton was "quite uncertain about

[the] final destination," even though they had been placed in Anne's "file [cabinet] beside *45 Mercy Street* and other poems intended for publication." Since these poems "never fit thematically into any book she worked on thereafter," Sexton may have been saving them for later publication. Or, "although written in the later years of her career, these poems often return to the stricter form, rhyme, and meter of her earlier work. Perhaps this return, coupled with the very personal content of these poems, made her initially uneasy about publishing them" (*WD,* v–vi).

The epigraph to these Scorpio poems is from Pushkin: "And reading my own life with loathing, I tremble and curse" (*WD,* 55). Anne Sexton was born on 9 November 1928 under the sign of Scorpio. The series opens with a letter from an astrologer: "*Dear Friend,* / *It may seem to you superstitious and childish to* / *consult the Forecast in your daily activities, but the* / *main object of reading your horoscope should be* / *self-training and knowledge of yourself and your* / *character traits*" (*WD,* 57). "Self-training and knowledge of yourself and your character traits" is the theme of the fifteen poems of the series, as the opening poem suggests: "Madame, I have a confusion, / will you take it away? / Madame, I have a sickness, / will you take it away? / Madame, I am the victim of an odor, / will you take it away? Take! For God's sake take! / Mend everything!" (*WD,* 57) The following fourteen poems follow similar form, each entitled with a date, and all but one opening with an italicized horoscope prediction (such as we might find in a newspaper). This structure is humorous in a typically Sexton, slant sort of way; the banality of the opening horoscope entry contrasts almost comically with the poem that follows.

Thematic unity here is achieved, loosely, by the shifting focus on "yourself and your character traits"; selection of subjects is various and wide-ranging. Since all, however, are subjects with which we are by now familiar, it is difficult to see which poems might have been so personal as to have made the poet "uneasy," at this point, "about publishing them." The theme suggested in the epigraph is evident here, although self-loathing seems strangely less evident here than in the poems of other volumes.

The poem "February 17th" can serve as an example:

> *Take nothing for granted.*

> Yes, I know.
> Wallace will be declared king.

For his queen, Shirley Temple Black.

. . . .

Yes, I know.
Death sits with his key in my lock
Not one day is taken for granted.
Even nursery rhymes have put me in hock.
If I die before I wake. Each night in bed.
My husband sings *Baa Baa black sheep* and we pretend
that all's certain and good, that the marriage won't end.

                                                    (*WD*, 69)

Surely there is genuine humor here ameliorating the self-loathing. Sexton's special brand of dark laughter is evident, facing the absurd in a matter-of-fact voice, projecting the comical through rhythms and tone.

The fourth and last section of *Words for Dr. Y.* contains, as Linda Gray Sexton tells us, "three horror tales. Anne enjoyed writing these stories perhaps more than anything else she ever produced and was proud of the result" (*WD*, vi). Each of these stories has a first-person narrator (as we might expect from a poet who personifies speakers so clearly in her verse). And each can be read as a gloss to major themes of Sexton's poetry. "Ghost," the first of the three, is indeed a kind of horror story. Its speaker is Anne's great-aunt Anna, who figures so largely in Sexton's poetry, especially the early work. Here, "Nana," as Anne called her, haunts Anne from beyond the grave, claiming responsibility both for many of Anne's difficulties and for some of her successes. What Anne experiences as madness is a result of that haunting, as is her broken hip: "She had at the time been committing a major sin" (*WD*, 83). Anne's poetic gift results as well from this ghost's influence; "it is . . . unfortunate that she did not inherit my gift with the English language. But here I do interfere the most, for I put *my* words onto her page, and . . . she . . . calls it 'a gift from the muse.' Oh how sweet it is!" (*WD*, 85) Sexton's poems document extensively Sexton's love for and guilt over the death of this great-aunt. It is interesting that in this story Sexton fancifully (and seriously?) explores the possibility that their relationship has continued.

"Vampire," the second story, belongs more firmly in the horror-story genre. Its speaker is a male insurance agent turned vampire who, having been captured and imprisoned by unknown assailants, goes out each night carrying a loaf of bread and an address book. His goal is to find one of the "girls" listed in his book and eat his bread in her bedroom while sucking her blood from her navel: "that which held her to her mother to her mother to her mother—back into the eternal" (*WD*, 91). He loves these sojourns and is completely insensible of the fact that he is killing the girls: "Do I only dream that she cries out in joy? . . . She is very still, but that is proper" (*WD*, 91). One is reminded of Sylvia Plath's daddy-husband: "If I've killed one man, I've killed two— / the vampire who said he was you / And drank my blood for a year."[6] One thinks also of Sexton's poem "Loving the Killer" (*LP*), or her lines (peculiarly echoing Plath's "oo" rhyme in "Daddy"): "You do / drink me. The gulls kill fish" ("Barefoot," *LP*). In Sexton's "Vampire," there is no angry retribution; the women-victims remain passive, dead. But somehow the anger vibrates around the edges of the story. In Plath's words at the conclusion of "Daddy," "There's a stake in your fat black heart / And the villagers never liked you. / They are dancing and stamping on you. / They always *knew* it was you. / Daddy, daddy, you bastard, I'm through."[7]

The third story, "The Bat," offers a surreal, nightmarish narrative. The narrator is a man who at first awaits his "verdict" in an atmosphere reminiscent of Kafka's *The Trial,* but with peculiar humor: called by his social security number to hear his verdict, the narrator exclaims, "Good God, . . . the same God-damned number even HERE!" (*WD*, 93) His verdict is reincarnation as a bat, with nine former human lives to remember. As he remembers fragments of these lives, however, an advertisement insistently interrupts, until he sees the entire "AD—a complete scenario" (*WD*, 97), which involves the narrator, now a man, rescuing a nameless girl from an attacker, trying to comfort her, and then following the attacker's instructions to, literally, crucify her against his closet wall. In this connection, one is reminded of similar imagery in many of Sexton's poems, where she, as speaker, is imaginatively crucified. One thinks also of her poem "Bat" (*45M*), where she likens herself to the ugly, "misshapen" creature who hangs upside down "in the cemetery," and where both, like witches, "[fly] at night" (*45M*, 27). In the complicated relationship established by this story between various victims and victimizers, Sexton expresses frustration at the absurdity of existence, anger at her own perceived ugliness and at helpless victimization, and (as in "Vampire") rage against the male victimizer.

"Last Poems," the six final poems of Sexton's *Complete Poems,* written between 14 March 1974 and 27 September 1974, are principally about love and death, which may have been the two great themes coursing through Sexton's thoughts in the seven months before her suicide. The first poem, "Admonition to a Special Person," offers a kind of valediction (to whom?) to "Watch out for power, . . . hate, . . . friends, . . . intellect, . . . games, . . . [and] love" (*CP*, 607):

> Watch out for love
> (unless it is true,
> and every part of you says yes including the toes)
> (*CP*, 607)

This poem sounds much like e. e. cummings's "dive for dreams":

> trust your heart
> if the seas catch fire
> (and live by love
> though the stars walk backward)[8]

The second poem, "In Excelsis," is a love poem to "Barbara" (mentioned also in the epigraph to *45 Mercy Street* and in its poem "There You Were"). As in "There You Were," Anne and Barbara stand on a beach in "In Excelsis." In this "Last Poem," Sexton imagistically links drowning (entering the sea) with sexual love, a linkage accomplished also in "The Consecrating Mother" (*45M*), as we have seen; it is interesting to note that in *45 Mercy Street*, "The Consecrating Mother" follows "There You Were." Several motifs may be at work simultaneously in this group of poems: the attractiveness of death, its possibility of offering new life, and (possibly homosexual) love. Yet this love-between-women theme is complex in itself; in another of Sexton's *45 Mercy Street* poems, "The Red Dance," the speaker refers to herself as "Sappho." Such a reference, we should remember, suggests love of women (a feminist company of women) *and* of art; Sappho the poet leaped into the sea both to pay the price of art and to express despair at unrequited love.

"Uses," "As It Was Written," and "Lessons In Hunger," the third, fourth, and fifth poems, explore the speaker's perception of victimization. In "Uses," she echoes Plath's Jew imagery (not for the first time in these late poems) and cadences ("I, alone, came through, / starved but making it by eating / a body or two" [*CP*, 610]). "As It Was Written" suggests some of the more successful apocalyptic imagery of other, slightly earlier poems ("Earth, earth, / riding your merry-go-round / toward extinction" [*CP*, 611]) but ends with the speaker victimized "each night," with the moon "with its hungry red mouth" sucking, vampirelike, "at my scars" (*CP,* 612). "Lessons in Hunger" recalls and continues the familiar motif of unsated hunger. In a Kafkaesque scene vaguely reminiscent of the beginning of "The Bat," the speaker confronts a faceless, bodiless "blue blazer" (*CP,* 612), to be answered only in silence.

Sexton wrote the final poem, "Love Letter Written in a Burning Building," one week before her death. The poem is addressed to "Dearest Foxxy"; the building of the title is a burning crate, and the crate is a coffin. Writes the speaker:

> I have on a mask in order to write my last words,
> and they are just for you, and I will place them
> in the icebox saved for vodka and tomatoes,
> and perhaps they will last.
> ....
> If my toes weren't yielding to pitch
> I'd tell the whole story.
>
> (*CP,* 613–14)

Seven days later, Anne Sexton removed her mask. And if she did not leave us with "the whole story," she left us with much that is valuable. Her poems will last.

Chapter Ten
The Experience Teller

Four months before her death, Anne Sexton wrote a letter to Erica Jong in which she summarized her creative intentions and stated her aesthetic credo:

The whole life of us writers, the whole product I guess I mean, is the one long poem. . . . It's all the same poem. It doesn't belong to any one writer—it's God's poem perhaps. Or God's people's poem. You have the gift—and with it comes responsibility—you mustn't neglect or be mean to that gift—you must let it do its work. It has more rights than the ego that wants approval. . . . if you can feel you are in touch with experience, if you've (so to speak) stuck your finger into experience and got it right and can put it down so that others (even experience tellers) can comprehend their own lives better, . . . then you must get on with it! . . . the listener awaits. (L, 414–15)

Clearly, the profession of poet carried with it, for Sexton, both a fulfillment of the need for self-expression and an awareness of the responsibility to develop her gift. It is probably true for most writers that the very act of creative expression is gratifying to some degree; indeed, one imagines that even pure need of expression can be its own reward. It is also the case, however, that for many poets, as for Sexton, writing poems (or letting her gift "do its work") fails to elicit universal approval.

Sexton risked, and often received, disapproval from precisely those colleagues and readers from whom she sought validation. In the course of expanding the boundaries and augmenting the definition of personal poetry, Sexton explored such subjects as madness, female physicality, love, and suicide in such original and honest ways that she frequently enough drew (and continues still to draw) the criticism that her work is merely narcissistic, that it is simply psychological documentation and not poetry at all. One critic, for example, writes that "Miss Sexton's verses often reach the point of unconscious self-parody. Her subsequent suicide does not relieve their self-indulgence but merely confirms the authenticity of its obsession."[1] Other poets have condemned her work as well. One thinks, for instance, of the now-famous remark by James Dickey, reviewing *To Bedlam and Part Way Back,* that Sexton's "poems so obviously come out of deep, painful sections of the author's life that one's literary opinions scarcely seem to matter; one feels tempted to drop them furtively into the nearest ashcan, rather than be caught with them in the presence of so much naked suffering."[2]

Both the evidence of Sexton's work and the content of her late letter (quoted above), however, reveal the superficiality and wrong-headedness of such views. Such "literary opinions" should not "matter," although they did, sometimes, to Sexton. Emotion is indeed compelling and forceful in her poems, but such emotion (rather than comfort) must be this experience teller's raw material. Sexton's own comment links expression with responsibility, and this dual intention is clearly achieved in her poetry.

It is particularly significant, in fact, to hear Sexton say that her artistic purpose transcends mere self-expression and to hear her suggest that the search for herself that her poetry documents should and must serve the wider purpose of helping her listeners to "comprehend their own lives better." Anne Sexton does achieve that aim through sheer force of emotion, through shock, and through humor. Many readers seem unwilling to recognize Sexton's wit; perhaps it seems incongruous to laugh with (not at) the speaker as she reveals intimate and terrible confidences. But many of these poems are funny, and it is often through humor that Sexton exposes the pretense that makes life unbearable. There are many fine poems in Sexton's canon; this poet's humor, insight, and technical mastery should insure their success. Because of and beyond these accomplishments, however, Sexton's poetry does reach the "listener" who "awaits." The poet's search for herself informs and enlightens our search; in the speaker's fears, difficulties, nightmares, failures, and achievements, we recognize echoes of our own.

The central question, as critic Sandra M. Gilbert phrases it, is this: "Does Sexton's continuing, 'confessional' search for Anne signify, to those of use who are searching for ourselves, anything beyond *Anne's* quest? Would this poet's voice be muffled or stifled if she enclosed herself more, set herself a few more formal limits?"[3] Although Gilbert speaks here particularly of Sexton's *The Death Notebooks,* the questions are relevant to Sexton's oeuvre. And Gilbert's answer is "Yes. She probably had to cultivate self-absorption, speak in a deliberately naive or flat tone, risk sentimentality and cuteness, in order to achieve the triumphs [and] grandeur" of her work.[4] Linda W. Wagner-Martin's assessment of Esther Greenwood in Sylvia Plath's *The Bell Jar* can be adapted to apply to Anne Sexton's impetus and method: this poet "is not ashamed of her descent into madness: she wants to tell about it, partly to rid herself of memories, partly to help other women faced with the same cultural pressure."[5]

One should add that Sexton's aim seems also to explore the possibilities of meaning and value for her life and, by extension, for the lives of others. Her poetry documents not only a search for self but also a search for God. Her work is, as she writes in that late letter, "all the same poem. . . . it's God's poem perhaps. Or God's people's poem." A need for spiritual significance runs through Sexton's poetry from beginning to end, an need that is largely frustrated in the early work. "Need is not quite belief," she writes in "With Mercy for the Greedy":

> My friend, my friend, I was born
> doing reference work in sin, and born
> confessing it. This is what poems are:
> with mercy
> for the greedy.
> They are the tongue's wrangle,
> the world's pottage, the rat's star.
>   (*PO*, 22–23)

The evidence of the whole range of Sexton's "pottage," of her "tongue's wrangle," tells us that need does finally become belief, even if it is perhaps tentatively achieved, and even if, as Maxine Kumin comments, "she found, or invented Him."[6] Sexton's last poems, especially those in *The Death Notebooks*, suggest that death has become for her not an act of nihilistic violence but of movement toward God's light; these poems are as much about new life beyond the grave as they are about death. This poet-rat is "blessed" in "O Ye Tongues": "For God did not forsake them but put the blood angel to look / after them until . . . they would enter their star" (*DN*, 100). And although the rats of "Rats Live on No Evil Star" "die before our time," we must note that Sexton's fascination with that palindrome affirms at least the possibility of her belief that the end is the beginning.

Many of Sexton's early critics failed to see Sexton's work for what it really was—an "hegira," as the first section of *45 Mercy Street* is entitled. Her whole canon records for us "a journey" that is "undertaken" both "as a means of escaping from an undesirable or dangerous environment" and "as a means of arriving at a highly desirable destination" (*45M,* 1). For Sexton, escape and arrival are identical conclusions. Suicide is an act of female triumph, for it is the ultimate affirmation of self and of freedom from male domination. "When . . . death takes you and puts you thru the wringer, it's a man," writes Sexton. "But when you kill yourself, it's a woman" (*L,* 231).

Power, control, and self-determination are the relevant issues here. The male Other accompanies Anne on every step of her journey, threatening to exploit her fears and sap her strength. He achieves temporary victories, most significantly, perhaps, in the conquering God of "The Rowing Endeth" (*AR*). As Diana Hume George points out:

> Sexton's search for the traditional Father-God in dozens of poems that may be failures in the feminist sense is an eloquent representation of an entire culture's quest for that same God. The loving and admonishing Father for whom she searches is the Father for whom we have all searched. . . . Even those of us who have rejected him outright in favor of no gods at all—or of gods that offend our sensibilities less, match our politics or gender better, or seem to us truer, more imaginative—catch ourselves wishing, or fearing, that he might exist. Sexton's failing Father-God is, in short, our own; I cannot see how it could be otherwise in a patriarchy as old and enduring as ours.[7]

Yet even though the accommodation realized in *The Awful Rowing toward God* suggests final subservience to the male Other, the poet's death itself declares the ultimate assertion of the female self. The carpenter is a persistent image in Sexton's poetry, a male role that the speaker comes to assume. In the *Love Poems,* the carpenter is the actor, builder, life-giver, and destroyer, a figure much like God in "The Rowing Endeth." But there is also evidence that the poet usurps this role, paradoxically overturning the traditional view of suicide as destruction and appropriating the metaphor of carpentry, so that it comes to signify female building and creation. In "The Death Baby" (*DN*) she has "made a pact / . . . / To build our death like carpenters." In "Wanting to Die," she writes, "But suicides have a special language. / Like carpenters they want to know *which tools.* / They never ask *why build*" (*LD,* 58).

The relevant question is not why, but how, and the tools clearly are created and employed in the poetry itself. Anne Sexton's canon is indeed, as she herself says, a record of the process of building by "[stick-ing her] finger into experience," "[getting] it right," and "put[ting] it down." From her first volume to her last, this process is manifested in her exploration of what we can finally recognize as a single, multifa-ceted biographical theme. Each new volume, with its shifting thematic emphasis and technical realization, evinces a newly imaginative at-tempt to "[get] it right." And what she gets right is a poetry both of her experience and of the female experience. She is searingly honest and uncompromisingly forthright. The poet Maxine Kumin reminds us that in assessing "Anne Sexton's place in the history of poetry . . . [w]e must first acknowledge the appearance in the twentieth century of women writing poetry that confronts the issues of gender, social role, and female life and lives viewed subjectively from the female per-spective." Anne Sexton "delineated the problematic position of women—the neurotic reality of the time—though she was not able to cope in her own life with the personal trouble it created" (CP, xxxiii, xxxiv). Perhaps not. But her canon, the history of her journey toward a "highly desirable destination" is finally "one long poem" that helps others to "comprehend their own lives better."

Notes and References

Chapter One

1. "Rowing," in *The Awful Rowing toward God* (Boston: Houghton Mifflin Co., 1975), 1; hereafter cited in the text as *AR*.
2. *Anne Sexton: A Self-Portrait in Letters,* ed. Linda Gray Sexton and Lois Ames (Boston: Houghton Mifflin Co., 1979), 43: hereafter cited in the text as *L*.
3. "Funnel," in *To Bedlam and Part Way Back* (Boston: Houghton Mifflin Co., 1960), 28–29; hereafter cited in the text as *TB*.
4. Diana Hume George, *Oedipus Anne: The Poetry of Anne Sexton* (Urbana: University of Illinois Press, 1987), 29.
5. "Those Times . . . ," in *Live or Die* (Boston: Houghton Mifflin Co., 1966), 29; hereafter cited in the text as *LD*.
6. George, *Oedipus Anne,* 14.
7. "The Truth the Dead Know," in *All My Pretty Ones* (Boston: Houghton Mifflin Co., 1962), 3; hereafter cited in the text as *PO*.
8. "Loving the Killer," in *Love Poems* (Boston: Houghton Mifflin Co., 1969), 18; hereafter cited in the text as *LP*.
9. "Gods," in *The Death Notebooks* (Boston: Houghton Mifflin Co., 1974), 1; hereafter cited in the text as *DN*.

Chapter Two

1. George, *Oedipus Anne,* 27.

Chapter Three

1. "Interview with Barbara Kevles," in *No Evil Star; Selected Essays, Interviews, and Prose,* ed. Steven E. Colburn (Ann Arbor: University of Michigan Press, 1985), 94.
2. Kevles interview, *No Evil Star,* 94.
3. "Interview with William Heyen and Al Poulin," in *No Evil Star,* 133.
4. M. L. Rosenthal, *The New Poets: American and British Poetry since World War II* (New York: Oxford University Press, 1967), 25.
5. Ibid., 26.
6. Charles Gullans, "Poetry and Subject Matter: From Hart Crane to Turner Cassity," *The Southern Review* 7 (Spring 1970): 497–98. Reprinted in *Anne Sexton: The Artist and Her Critics,* ed. J. D. McClatchy (Bloomington: Indiana University Press, 1978), 132.

7. Ralph J. Mills, Jr., *Contemporary American Poetry* (New York: Random House, 1965), 156.

8. A. R. Jones, "Necessity and Freedom: The Poetry of Robert Lowell, Sylvia Plath, and Anne Sexton," *Critical Quarterly* 7 (Spring 1965): 14.

9. Kevles interview, *No Evil Star,* 89.

10. Rosenthal, *The New Poets,* 79.

11. T. S. Eliot, "Tradition and the Individual Talent," *The Sacred Wood* (London: Methuen & Co., 1920), 58.

12. As Diana Hume George reminds us, "Not only was Sexton among the original members of the confessional school; she might legitimately be said to be its mother." Sexton finished *Bedlam* "while Lowell was completing *Life Studies,* the publication of which is usually said to mark the beginning of the confessional movement." Furthermore, she worked on *Bedlam* without Lowell's influence, since *Bedlam* was "substantially complete" when she worked with Lowell, and "she read none of Lowell's own new work" during that time (George, *Oedipus Anne,* 90).

13. Ibid., 91.

14. Rosenthal, *The New Poets,* 130.

15. M. L. Rosenthal, "Sylvia Plath and Confessional Poetry," *The Art of Sylvia Plath,* ed. Charles Newman (Bloomington: Indiana University Press, 1970), 74.

16. "Interview with Patricia Marx," in *No Evil Star,* 71.

17. Donald Sheehan, "An Interview with James Merrill," *Contemporary Literature* 9 (Winter 1968): 1–2.

18. Robert Lowell, *Paris Review* interview, in *Writers at Work: The Paris Review,* ed. Malcolm Cowley (New York: Viking Press, 1963), 349.

19. Marx interview, *No Evil Star,* 75.

20. Rosenthal, *The New Poets,* 131–32.

21. Marjorie G. Perloff, *The Poetic Art of Robert Lowell* (Ithaca, N.Y.: Cornell University Press, 1973), 86, 88, 99.

22. Kevles interview, *No Evil Star,* 90.

23. Marx interview, *No Evil Star,* 75.

24. Rosenthal, *The New Poets,* 26, 79.

25. "Interview with Harry Moore," in *No Evil Star,* 50.

26. Rosenthal, *The New Poets,* 25.

27. Perloff, *The Poetic Art of Robert Lowell,* 99.

28. Lowell, *Writers at Work,* 349.

29. Marx interview, *No Evil Star,* 75.

30. George, *Oedipus Anne,* 30–31.

31. Marx interview, *No Evil Star,* 72–73.

32. Moore interview, *No Evil Star,* 43.

33. Kevles interview, *No Evil Star,* 94.

34. Ibid., 95.

35. Ibid.

36. Moore interview, *No Evil Star,* 43–47.
37. Ibid., 54.
38. Ibid., 49.
39. Ibid., 64.
40. Kevles interview, *No Evil Star,* 94.
41. Maxine Kumin, "How It Was: Maxine Kumin on Anne Sexton," introduction to *The Complete Poems* (Boston: Houghton Mifflin Co., 1981), xxvi; hereafter cited in the text as *CP.*
42. Kevles interview, *No Evil Star,* 94.

Chapter Four

1. Kevles interview, *No Evil Star,* 95–96.
2. Robert Boyers, *"Live or Die:* The Achievement of Anne Sexton," in McClatchy, *Anne Sexton,* 204.
3. Kevles interview, *No Evil Star,* 94.
4. Gullans, "Poetry and Subject Matter," in McClatchy, *Anne Sexton,* 131–32.
5. Boyers, *"Live or Die,"* 204–205.
6. Kevles interview, *No Evil Star,* 94.
7. Ibid., 95.
8. "The Barfly Ought to Sing," *Tri-Quarterly* 7 (Fall 1966): 89–93. Reprinted in Newman, *The Art of Sylvia Plath,* 175.
9. Kevles interview, *No Evil Star,* 93–94.
10. Sylvia Plath, "Daddy," in *Ariel* (New York: Harper & Row, 1966), 51.
11. Sylvia Plath, "Lady Lazarus," in *Ariel,* 7.
12. Robert Lowell, "Man and Wife," in *Life Studies and for the Union Dead* (New York: Farrar, Straus and Giroux, 1959), 87.
13. Kevles interview, *No Evil Star,* 97.

Chapter Five

1. Kevles interview, *No Evil Star,* 94.
2. Charles Gullans, review of *Live or Die,* in McClatchy, *Anne Sexton,* 131.
3. Weeks interview, *No Evil Star,* 114, 117.
4. Kevles interview, *No Evil Star,* 86.
5. Adrienne Rich, "Three Conversations," in *Adrienne Rich's Poetry,* ed. Barbara Charlesworth Gelpi (New York: W. W. Norton & Co., 1975), 111.
6. Alicia Ostriker, "The Thieves of Language: Women Poets and Revisionist Mythmaking," in *The New Feminist Criticism,* ed. Elaine Showalter (New York: Pantheon Books, 1985), 331.
7. Kevles interview, *No Evil Star,* 93.
8. Kumin, "How It Was," xxix.

9. Kevles interview, *No Evil Star,* 94.

10. Kumin, "How It Was," xxxiv.

11. Kevles interview, *No Evil Star,* 84.

12. Jane McCabe, "'A Woman Who Writes': A Feminist Approach to the Early Poetry of Anne Sexton," in McClatchy, *Anne Sexton,* 218.

13. Annette Kolodny, "Dancing Through the Minefield: Some Observations on the Theory, Practice, and Politics of a Feminist Literary Criticism," in Showalter, *The New Feminist Criticism,* 144.

14. Elaine Showalter, "Toward a Feminist Poetics," in Showalter, *The New Feminist Criticism,* 132.

15. Kumin, "How It Was," xxix.

16. Rich, "Three Conversations," 112.

17. Ibid., 105.

18. Kevles interview, *No Evil Star,* 93.

19. Showalter, "Toward a Feminist Poetics," 134–35.

20. Ostriker, "Thieves of Language," 315.

21. Ibid., 318.

22. Ibid., 321.

23. Mary Ellmann, *Thinking about Women* (New York: Harcourt Brace Jovanovich, 1968), 150.

24. Ostriker, "Thieves of Language," 323.

25. Ibid., 331.

26. Ellman, *Thinking About Women,* 55–145.

27. McCabe, "'Woman Who Writes,'" 223–24.

28. Kevles interview, *No Evil Star,* 86.

29. "Interview with Maxine Kumin, Elaine Showalter, and Carol Smith," in *No Evil Star,* 173.

Chapter Six

1. Maxine Kumin, "A Friendship Remembered," in McClatchy, *Anne Sexton,* 108.

2. Heyen and Poulin interview, *No Evil Star,* 145.

3. Jack Zipes, ed., *The Complete Fairy Tales of the Brothers Grimm* (New York: Bantam Books, 1987), xxviii.

4. Bruno Bettelheim, *The Uses of Enchantment* (New York: Random House, 1977), 8, 14, 18.

5. Ibid., 11.

6. William Mark Dean, "The Psychological Relevance of Fairy Tales," unpublished paper, 4.

7. Heyen and Poulin interview, *No Evil Star,* 145.

8. Anne Sexton, "Rumpelstiltskin," in *Transformations* (Boston: Houghton Mifflin Co., 1971), 17–18; hereafter cited in the text as *T.*

9. Sigmund Freud, "The Occurrence in Dreams of Material from Fairy

Tales," *The Standard Edition of the Complete Psychological Works of Sigmund Freud,* ed. and trans. James Strachey et al., vol. 12 (London: Hogarth Press, 1925), 281.

10. Freud, "The Interpretation of Dreams," in Strachey et al., *Standard Edition,* vol. 4, 246.

11. "Little Red Cap," in Zipes, *Complete Fairy Tales,* 101.

12. "Snow White," in Zipes, *Complete Fairy Tales,* 196–204.

13. Christopher Lehmann-Haupt, "Grimm's Fairy Tales Retold," *New York Times,* 27 September, 1971, 37. Reprinted in McClatchy, *Anne Sexton,* 147.

14. Bettelheim, *Uses of Enchantment,* 202.

15. Ibid., 199–215.

16. Ibid., 207.

17. Freud, "Interpretation of Dreams," 309n.

18. "Rapunzel," in Zipes, *Complete Fairy Tales,* 49.

19. Bettelheim, *Uses of Enchantment,* 236.

20. Ibid., 232.

21. Heyen and Poulin interview, *No Evil Star,* 145.

Chapter Seven

1. Robert Frost, "Fire and Ice," in *Complete Poems of Robert Frost* (New York: Henry Holt and Co., 1949), 268.

2. "The Ambition Bird," in *The Book of Folly* (Boston: Houghton Mifflin Co., 1972), 3; hereafter cited in the text as *BF.*

3. Sylvia Plath, "The Applicant," in *Ariel,* 5.

4. Estella Lauter, *Women as Mythmakers: Poetry and Visual Art by Twentieth-Century Women* (Bloomington: Indiana University Press, 1984), 25.

5. Plath, "Lady Lazarus," 8–9.

6. J. D. McClatchy, "Anne Sexton: Somehow To Endure," in McClatchy, *Anne Sexton,* 282.

7. Lauter, *Women as Mythmakers,* 26–27.

8. Barbara Swan, "A Reminiscence," in McClatchy, *Anne Sexton,* 84.

9. Lauter, *Women as Mythmakers,* 26.

10. Sylvia Plath, "Tulips," in *Ariel,* 11.

11. "The Barfly Ought to Sing," 177.

Chapter Eight

1. Heyen and Poulin interview, *No Evil Star,* 155.

2. Kevles interview, *No Evil Star,* 107–8.

3. Ibid., 92.

4. Heyen and Poulin interview, *No Evil Star,* 155–56.

5. Kevles interview, *No Evil Star,* 105.

6. Christopher Smart, *Rejoice in the Lamb: A Song from Bedlam,* ed. William Force Stead (London: J. Cape, 1939), 13–14.

7. Ibid., 17.

8. Sophia B. Blaydes, *Christopher Smart as a Poet of His Time: A Re-Appraisal* (The Hague: Mouton, 1966), 102.

9. Smart, *Rejoice in the Lamb,* 296–97.

10. Blaydes, *Christopher Smart,* 103.

11. Smart, *Rejoice in the Lamb,* line 41, p. 79.

12. Ibid., line 30, p. 99.

13. Ibid., line 51, p. 123.

14. *Rejoice in the Lamb,* 49.

Chapter Nine

1. Heyen and Poulin interview, *No Evil Star,* 143.

2. George, *Oedipus Anne,* 53.

3. "Interview With Gregory Fitzgerald," in *No Evil Star,* 192.

4. *45 Mercy Street,* ed. Linda Gray Sexton (Boston: Houghton Mifflin Co., 1976), vii; hereafter cited in the text as *45M.*

5. *Words for Dr. Y.,* ed. Linda Gray Sexton (Boston: Houghton Mifflin Co., 1978), v; hereafter cited in the text as *WD.*

6. Plath, "Daddy," 51.

7. Ibid., 51.

8. e. e. cummings, "dive for dreams," in *95 Poems* (New York: Harcourt, Brace & Co., 1958), 60.

Chapter Ten

1. Edward Butscher, *Sylvia Plath: Method and Madness* (New York: Seabury Press, 1976), 375n.

2. James Dickey, "Five First Books," *Poetry* 97 (February 1961): 318.

3. Sandra M. Gilbert, "On *The Death Notebooks,*" in McClatchy, *Anne Sexton,* 164.

4. Ibid., 164–65.

5. Linda W. Wagner-Martin, *Sylvia Plath: A Biography* (New York: Simon and Schuster, 1987), 186.

6. Maxine Kumin, "Reminiscence Delivered at Memorial Service for Anne Sexton in March Chapel, Boston University," in *To Make a Prairie* (Ann Arbor: University of Michigan Press, 1979), 82.

7. George, *Oedipus Anne,* 48.

Selected Bibliography

PRIMARY WORKS

Poetry

All My Pretty Ones. Boston: Houghton Mifflin Co., 1962.
The Awful Rowing toward God. Boston: Houghton Mifflin Co., 1975; London: Chatto and Windus, 1977.
The Book of Folly. Boston: Houghton Mifflin Co., 1972; London: Chatto and Windus, 1974. (Poems and stories)
The Complete Poems. Boston: Houghton Mifflin Co., 1981.
The Death Notebooks. Boston: Houghton Mifflin Co., 1974; London: Chatto and Windus, 1975.
45 Mercy Street. Edited by Linda Gray Sexton. Boston: Houghton Mifflin Co., 1976; London: Martin Secker and Warburg, 1977.
Live or Die. Boston: Houghton Mifflin Co., 1966; London: Oxford University Press, 1968.
Love Poems. Boston: Houghton Mifflin Co., 1969; London: Oxford University Press, 1969.
Poems (with Thomas Kinsella and Douglas Livingstone). London: Oxford University Press, 1968.
Selected Poems. London: Oxford University Press, 1964.
To Bedlam and Part Way Back. Boston: Houghton Mifflin Co., 1960.
Transformations. Boston: Houghton Mifflin Co., 1971; London: Oxford University Press, 1972.
Words for Dr. Y: Uncollected Poems with Three Stories. Edited by Linda Gray Sexton. Boston: Houghton Mifflin Co., 1978.

Children's Books

Co-authored with Maxine Kumin:
Eggs of Things. New York: Putnam, 1963.
Joey and the Birthday Present. New York: McGraw-Hill, 1971.
More Eggs of Things. New York: Putnam, 1964.
The Wizard's Tears. New York: McGraw-Hill, 1975.

Nonfiction

Anne Sexton: A Self-Portrait in Letters. Edited by Linda Gray Sexton and Lois Ames. Boston: Houghton Mifflin Co., 1979.

No Evil Star: Selected Essays, Interviews and Prose. Edited by Stephen E. Colburn. Ann Arbor: University of Michigan Press, 1985. This is a useful
collection of essays, short stories, and interviews by Anne Sexton, most
of which appeared originally in journals and are reprinted here. These
are not listed elsewhere in this bibliography. Contents: Essays and Prose:
"Classroom at Boston University," 3–5; "The Barfly Ought to Sing" (6–
13); "Comment on 'Some Foreign Letters,'" 14–17; "The Last Believer,"
18–22; "All God's Children Need Radios," 23–32; "The Freak Show,"
33–38. Interviews (arranged chronologically): "With Harry Moore," 41–
69; "With Patricia Marx," 70–82; "With Barbara Kevles," 83–111;
"With Lois Ames," 119–29; "With William Heyen and Al Poulin,"
130–57; "With Maxine Kumin, Elaine Showalter, and Carol Smith,"
158–79; "With Gregory Fitzgerald," 180–206.

SECONDARY WORKS

Bibliographies

George, Diana Hume. "Selected Bibliography." In *Oedipus Anne: The Poetry of
Anne Sexton,* 197–203. Urbana: University of Illinois Press, 1987. A
listing of primary sources and a plentiful listing of secondary sources to
1987.
McClatchy, J. D. "Selected Bibliograpy." In *Anne Sexton: The Artist and Her
Critics,* edited by J. D. McClatchy, 291–94. Bloomington: Indiana University Press, 1978. A useful listing of primary sources and secondary
sources to 1976.
Northouse, Cameron, and Thomas P. Walsh. *Sylvia Plath and Anne Sexton: A
Reference Guide.* Boston: G. K. Hall & Co., 1974. Complete bibliography
through 1973, including chronological listings of poems' publication in
magazines.

Books

Bettelheim, Bruno. *The Uses of Enchantment: The Meaning and Importance of
Fairy Tales.* New York: Random House, 1977. An examination of the
cultural, psychological, and emotional sources and uses of fairy tales,
especially useful in studying Sexton's *Transformations.*
Bixler, Frances, ed. *Original Essays on the Poetry of Anne Sexton.* Conway: University of Central Arkansas Press, 1988. A useful and wide-ranging collection of excellent critical essays that appear originally or only in this
volume. Contents: Diane Wood Middlebrook, "Anne Sexton and Robert
Lowell," 5–21; Kay Ellen Merriman Capo, "'I Have Been Her Kind':
Anne Sexton's Communal Voice," 22–45; Ann Marie Seward Barry, "In

Praise of Anne Sexton's *The Book of Folly*: A Study of the Woman / Victim / Poet," 46–65; Jenny Goodman, "Anne Sexton's *Live or Die*: The Poem as the Opposite of Suicide," 71–80; Brenda Ameter, "'Put Your Ear Down to Your Soul and Listen Hard': Anne Sexton's Theory and Practice of Archetypal Poetry," 81–91; Frances Bixler, "Anne Sexton's 'Motherly' Poetics," 92–101; Caroline King Barnard Hall, "*Transformations*: A Magic Mirror," 107–29; Michael Burns, "Confession as Sacrament," 130–37; Lynette McGrath, "Anne Sexton's Poetic Connections: Death, God, and Form," 138–63; Diana Hume George, "Anne Sexton's Island God," 169–83; Margaret Scarborough, "Anne Sexton's 'Otherworld Journey,'" 184–202; Frances Bixler, "Journey Into the Sun: The Religious Pilgrimage of Anne Sexton," 203–37; Diana Hume George, "Itinerary of an Obsession: Maxine Kumin's Poems to Anne Sexton," 243–66.

Colburn, Steven E., ed. *Anne Sexton: Telling the Tale.* Ann Arbor: University of Michigan Press, 1988.

George, Diana Hume. *Oedipus Anne: The Poetry of Anne Sexton.* Urbana: University of Illinois Press, 1987. An impressive study of Sexton as "a contemporary Oedipus," a "truth-seeker," connecting Sexton's work both with contemporary psychoanalysis and with feminism.

————, ed. *Sexton: Selected Criticism.* Urbana: University of Illinois Press, 1988.

McClatchy, J. D., ed. *Anne Sexton: The Artist and Her Critics.* Bloomington: Indiana University Press, 1978. A useful collection of articles about Sexton, including critical essays about her poetry, interviews, worksheets, personal reminiscences, and reviews. Many excellent critical essays on Sexton, which appeared originally in journals, are reprinted in this book; these are not listed in "Articles and Parts of Books." Contents: Barbara Kevles, "The Art of Poetry: Anne Sexton (1968)," 3–29; Patricia Marx, "Interview with Anne Sexton (1965)," 30–42; William Packard, "Craft Interview with Anne Sexton (1970)," 43–47; "Worksheets for 'Elizabeth Gone,'" 51–68; Robert Lowell, "Anne Sexton," 71–73; Denise Levertov, "Light Up the Cave," 74–80; Barbara Swan, "A Reminiscence," 81–88; Charles Maryan, "The Poet on Stage," 89–95; Polly C. Williams, "Sexton in the Classroom," 96–101; John Malcolm Brinnin, "Offices (Boston University)," 102; Maxine Kumin, "A Friendship Remembered" 103–10; Lois Ames, "Remembering Anne" 111–14; James Dickey, Geoffrey Hartman on *To Bedlam and Part Way Back* 117–21; May Swenson, Thom Gunn, Louise Bogan, Ian Hamilton on *All My Pretty Ones*, 122–29; Hayden Carruth, Charles Gullans, Thomas P. McDonnell on *Live or Die* 130–38; Mona Van Duyn, Daniel Hughes, Joyce Carol Oates on *Love Poems*, 139–45; Christopher Lehmann-Haupt, Vernon Young on *Transformations*, 146–51; Arthur Oberg, Muriel Rukeyser on *The Book of Folly*, 152–61; Sandra M. Gilbert on *The Death Notebooks*, 162–67; Joyce Carol

Oates, Robert Mazzocco, Ben Howard on *The Awful Rowing toward God*,
168–85; Patricia Meyer Spacks on *45 Mercy Street*, 186–89; Richard
Howard, "Anne Sexton: 'Some Tribal Female Who Is Known but For-
bidden,'" 193–203; Robert Boyers, "*Live or Die*: The Achievement of
Anne Sexton," 204–15; Jane McCabe, "'A Woman Who Writes': A
Feminist Approach to the Early Poetry of Anne Sexton," 216–43; J. D.
McClatchy, "Anne Sexton: Somehow to Endure," 244–90.

Middlebrook, Diane Wood. *Anne Sexton: A Biography*. Forthcoming.

Wagner-Martin, Linda W., ed. *Critical Essays on Anne Sexton*. Boston: G. K.
Hall, 1989.

Articles and Parts of Books

Dickey, James. "Five First Books." *Poetry* 97 (February 1961): 316–20. A
review of *To Bedlam and Part Way Back* in which Dickey criticizes Sexton's
handling of an "extremely painful subject": "One feels tempted to drop
[her poems] furtively into the nearest ashcan."

Gallagher, Brian. "The Expanded Use of Simile in Anne Sexton's Transformations." *Notes on Modern American Literature* 3 (Summer 1979): 9–13.
An examination of how simile in the narrative sections of the *Transformations* poems provides "modern parallels" to, extends the meaning of,
and emphasizes latent sexual content in the Grimm tales.

Hoffmann, Nancy Jo. "Reading Women's Poetry: The Meaning and Our
Lives." *College English* 34 (October 1972): 48–62. Hoffmann discusses
the potential of feminist poetry to offer positive role models in the classroom and considers, among other poems, Sexton's "Live."

Howard, Richard. "Five Poets." *Poetry* 101 (March 1963): 412–18. A review
of *All My Pretty Ones*, along with new volumes by Plath, Levertov,
Dickey, and Koch.

Jones, A. R. "Necessity and Freedom: The Poetry of Robert Lowell, Sylvia
Plath, and Anne Sexton." *Critical Quarterly* 7 (Spring 1965): 11–30. Of
major significance in this essay is Jones's use and definition of the term
"confessional" and his early consideration of a "confessional" movement
in modern American poetry.

Juhasz, Suzanne. "'The Excitable Gift': The Poetry of Anne Sexton." In *Naked
and Fiery Forms: Modern Poetry by Women, a New Tradition*. New York:
Harper and Row, 1976.

———. "Seeking the Exit or the Home: Poetry and Salvation in the Career
of Anne Sexton." In *Shakespeare's Sisters: Feminist Essays on Women Poets*,
edited by Sandra M. Gilbert and Susan Gubar, 261–68. Bloomington:
Indiana University Press, 1979. A cogent consideration of Sexton's
sources of inspiration and of the reasons why "sanity might bring peace
to the woman, but it would destroy the poet."

Johnson, Greg. "The Achievement of Anne Sexton," *The Hollins Critic* 21
(June 1984): 1–13. An examination of Sexton's early volumes as they

reveal the poet's "search for identity" and the "poetry of life" that that search produces.

Kumin, Maxine. "Reminiscence Delivered at Memorial Service for Anne Sexton in Marsh Chapel, Boston University" and "Sexton's *The Awful Rowing toward God.*" In *To Make a Prairie*, 76–80, 81–82. Ann Arbor: University of Michigan Press, 1979. Brief and valuable reminiscences, with commentary about Sexton's need for God "as a sure thing."

Lauter, Estella. "Anne Sexton's Radical Discontent." In *Women as Mythmakers: Poetry and Visual Art by Twentieth-Century Women.* Bloomington: Indiana University Press, 1984. An original and valuable examination of the "quest" and image-making of a visionary poet.

Legler, Philip. "O Yellow Eye." *Poetry* 110 (May 1967): 125–27. A review of *Live or Die* that focuses on "a few of the finest" poems of that volume.

Middlebrook, Diane. "Becoming Anne Sexton." *Denver Quarterly* 18 (Winter 1984): 23–34. An intriguing study of ways Sexton's poetry furnishes the poet a creative way to "unit[e] the buried self wtih her social stereotype, the suburban housewife" while separating herself from her mother's influence.

Middlebrook, Diane Wood. "Housewife into Poet: The Apprenticeship of Anne Sexton." *New England Quarterly* 56 (December 1983): 483–503. A valuable sketch of Sexton's literary "apprenticeship," from the beginning of her career in 1957 to her "genuine separation from all her early mentors" in 1962.

———. "Three Mirrors Reflecting Women: Poetry of Sylvia Plath, Anne Sexton, and Adrienne Rich." In *Worlds into Words: Understanding Modern Poems*, 65–96. New York: W. W. Norton, 1978.

Mills, Ralph J., Jr. "Anne Sexton." In *Contemporary American Poetry*, 218–34. New York: Random House, 1965.

Nichols, Kathleen L. "The Hungry Beast Rowing toward God: Anne Sexton's Later Religious Poetry." *Notes on Modern American Literature* 3 (Summer 1979): 13–16. A study of *The Awful Rowing toward God* as a journey "to find in death the ideal mother and father."

Ostriker, Alicia. "That Story: The Changes of Anne Sexton." In *Writing Like a Woman*, 59–85. Ann Arbor: University of Michigan Press, 1983. An interesting examination of Sexton's late volumes, beginning with *Transformations*, in which Sexton "set the uninhibited self to work interpreting prior, external, shared cultural traditions."

Phillips, Robert. "Anne Sexton: The Blooming Mouth and the Bleeding Rose." In *The Confessional Poets*, 73–91. Carbondale: Southern Illinois University Press, 1973. A study of Sexton's "poetry of misfortune."

Rosenthal, M. L. "Other Confessional Poets." In *The New Poets: American and British Poetry since World War II*, 131–38. New York: Oxford University Press, 1967. An early placement of Sexton within the confessional movement by the critic who popularized the term "confessional."

Shurr, William H. "Anne Sexton's *Love Poems:* The Genre and the Differ-

ences." *Modern Poetry Studies* 10 (1980): 58–68. A study of specific love
poems as they present "the record of a love affair which . . . lasted about
four years."

Wagner, Linda W. "45 Mercy Street and Other Vacant Houses." In *American
Literature: The New England Heritage,* edited by James Nagel and Richard
Astro, 145–65. New York: Garland Publishing Inc., 1981. An examination of the effect on Sexton's poetic female imagination of having to
create her work within a male tradition.

Index

African safari, 8, 78
American Academy of Arts and Letters traveling fellowship, 7, 54
American Place Theater, 9
Ames, Lois, 154
"Anne Sexton and Her Kind," 73
Antioch Summer Writers' Conference, 6
"Applicant, The," 115
Ariel, 33, 65, 78, 84, 115, 118, 119
"Ariel," 136
Atwood, Margaret, 88

Bart, Lily, 84
Barth, John, 9
"Because I Could Not Stop for Death," 64
Bell Jar, The, 172
Bellow, Saul, 54–55, 114
Berryman, John, 33
Bettelheim, Bruno, 94, 95, 103, 104, 110
Blaydes, Sophia B., 142
Boston University, 5, 9, 81
Boyers, Robert, 55, 56
Bread Loaf Writers Conference, 7
Brinnin, John Malcolm, 9
Byron, Lord, 34

Charles Playhouse, 8
Chopin, Kate, 84
Cinderella, 93, 94
"Colossus, The," 135
Congress for Cultural Freedom travel grant, 7, 78
cummings, e. e., 168

"Daddy," 65, 66, 167
Daedalus, 52
Dean, William Mark, 95
Dickey, James, 171
Dickinson, Emily, 34, 64, 87
"Digging for China," 14

Dingley, Anna Ladd ("Nana"), 1, 3, 5, 10, 22, 23, 42, 119, 155, 166
Dingley, Nelson, 1
"Directive," 14
"dive for dreams," 168
Dream Songs, 33

Eliot, T. S., 34, 137, 140
Ellmann, Mary, 82, 88, 89

Fairfield University, 9
Far Field, The, 33
"Fire and Ice," 113–14, 126, 129
Ford Foundation, 8
Freud, Sigmund, 97, 105
Frost, Robert, 14, 113, 126, 129

Garland School, 3
George, Diana Hume, 2, 4, 34, 42, 151, 173
Gilbert, Sandra M., 171
Gilman, Charlotte Perkins, 84
Ginsberg, Allen, 33, 89
"Golden Key, The," 95
Green Hornet, The, 58
Greenwood, Esther, 84, 172
Grimm fairy tales, 92–112, 124
Griffin, Susan, 88
Guggenheim Fellowship, 9, 73
Gullans, Charles, 55

Hansel and Gretel, 94, 95
Harvard University, 8, 9, 73
Harvey, Blanche, 2
Harvey, Jane, 2
Harvey, Mary Gray Staples, 1, 6, 42
Harvey, Ralph Churchill, 1, 6, 42
H. D., 88
Heart's Needle, 33
"Helen in Egypt," 88
Hemingway, Ernest, 131
Henderson the Rain King, 114

Herzog, 54–55, 69, 114
Holmes, John, 6, 12, 13, 14, 16, 34, 60, 61
Howl, 33
Hughes, Ted, 8

Icarus, 51, 52, 115–16

Jocasta, 13
Jones, A. R., 34
Jong, Erica, 170
Jubilate Agno, 141, 142, 145, 146

Kafka, Franz, 42, 44, 167
Kevles, Barbara, 54, 132
Kierkegaard, Sören, 10, 152
Kizer, Carolyn, 12, 81, 82
Kolodny, Annette, 82
Kumin, Maxine, 6, 12, 42, 79, 80, 83, 91, 92, 172, 174
Kunitz, Stanley, 110

"Lady Lazarus," 66, 118–19
Lauter, Estella, 118, 122, 127
Lehmann-Haupt, Christopher, 101
Life Studies, 33, 35, 36, 67
"Little Red Cap," 99
"Love Song of J. Alfred Prufrock, The," 137
Lowell, Robert, 6, 12, 31, 32, 33, 34, 35, 41, 55, 67, 81, 82, 89

Macbeth, 42
"Man and Wife," 67
Martin, Doctor Sidney, 5, 12
Marx, Patricia, 90
McCabe, Jane, 82, 89
McLean Hospital, 9, 10
Merrill, James, 35
Millay, Edna St. Vincent, 81
Miller, Nolan, 12, 15
Mills, Ralph J. Jr., 33
Minnesota Opera Company, 9
"Muse of Water, A," 82

National Book Award, 7, 54
National Endowment for the Humanities, 73

New Criticism, 36
Newman, Charles, 63, 64, 128
nursery rhymes, 21

Oberlin College, 9
Oedipus, 13, 109, 120, 126
Ostriker, Alicia, 77, 87, 88

Perloff, Marjorie, 36, 41
Phi Beta Kappa, 9, 73
Plath, Sylvia, 6, 7, 8, 12, 33, 63, 64, 65, 66, 71, 78, 84, 88, 115, 118, 119, 127, 128, 135, 136, 137, 164, 167, 168, 172
Poetry, 8
Pontellier, Edna, 84
Pulitzer Prize for Poetry, 8, 54, 73
Pushkin, Alexander, 165

Radcliffe College, 8, 9, 73
Rapunzel, 94, 109
Regis College, 9
Rich, Adrienne, 76, 84
Roethke, Theodore, 33
Rogers Hall School, 3, 4
Rosenthal, M. L., 33, 34, 35, 36, 41
Royal Society of Literature Fellow, 7

Schopenhauer, Arthur, 13
Sexton, Alfred Muller II ("Kayo"), 4, 5, 7, 8, 10
SEXTON, Anne
  birth, 1, 165; childhood and adolescence, 1–4; as confessional poet, 13–14, 25, 33–53, 55–56, 62, 74, 80, 82, 85, 110–11, 125, 131, 132, 134, 154, 155, 170–74; and daughters, 4–5, 10, 26, 81, 85; death, 11, 147, 152, 153, 168; divorce, 10, 153, 157; and father, 6, 10, 45–48, 120–22, 155; as feminist, 81, 82–91; humor, 9, 89, 96, 98, 100, 101, 112, 159, 160, 171; and husband, 4–5, 7–8, 10, 78, 81; marriage, 4, 12; and mother, 6, 10, 22, 29, 30, 37–41, 69, 85–86, 108, 119, 155; New England

background, 1–2, 74, 105; operation, 7, 37–41; religious belief, 9, 10, 49, 122, 125, 131–46, 148–52, 172; "sealed hotel," "summer hotel," 6, 12; witch, 90–91, 93, 94, 95, 105, 106, 124, 150, 156; as woman writer, 8, 34–35, 71, 73–91, 124, 167, 173

WORKS—POETRY:
"Abortion, The," 43
"Addict, The," 65, 66, 78
"Admonition to a Special Person," 168
"Again and Again and Again," 77–78, 84
"All My Pretty Ones," 6, 44–49, 55
All My Pretty Ones, 7, 32–53, 54, 62, 73, 80
"Ambition Bird, The," 114–16
"And One for My Dame," 63
"Angels of Blizzards and Blackouts," 126
"Angels of the Love Affair," 129
"Anna Who Was Mad," 119
"As It Was Written," 168–69
"Assassin, The," 113, 126
"Author of the Jesus Papers Speaks, The," 123, 125
Awful Rowing Toward God, The, 1, 9, 10, 147–52, 153, 154, 164, 173
"Baby Picture," 133
"Barefoot," 75, 167
"Bat," 156, 167
"Bayonet," 157
"Begat," 122
"Beginning the Hegira," 154–55
"Bells, The," 23
"Bestiary U.S.A.," 155–56
"Big Boots of Pain, The," 159
"Black Art, The," 90, 105
"Boat, The," 120–21
Book Of Folly, The, 9, 113–29, 130, 161, 162
"Break, The," 8, 76–77, 78, 79, 84, 88, 89
"Break Away, The," 157
"Breast, The," 75, 79

"Briar Rose (Sleeping Beauty)," 109–10
"Buying the Whore," 164
"Children, The," 149–50
"Christmas Eve," 68, 85, 119
"Cigarettes and Whiskey and Wild, Wild Women," 160
"Cinderella," 106, 111
"Civil War, The," 149
"Clothes," 133
Complete Poems, The, 161, 167
"Consecrating Mother, The," 159, 168
"Consorting with Angels," 61
"Cripples and Other Stories," 63, 65–66, 78, 87, 116–17
"Crossing the Atlantic," 67
"Daddy Warbucks," 159
"Death Baby, The," 133, 173
Death Notebooks, The, 9, 125, 130–46, 148, 150, 153, 154, 161, 164, 171, 172
"Death of the Fathers, The," 115, 120–22, 126, 127
"December 2nd," 78
"Despair," 157
"Division of Parts, The," 23, 131
"Divorce," 157–58
"Divorce Papers, The," 156–58
"Divorce, Thy Name Is Woman," 158
"Doctor of the Heart, The," 115, 116–19, 125
"Double Image, The," 5, 25–31, 69, 83, 85, 119, 131
"Dreaming the Breasts," 119, 123
"Earth Falls Down, The," 150
"Eating the Leftovers," 158–60
"Eighteen Days Without You," 78, 87
"Elizabeth Gone," 23, 119
"Expatriates, The," 23
"Faustus and I," 133
"February 17th," 165–66
"Firebombers, The," 113
"Flee on Your Donkey," 56–59, 61, 62, 67, 68, 131
"Flight," 43

"Food," 155
"For Eleanor Boylan Talking with
     God," 49
"For God While Sleeping," 49
"For John, Who Begs Me Not To
     Enquire Further," 13–14, 15, 83
"For Johnnie Pole on the Forgotten
     Beach," 23
"For Mr. Death Who Stands with His
     Door Open," 132
"For My Lover, Returning to His
     Wife," 79
"For the Year of the Insane," 61, 62
"45 Mercy Street," 154–55, 164
45 Mercy Street, 152–61, 161, 165,
     168, 172
"Frenzy," 148
"Friends," 121–22
"Frog Prince, The," 105, 107, 108
"Funnel," 2, 23
"Furies, The," 134–37, 139, 141,
     146, 154
"Fury of Abandonment, The," 136
"Fury of Beautiful Bones, The," 134
"Fury of Cocks, The," 136
"Fury of Cooks, The," 135–36, 139
"Fury of Earth, The," 135, 136
"Fury of Flowers and Worms, The,"
     136
"Fury of God's Good-bye, The," 136
"Fury of Guitars and Sopranos, The,"
     134–35
"Fury of Hating Eyes, The," 134,
     135
"Fury of Jewels and Coal, The," 135
"Fury of Overshoes, The," 136
"Fury of Rainstorms, The," 136
"Fury of Sundays, The," 136
"Fury of Sunrises, The," 136, 150,
     163
"Fury of Sunsets, The," 136
"Godmonger, The," 148
"Gods," 10, 132
"God's Backside," 133
"Going Gone," 113, 115
"Gold Key, The," 95, 96, 98, 105,
     116

"Grandfather, Your Wound," 133
"Gull," 156
"Hansel and Gretel," 97, 108
"Her Kind," 90, 105
"Hex, The," 119–21
"Hog," 156
"Hornet," 156
"Housewife," 85
"How We Danced," 120
"Hurry Up Please It's Time," 137–
     41, 149, 154
"Imitations of Drowning," 61, 62, 63
"In Celebration of My Uterus," 80
"In Excelsis," 168
"In the Deep Museum," 49
"I Remember," 43, 49
"Iron Hans," 97, 105, 109
"Is It True?" 149
"Jesus, the Actor, Plays the Holy
     Ghost," 150–51
"Jesus Asleep," 123
"Jesus Awake," 123
"Jesus Cooks," 123, 124–25
"Jesus Dies," 123
"Jesus Papers, The," 122–25
"Jesus Raises Up the Harlot," 123
"Jesus Suckles," 123
"Jesus Summons Forth," 123
"Jesus Unborn," 123
"Killing the Love," 158
"Kind Sir, These Woods," 14–16, 57
"Kiss, The," 75, 79
"Kite, The," 23
"Lament," 43
"Landscape Winter," 157
"Last Poems," 167–69
"Leaves That Talk," 159
"Lessons in Hunger," 168, 169
"Letters to Dr. Y.," 161–64
"Letter Written During a January
     Northeaster," 49
"Letter Written on a Ferry While
     Crossing Long Island Sound," 49–
     50, 86
Life Notebooks, The, 153, 154, 160
"Little Girl, My String Bean, My
     Lovely Woman," 69

"Little Peasant, The," 97
"Little Uncomplicated Hymn, A," 69
"Live," 69–72
Live or Die, 8, 33, 54–72, 73, 74, 78, 114, 136
"Lobster," 156
"Love Letter Written in a Burning Building," 169
"Love Plant, The," 158
Love Poems, 9, 55, 59, 73–91, 108, 114, 158, 173
"Love Song for K. Owyne," 49
"Loving the Killer," 8, 78, 87, 158, 167
"Lullaby," 21
"Maiden Without Hands, The," 106
"Making a Living," 132, 134
"Man and Wife," 66–67
"Menstruation at Forty," 62–63
"Mercy Street" (unpublished play), 9
"Moon Song, Woman Song," 75, 79
"Moss of His Skin, The," 23
"Mother and Jack and the Rain," 61, 63, 72
"Mr. Mine," 75, 79
"Music Swins Back to Me," 19–20, 21, 83, 88
"My Lai Soldier," 163
"Noon Walk on the Asylum Lawn," 20, 21
"Oh," 127–29
"One-Eye, Two-Eyes, Three-Eyes," 97, 108
"One-Legged Man, The," 115
"Operation, The," 7, 36–41, 43, 119
"Other, The," 115
"O Ye Tongues," 141–46, 154, 172
"Oysters," 120
"Passion of the Mad Rabbit, The," 159–60
"Poems 1971–1973," 164
"Poet of Ignorance, The," 149
"Praying on a 707," 133
"Protestant Easter," 68
"Rapunzel," 97, 108–9
"Rats Live on No Evil Star," 133–34, 151, 172

"Red Dance, The," 158, 168
"Red Riding Hood," 99, 105
"Red Shoes, The," 126
"Riding the Elevator into the Sky," 150
"Ringing the Bells," 21
"Road Back, The," 23
"Rowing," 1, 151
"Rowing Endeth, The," 11, 151, 152, 154, 173
"Rumpelstiltskin," 96, 97, 115
"Santa," 121
"Scorpio, Bad Spider, Die," 164–66
"Seal," 156
Selected Poems, 7
"Self in 1958," 63, 68
"Sickness Unto Death, The," 150
"Silence, The," 127, 129
"Snail," 156
"Snow White and the Seven Dwarfs," 97, 101–5, 106, 108, 109, 111, 126, 158
"Some Foreign Letters," 13, 23–25, 119
"Somewhere in Africa," 60–61, 62, 63, 67
"Stand-Ins, The," 157
"Starry Night, The," 43
"Story for Rose on the Midnight Flight to Boston, A," 23
"Suicide Note," 63
"Sun, The," 62
"Surgeon, The," 164
Survivor, The, 43
"Sweeney," 129
"Sylvia's Death," 63–65
"Talking to Sheep," 155
"There You Were," 168
"Those Times . . .," 3, 68
"Three Green Windows," 59–60, 62, 67
"To a Friend Whose Work Has Come to Triumph," 51–53, 115–16
To Bedlam and Part Way Back, 7, 12–31, 32, 33, 44, 49–50, 55, 59, 62, 69, 73, 80, 147, 171
"To Like, To Love," 164

"To Lose the Earth," 61
"Touch, The," 74–75, 77, 79, 83
Transformations, 9, 75, 88, 92–112,
    114, 116, 122, 123, 124, 125,
    130, 158
"Truth the Dead Know, The," 6, 43
"Twelve Dancing Princesses, The,"
    106–7, 114, 115
"Two Sons," 63
"Unknown Girl in the Maternity
    Ward," 23, 69
"Uses," 168
"Venus and the Ark," 87
"Waiting Head, The," 23
"Waking Alone," 157, 158
"Walking in Paris," 72, 119
"Wall, The," 150
"Wanting to Die," 63, 64, 88, 128,
    173
"Wedding Night, The," 67
"Wedlock, The," 157
"Welcome Morning," 150
"When the Glass of my Body Broke,"
    157
"Where I Live in This Honorable
    House of the Laurel Tree," 23
"Where It Was Back Then," 157
"White Snake, The," 111
"Wifebeater, The," 115, 126
"Witch's Life, The," 150
"With Mercy for the Greedy," 49,
    131, 172
"Wonderful Musician, The," 108
"Words," 148
Words for Dr. Y., 161–67
"You, Doctor Martin," 16–19, 21,
    56, 57, 59, 83, 116–17
"You All Know the Story of the Other
    Woman," 79
"Young," 43, 49

WORKS—PROSE:
"Bar Fly Ought To Sing, The," 64,
    128
"Bat, The," 167, 169
"Ghost," 166
novel (unfinished), a, 8
"Vampire," 166–67

Sexton, Joyce Ladd, 5, 25, 69, 83
Sexton, Linda Gray, 4, 5, 69, 92, 153
Shadow, The, 58
Showalter, Elaine, 83, 85, 91
Simpson, Louis, 36, 40
"Skunk Hour," 31
Smart, Christopher, 141, 142, 143,
    144, 146
Snodgrass, W. D., 6, 12, 13, 21, 30,
    33, 51, 81
Snow White, 93, 94, 100–105
Staples, Arthur Gray, 1
Starbuck, George, 6, 9, 12
Stead, William Force, 142
Swan, Barbara, 97, 125–26

"Tell all the Truth but tell it slant," 87
Thinking About Women, 82
Thorazine, 62
Thoreau, Henry David, 14
"Tradition and the Individual Talent,"
    34
Trial, The, 167
Tri-Quarterly, 63, 128
Tufts University, 9
"Tulips," 127

Vonnegut, Kurt, 99

Wagner-Martin, Linda W., 172
Walden, 14
Waste Land, The, 137, 140, 141
Wellesley College, 1
Wharton, Edith, 84
Whitman, Walt, 34, 89
Wilbur, Richard, 14
Williams, William Carlos, 89
*Woman and Nature: The Roaring Inside
    Her,* 88
Wordsworth, William, 89

"Yellow Wallpaper, The," 84

Zipes, Jack, 93